Walter Chamberlain

A plain reply to Bishop Colenso : respectfully addressed to the laymen of England

Walter Chamberlain

A plain reply to Bishop Colenso : respectfully addressed to the laymen of England

ISBN/EAN: 9783337305741

Printed in Europe, USA, Canada, Australia, Japan

Cover: Foto ©Lupo / pixelio.de

More available books at **www.hansebooks.com**

A PLAIN REPLY

TO

BISHOP COLENSO.

RESPECTFULLY ADDRESSED TO THE LAYMEN OF ENGLAND.

BY

WALTER CHAMBERLAIN, M.A.,

INCUMBENT OF ST. JOHN'S, BOLTON, LANCASHIRE,
AUTHOR OF "THE CHRISTIAN VERITY STATED," ETC., ETC.

LONDON:

WERTHEIM, MACINTOSH, AND HUNT,
24, PATERNOSTER-ROW,
AND 23, HOLLES-STREET, CAVENDISH-SQUARE.

1863.

"FOR THE PRIEST'S LIPS SHOULD KEEP KNOWLEDGE, AND THEY SHOULD SEEK THE LAW AT HIS MOUTH; FOR HE IS THE MESSENGER OF THE LORD OF HOSTS."—MAL. II. 7.

TO THE LAYMEN OF ENGLAND.

My Brethren,

A Bishop of our beloved, National, Church has published a dreadful book. It denies the historical veracity of the first six books of the Holy Bible; those which we are wont to call the Pentateuch, or Five Books of Moses, and the Book of Joshua.

He has especially commended his work to your attention; and, certainly, by an ostentatious use of figures, it has a practical and business-like appearance, very well fitted to win your confidence.

I have had occasion, in the discharge of public duty, to read it, and must say that, though not neglectful of its figures, my attention was rivetted by its Hebrew words, and its principles. Upon a close examination, I find it full of errors; which this book (to which I invite your kind attention) professes to expose.

To you, men of law, and men of commerce, I especially appeal; and am content to abide by your decision. If the arguments in this book be sound, as I submit they are, then Bishop Colenso becomes utterly unworthy of any future attention, on similar subjects.

Allow me the honour of remaining,

My Brethren,

Your respectful, humble Servant,

WALTER CHAMBERLAIN.

Bolton, Lancashire, January 13, 1863.

PREFACE.

Soon after Dr. Colenso's book was published it was suggested to the writer of the following pages that, owing to a particular course of reading, he might possibly be able to say a word or two in reply. By return of post he had become painfully conscious how it was he had so soon parted with six bright silver shillings; and, in the course of the day, he had ascertained the value of the production he had received for his money.

One was tempted to conclude that the book itself deserved no answer; but others seemed to think that it did. And if Dr. Colenso has done no other kind of good by its publication, he has certainly contributed very handsomely to the entertainments of the past Christmas season. Editors of periodical journals are especially indebted to him; they have been provided with leading articles for weeks. Till, at last, it is impossible not to feel a sort of pity for this erring Bishop; he has dropped, like a kid, into a herd of peccaries, who, naturally, enjoy the exhilaration of tearing him to pieces. One newspaper attacks him on the left, another shakes him cruelly (but cleverly) on the right, a third comes down with a ponderous article on his front, and a host of other papers administer much-deserved discipline behind. One gentleman takes up the Bishop upon his Hebrew. It is publicly stated, that a precise Irishman will conduct an assault (very desperate) upon Dr. Colenso's arithmetic. And now the author of these pages has arrested him for inaccuracy in the larder; a mere matter, among other questions, of sheep and pigeons. Indeed, whole communities of clergymen have been grievously moved. Rochester has burst into one universal groan, not unmixed with tears, on the attractive banks of Thames; and the sunny diocese of Winchester, with a haziness of view, like that which lends enchantment to the fields of Hampshire, has expressed a conviction, promiscuously, that the Bishop of Natal is sure to be refuted everywhere.

Yet, amid all this clamour, one thing is very noticeable—all these defences of the truth are *ad clerum*. And what need of them? The author will undertake to show, in the course of any one year, just 150 solid reasons, stamped with the Queen's authority, for believing that nothing can be right which assails those doctrines, for preaching which, the revenues of the Church of England are "dispersed abroad, and given to the poor" (clergy?). And he has such implicit confidence in the acquisitions of the Right Reverend Bench, that he is convinced every gentleman among them could produce, in the same short time, several thousands of reasons, equally good, for believing that Dr. Colenso must be wrong. The clergy do not require conviction; and we may all take comfort in the assurance, that, notwithstanding the Bishop of Natal's considerate and soothing appeal on behalf of his brethren, at p. xxxvi of his naughty book, not six among them all will there be, without sense enough to see the hollowness, and the wickedness, and the ignorance, of Dr. Colenso's attack upon the Pentateuch.

Under this conviction, the Author has prepared this "Plain Reply," not for the clergy, but for the laity—especially for the laity. Indeed, he understands, that two eminent divines (to the Hebrew learning of one of whom, all will pay respect) have announced their intention of replying to, and, no doubt, of refuting, Bishop Colenso. It is well, that, at least, one Bishop, should show himself quite a match for another, to the edification of all the clergy. So, stepping gently aside, and leaving these eminent men to those mutual amenities which characterize the affectionate little differences of distinguished clerics, the Author commends the pages of his "Plain Reply" to the consideration of laymen.

It will be found *very* plain. And "is there not a cause?" There are among the laity those who entertain, as they ought, sincere and profound respect for the name, and character, and position, and attainments, of an English Bishop. Whatever comes from the pen of any one such is likely to produce a serious, and lasting, impression upon their minds. They are prepared to give it implicit credence, because it was written by a Bishop. Or else, upon the assumption that even a bishop may be wrong, they begin to entertain in their minds certain deep questions, touching the strength and solidity of the bench upon which the prelates sit, to which it may, perhaps, be as well to make no further allusion. For this class of laymen a plain reply is wanted. There is another class, which entertains such incorrect ideas concerning the state of the Church of England, that it verily believes the clergy generally are not competent to refute notions so unscriptural as those which have lately been published among them; or that, if they can, motives of self-interest, or the trammels of a complicated ecclesiastical system, prevent their doing so. For these a still plainer reply, to Dr. Colenso, is desirable.

The squabblings of Ecclesiastical Courts over matters of religious doctrine are much too tedious to retain the interest of stirring men of the world; and are notoriously distasteful, as well they may be, to all laymen.

Thus, addressing himself to laymen, the Author has been careful to frame his reply in such a way as seems most likely to induce them to read it; which reading he apprehends to be necessary to the utility of his undertaking. He hopes it will be found accurate, and critical enough, without being too laboured; and he trusts also, that it will prove to be so matter-of-fact, and homely, as to be felt convincing. It will, possibly, be thought that, in some places, his style is not becoming the gravity of the occasion. The Author protests that he is not able to regard Dr. Colenso's, as a serious attack upon the Pentateuch. Nor does he think it should be treated as such. It is desirable the laity should know this, and feel it. Such an attack proceeding from any one but a bishop, and an arithmetical bishop, would have been laughed to scorn. It would have been passed round slyly behind people's backs at evening parties; and when the unhappy delinquent made his bow, there would have been an universal titter. If any unfortunate "working" curate had sent out such a book, it would have made him ridiculous in his diocese; have laid heavily on his publisher's shelves; and, perhaps, have introduced him to what Lancashire lads call "the " stone jug," *videlicet*, a gaol. In this case, for debt.

Now, "the Rule of Three" is an excellent domestic apparatus; and Dr. Colenso knows that as well as any man, but not better than most. Yet, before you can apply the Rule of Three to any author's statements, you must first be sure you quite understand him. Dr. Colenso has applied the Rule of Three to the Books of Moses. His misfortune is that he does not understand what Moses has said; so that, while his sums are all right, his calculations are all wrong.

When the Author first received Dr. Colenso's book, he trembled; for he supposed that the Bishop must have brought mathematical science (to which, unhappily! the Author must make no pretensions) to bear upon the Pentateuch, in such a way that a reply would be beyond the powers of any ordinary reader. How great was his relief when he discovered that a comprehensive view of the first four rules of arithmetic, a little Rule of Three, and a small taste of Fractions, was all that was required to enable any one to do the Bishop's sums over again. Let not laymen be deceived on this matter, nor dazzled by a name. This is all that is necessary; and the Author doubts not that many promising young infidels, in certain counties, have been marking down Bishop Colenso's sums upon the tavern-table! This, no doubt, is serious, and the business is serious, also, as regards Dr. Colenso; but, as an assault upon the Holy Bible, and upon the Pentateuch in particular, the Author denies that Dr. Colenso's book is serious at all. The Bishop has been simply, to the horror of his brethren, dashing the favoured casket of his brains against that holy stone of which it has been said, "He that falls upon this stone shall "be broken; but upon whomsoever it shall fall it shall grind him to "powder." May a gracious Saviour turn, and look upon Peter!

But, supposing that, now and then, the Author has been a little jocose, it is not easy to laugh, just now, in Lancashire; and surely no one, of common humanity, will grudge the Author a little pleasantness, after undergoing the painful discipline of minutely examining Dr. Colenso's book. Besides, there is a little something else to be said on this matter. Doctors of Divinity must really discover some means of disguising their physic, or their patients will rather die than take it. It is notorious that laymen never read books of deep divinity; and they are right. Those books are, generally, not readable. It may be questioned how much most of the clergy read them, after they have been dragged through the usual examinations. Is there no style on which the laity may rest between the flowery, but deceptive, meadows of the religious novel, and the woody productions of standard divines?

The Author confesses for himself that he scarcely ever read a book of divinity, but he put it down, convinced that he would have been a happier, and possibly a wiser, man if he had let it alone. One consequence, no doubt, is, that he cannot come up to the height of any great argument in the style usually adopted, and supposed to be approved. He can only hope that, if here and there he falls short of the dignity of the subject, some of his readers will be able to perceive there is some effect, and very much method, in his indiscretion.

The subject is, however, very serious as regards Dr. Colenso, who has cast a passing shadow of disgrace upon the episcopal benches. Yet the Author, while publishing this reply, would take the opportunity of assuring the Bishop of Natal, that he yields to none in the sincere and earnest respect which he feels for all those distinguished in the schools. It is such a man as Dr. Colenso that he, like other clergymen, loves to see made a Bishop, when his heart is right towards God, and his powerful, and well-disciplined mind kept straight in the intricate passages of theology. Oh! what a blessing, what a triumph for Christians, it will be! when that day comes (as come we hope it will, by the grace of Jesus), when Dr. Colenso publicly avows his error, and resumes that place at the head, and in the hearts, of numbers of his brethren to which he is so well entitled!

It is desirable that laymen should not draw any false conclusions from the fact that such a book has been published by a Bishop. They may rely upon it this passing shadow will soon be dispelled. The clergy, as a body, have confidence in the truth, and are able to defend it. If the suppressed utterances which careful listeners may hear in some quarters indicate what may be heard in all, the Bishop of Natal will find very little encouragement among the working clergy. They feel that the dishonour is not theirs; but they are not the less sensible of the dishonour. The laity may be assured with truth that the clergy, as a body, are deeply attached to their Church and to its doctrines; as also to its order, and to its discipline; they are jealous of its honour; and seldom have occasion to feel ashamed of its prelates. The Church stands too well in the hearts of the people, and the learning and the character of her clergy and her bishops are too correctly, and too thoroughly, appreciated by the laity, for her to suffer more than temporary vexation from the wretched publication of Bishop Colenso.

ERRATA.

Page 7, *line* 17, *for* John vi., *read* John v.
,, 50, *note, for* Nolden *read* Noldius.
,, 55, *line* 20, *for* April—May, *read* March—April.
,, 61, *line* 33, *for* aspect, *read its* aspect.
,, 184, *line* 6, *for* caps, *read* cups.

SECTIONS.

No.		PAGE
1.	The Object of Dr. Colenso's Book	2
2.	The Saviour's Opinion of Moses' Writings	6
3.	The Evidence of Apostles and Prophets	9
4.	Hezron and Hamul	10
5.	The Whole Assembly	16
6.	Moses and Joshua addressing all Israel	20
7.	The Extent of the Camp. The Priests' Duties	22
8.	On Reading Holy Scripture	27
9.	Israel "Armed," and Dwelling "in Tents"	29
10.	The Israelites "borrowed"	35
11.	The Israelites in Tents	37
12.	The Israelites Polled	42
13.	The Institution of the Passover	47
14.	Bishop Colenso as Chief Pastor of a Flock	52
15.	The March out of Egypt	56
16.	"Between the Two Evenings"	68
17.	The Number of the Priests, and their Perquisites	79
18.	The Clergy Reserves	89
19.	The Exodus in the "Fourth Generation"	90
20.	The Number of Israelites at the Exodus	100
21.	The Number of the Danites	113
22.	The Number of Levites at the Exodus	115
23.	The Number of the Firstborn	132
24.	The Number of the People, and the Extent of Canaan	145
25.	The War on Midian	148
26.	Israel in the Desert	162
27.	The Scriptural Account of the Desert	164
28.	The Desert of EL TYH	168
29.	Dr. Colenso's Authorities on the Desert	172
30.	His strange Mistake about the Desert	175
31.	The Route of European Travellers	179
32.	Scripture Allusions to the Route in the Desert	181
33.	The Resources of Mount Sinai	188
34.	Israel's Intercourse with Inhabitants of the Desert	191
35.	General Aspect of the Desert	194
36.	Mode of Living in the Desert	199
37.	Conclusion	201

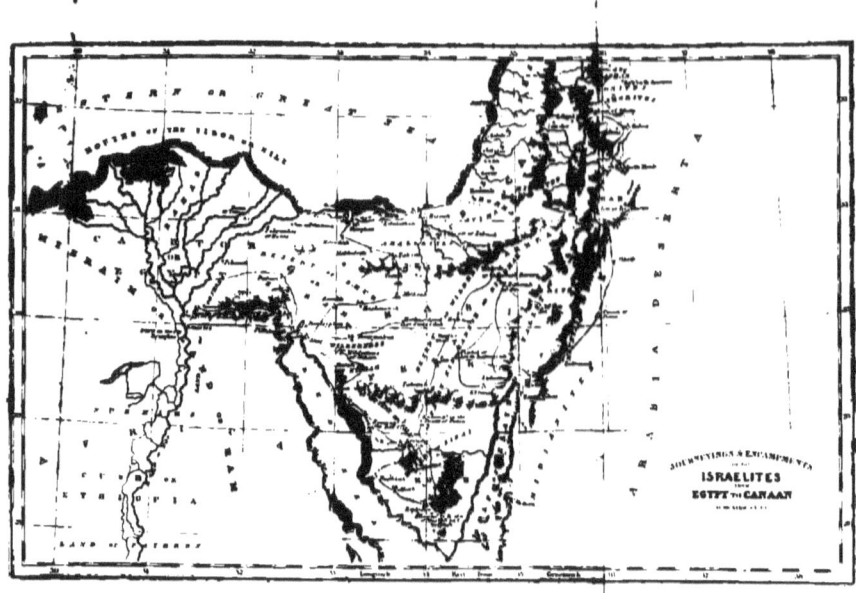

A

PLAIN REPLY

TO

BISHOP COLENSO,

ETC., ETC.

WHEN public servants, of established reputation, who have also conferred great benefits upon their employers, are accused of such confusion and inaccuracy in their accounts as indicate either incompetency or dishonesty, it is no wonder if people are surprised and alarmed. It is hard to believe the charges made against such men; and yet the temerity or the wickedness of those who make them, if false, seems incredible. In such cases they, who undertake the defence of the accused, are accustomed to publish as soon as possible a brief request, joined to some reasons for complying with it, that the public would not too hastily conclude that there are substantial grounds for the accusation. This is all the writer of the present pages undertakes to do. And he would remind all those to whom he appeals, but especially the conductors of certain portions of the daily press, that in the commonest affairs of even secular business it is considered unhandsome, or something worse, to join in open reproaches, or in ridicule or scorn, as if the suspected parties had already been proved guilty.

Dr. Colenso, Bishop of Natal, having previously reposed implicit confidence in the writers of the Pentateuch, and of the book called

Joshua's, has at last detected them either in gross stupidity or in fraud. Whoever those writers were, they have for a short space of three thousand years, at the least, enjoyed a handsome reputation. Though often assailed before, they have hitherto kept their situations with characters unblemished; and have, indeed, obtained to an extraordinary degree the esteem and confidence of most learned and cultivated people. The blessings, too, which they have brought upon all who trusted them are incalculable. But now the Doctor has caught them! By an adroit application of the first four rules of Arithmetic (with a terrible reference, at p. 111, to *logs*) he has entangled them beyond escape. To be sure, that pitiless science of Arithmetic has been understood, far enough for Dr. Colenso's purpose, ever since Adam had teeth and lost them; but then it was never brought to bear, in such a searching way, upon these suspicious and questionable books!

Yet, if the writers of these books have been guilty of the enormous blunders charged against them, they were very clumsy rogues indeed; or, if not rogues, must have belonged to that unhappy class whom most people consider more troublesome, though not so guilty. If they have really made these shocking arithmetical mistakes, it is strange they were not found out long ago; for any one, knowing little more than the figures, might do Dr. Colenso's sums with a piece of chalk on the back of a door. Every layman of common sense (and, like[1] the Bishop, " I commend this subject " more especially to the laity ") will feel that the grossness of the errors, of which the authors of these books are accused, is the best reason we could have for suspecting that the Bishop's calculations are made upon incorrect assumptions. Moreover, *divinity* cannot be learned by figures; and there may be considerations touching the Hebrew language, (of which the Bishop is, evidently, all but ignorant) which vitiate his arithmetical reasoning, by putting him wrong at the commencement.

§ I. THE OBJECT OF DR. COLENSO'S BOOK.

What result does the Bishop seek by this unmasked attack upon the first six books of the Holy Bible? He[2] has " decided that it

---

[1] Dr. Colenso's *Preface*, p. xxxv. [2] *Ibid* p. xx.

"was his duty to give no 'uncertain sound,' but to set down openly at the outset the nature of the issue involved." There is no doubt that he will shock the faith, in Christianity itself, of all those who listen to him with approbation; if they understand the real character of his work. But it is far from being his intention to do so. He only wishes to convince us that, as to supposed historical facts, we none of us rightly understand the Pentateuch; and are altogether mistaken as to its author's name. He suggests that neither Jews nor Christians, neither Prophets nor Apostles, nor (as we shall see) even the Son of God, ever have understood that Pentateuch; nor have they had the slightest just idea who its author was. And he is extremely anxious to give us information. It is on his conscience to do so.

Dr. Colenso has[1] become "convinced of the unhistorical character "of very considerable portions of the Mosaic narrative." He uses "the expression 'unhistorical,' or 'not historically true,' throughout, "rather than 'fictitious,' since the word fiction is frequently under- "stood to imply *a conscious dishonesty* on the part of the writer, an "*intention* to deceive. Yet, in writing the story of the Exodus, from "the ancient legends of his people, the Scripture writer may have had "no more consciousness of doing wrong, or of practising historical "deception, than Homer had, or any of the early Roman annalists;" *i.e.*, the Exodus is a story, or tale; a tale, too, very likely to deceive, but its author was not guilty of any intended deception. Hence, with an offensive pertinacity, he habitually all through his[2] book speaks of "the story," "according to the story," "what the story requires," &c., &c. Not that he denies either the Divine authority, or the inspiration, of the Pentateuch. On the contrary, his conclusion is[3] only "that the Pentateuch, as a whole, cannot "possibly have been written by Moses, or by any one acquainted "personally with the facts which it professes to describe, and further "that the (so called) Mosaic narrative, by whomsoever written, and "though imparting to us, as I fully believe it does, revelations of the "Divine will and character, cannot be regarded as historically true;" but that "it does not, therefore, cease to 'contain the true Word of "'God,' with 'all things necessary to salvation,' to be 'profitable for

---

[1] Dr. Colenso's *Preface*, p. xvii.
[2] See pp. 13, 17, 19, 24, 25, 37, 51, 55, 57, 58, 60, 61, 62, 65, 66, 68, 69, 70, 71, 72, 86, 88, 97, &c., &c.
[3] See pp. 8, 13.

"doctrine, reproof, correction, instruction in righteousness.' It still
"remains an integral portion of that book, which, whatever intermix-
"ture it may show of human elements—of error, infirmity, passion,
"and ignorance—has yet, through God's providence, and the special
"working of His Spirit on the minds of its writers, been the means
"of revealing to us His true name."

The last extract, it will be noticed, expresses Dr. Colenso's opinion of the Holy Bible at large; but, keeping our attention fixed upon the Pentateuch, we may ask, 'How could the God of all truth inspire, by the Holy Ghost, in any degree any man to put together "a story" which He knew to be false, but knew also that men would believe to be true; and which, as matter of fact, they have believed to be true?'

Of course the entire theory of "Scripture inspiration" is thus shivered to pieces at a blow. And writers, who express such sentiments, know this, and intend this; and also feel that the whole question of Scripture-Inspiration must be reconsidered and remodelled—to suit their purpose. Accordingly Dr. Colenso believes[1] that "There are others, doubtless, in the Christian ministry,
"who have attained to wider views of Scripture-Inspiration, and who
"do not suppose that those narratives are historically true, and yet
"'believe unfeignedly' in the Divine authority of the Scriptures."
Under this conviction he proposes to inculcate new ideas of the nature of Inspiration; for, says he, "in order that we may give due
"honour to the Bible, as containing a message of God to our souls,
"it is surely necessary that we take, ourselves, in the first place, and
"teach others to take, a right and true view both of the contents of
"the Book and the nature of Inspiration."

"Of the contents of the Book," as well as of "the nature of
"Inspiration." For a new theory of Inspiration is, in effect, a new mode of Interpretation. To discover, and publish, which the Bishop thinks "may be the step, which God in His providence calls us to
"take in the present age, in advance of the past generation."

Unfortunately, however, for us working clergymen, and for our congregations, the laity, this new mode of interpretation has not yet been fixed on, nor is it likely to be. Men like Dr. Colenso have long and often tried to invent one, but, in the opinion of able judges, have as often failed. What are we poor souls to do meanwhile? We are

[1] See pp. 150, 151, 152.

panting for instruction. Are people to forsake their churches, clergymen their pulpits, pastors their flocks? Is the distant mission-field to be left to the lion and the bear until all obscurities in the books of Moses are cleared away? Are we to take our hands off the plough every moment some nervous, or eccentric, or wicked shepherd boy cries, Wolf? Are the operations of the Christian Church, and our laymen's confidence in its doctrines and teaching, to be suspended, until a score or two of wrong-headed gentlemen have agreed upon a new mode of interpretation? They have been trying long enough, and are farther from agreeing than ever. Besides, if their precious theory, for which they give us paper, were really reduced to a system, and published, perhaps it might not prove convincing to the rest of their brethren. And, if not, are we all to bate breath, and gaze eagerly for another? These gentlemen wish to shatter the Portland vase, and, like greedy jobbers, blandly tell us they can make it stronger and more elegant than it was before. But the strong sense of our laity, sustained by the grace of God, will enable them to see through the folly of such pretensions. Men of business will hold fast the currency of gold until a more precious metal has been proved fit for practical circulation. They will feel instinctively how unlikely it is that the oldest national history in the world, which inspired Apostles[1] numbered among "the oracles of God," should be proved full of contradictions, absurdities, and impossibilities,[2] by a few little sums in addition and subtraction.

No new theory of Interpretation can be received, unless it submit to two conditions—*first*, that Moses wrote the Pentateuch; *second*, that its miracles are "historically true." For,[3] in several places, itself claims to have had Moses for its author, and itself maintains that certain recorded events were miraculous. Dr. Colenso cannot help us in the least. There is an irreconcilable enmity between the Pentateuch and him. For he emphatically denies that Moses wrote the Pentateuch; and if he admit one miracle, he may as well admit all, and then his book falls to pieces. We have but one alternative. If we believe Dr. Colenso, we must utterly reject the Pentateuch.

[1] Acts vii. 38; Rom. iii. 2, 9; iv. 5.
[2] Dr. Colenso's book, pp. 61, 90, 113, 138, 143.
[3] Exod. xvii. 14; xxiv. 4; Num. xxxiii. 2, &c., &c. For the whole argument see Macdonald's Pentateuch, vol. i., pp. 317—359. Clarks, Edinburgh. 1861.

§ II. THE SAVIOUR'S OPINION OF MOSES' WRITINGS.

The Bishop has correctly apprehended the serious nature of his undertaking, and has not failed to anticipate some of its possible consequences. He thinks it probable that some persons may be of opinion that the truth of Christianity depends, in a considerable degree, upon the historical truth of the Pentateuch. They may feel convinced that Christ, as the Son of God, and the apostles (at moments when their fullest inspiration cannot safely be denied), did say, in various ways, that Moses wrote the Pentateuch, and that its narratives are historically true. If so, what becomes of the Christian religion, supposing Dr. Colenso's book to be sound?

He has not lost sight of this argument; but does it no real justice; apparently, through the faintness of his perception, as to how great an extent the New Testament depends, for correct interpretation, upon the Old. Take, for example, that remarkable passage (John v. 46, 47), to which Dr. Colenso himself alludes, "For had ye believed Moses, ye would have believed me: for he wrote of me. But if ye believe not his writings, how shall ye believe my words?" The Saviour speaks in this place, not merely as man, but as God. It was on this occasion that the Jews sought to kill Him, "because he not only had broken the sabbath, but said also that God was his Father, making himself equal with God." Let that discourse be read carefully, from ver. 17 to ver. 47, and none can fail to perceive that, throughout it, Jesus professes to speak in His Divine character, as the Son of God. He speaks there on doctrines pertaining to everlasting life; of the resurrection of the dead, and of eternal judgment. And being such a discourse, and referring (as it repeatedly does) to His Divine nature, He concludes it with the solemn words referred to by Bishop Colenso. He had warned them to "search the Scriptures," for they testified of Him in His Divine character; and, in the same sense, He adds of Moses, "for he wrote of me." When Jesus said, in that discourse, "that all men should honour the Son, even as they honour the Father," or that "the dead shall hear the voice of the Son of God, and they that hear shall live," he spake avowedly as the Son of God. How can we separate His declaration concerning Moses, "he wrote of me," from that Divine character, as the Son of God, in which all along he had professed to be speaking?

Similar remarks might be made on our Lord's discourse with Nicodemus (John iii. 1—21), in which He refers to Moses lifting up the serpent in the wilderness, and the Jews being miraculously healed in consequence. And to that other beautiful discourse (John vi. 30—58), in which He calls Himself the true bread from heaven, and refers to the miraculous supply of manna. In these two cases, also, he speaks as the Son of God, and bears his own testimony to two of the greatest miracles in the Pentateuch, as to "historical fact."

Dr. Colenso has attempted (Preface, p. xxx.) to set aside such Scriptures by hinting that we can scarcely tell when our Saviour speaks merely in his human character, and when in his Divine. This is an old Unitarian device, but cannot avail in the instances referred to. Our Saviour speaks, in John vi. 45, 47, avowedly as the Son of God; and his hearers felt that he did. So, too, He did to Nicodemus, as the verses John iii. 16, 17, testify. And so, also, He did when discoursing on the manna. Moreover, the attempt made by the Bishop to mix up, with this discussion, a question of the knowledge possessed by Jesus, in his humanity, of matters of a scientific, psychological (or philological) character is nothing to the purpose. The blessed Saviour is solemnly discoursing to the Jews of salvation, and as solemnly, and openly, speaks as the Son of God, on the occasions above mentioned.

No doubt, our Saviour did accommodate Himself to the popular ideas of the Jews on various occasions; but not evilly or falsely so. Nor do I venture to suppose that Dr. Colenso would adopt the idea of such 'accommodation' in the bad sense intended by certain writers of the present day. Our Saviour, as the Son of God spake of Moses' writings, in the Jewish popular sense; as though He had said, "You know what books you call Moses' writings—read them—he wrote of Me;"—where the Son of God assures the Jews, and us, that Moses wrote those books they thought were his—viz., The Law, contained in Genesis, Exodus, Leviticus, Numbers, and Deuteronomy—and that, in such books, Moses wrote of Him. So, too, on other occasions,[1] the Son of God was wont to

[1] Matt. xxii. 40; Luke xvi. 16; xxix. 31, &c., &c.

speak of "the law and the prophets," or "Moses and the prophets," in the Jewish popular sense;—thus ascribing, as we just now said, the five books of the law to Moses, and also ascribing the book of Joshua to him whose name it bears. For the Jews imputed the various books of the prophets to those persons whose names they severally bear; and among those prophets they reckoned Joshua, and assigned to him that book which we call his.

But where did Moses write of Christ? In the Pentateuch, nearly everywhere; as the places referred to below will prove.[1] Surely, the promise in Eden was of Christ; Abel's sacrifice had reference to Christ; the promise to Abraham was concerning Christ; so also was Abraham's intended sacrifice of Isaac; the promises to Isaac and to Jacob were of Christ; the Angel in the bush, and in the fiery-cloudy pillar, "the Angel of the Covenant," was Christ; the paschal sacrifice in Egypt, and the Levitical sacrifices, and High Priesthood, had reference to Christ; the manna for forty years typified Christ; so did the lifting up of the serpent; so did the rock from which the water flowed miraculously: what can we exclude? If we take these references, which the New Testament abundantly sanctions; and if we take also those contexts, which the construction of the books shows to be inseparable from them; we shall have, undoubtedly, the great mass of the first four books of the Pentateuch. And as for Deuteronomy, Dr. Colenso will not care to dispute about that, seeing it is but a republication of the leading parts of the law contained in Exodus, Leviticus, and Numbers.

Also let it be particularly noticed that our Saviour, as the Son of God, does bear His personal testimony to the literal "historical truth" of two of the most astounding miracles recorded by Moses, viz., the miraculous healing of the people, who looked to the serpent which Moses lifted up; and to the forty years' fall of manna. Having the Son of God's testimony to these, as to historical facts, what else is there in the Pentateuch we need hesitate to believe? Nor is this the whole case; for when the Son of God refers, generally, to Moses' writings, in the popular Jewish sense, He not only asserts them to have been written by Moses, but also to be,

---

[1] Gen. iii. 15; iv. 4; xxii. 10—18; xxvi. 2—5; xxviii. 13—15; and xlix. 10. Exod. iii. 2; xii. 5; xiv. 19; xvii. 5; xxiii. 20; xxviii. 30—36. Levit., *passim, as to the sacrifices and High-priesthood*; Numb. ix. 15; xx. 11; xxi. 9.

what the Jews thought them, viz., narratives "historically true." Admitting possible miscopies in manuscripts; admitting difficulties, or obscurities, of construction; the broad, general fact must also be admitted—viz., that we possess the Pentateuch now, in the main, as the Jews possessed it in our Saviour's days; and that, as such, He gave Divine testimony, as the Son of God, that Moses wrote it, and that it is historically true.

§ III. THE EVIDENCE OF APOSTLES AND PROPHETS.

After the above, it is of little consequence to observe that the Prophets, the Evangelists, and the Apostles, at moments when their inspiration by the Holy Ghost cannot be rationally doubted, bore to Moses the same testimony as their Master. But the places, referred to below,[1] may be consulted, as especially adapted to fix this argument upon our minds. For the allusions to Moses, and the books which he wrote, are all through the rest of Holy Scripture so habitual, multitudinous, and minute, that only a very small selection of such places can be permitted us.

If these places, and others which the reader can select for himself, be reflected on, it must become apparent, beyond reasonable contradiction, that the sacred writers habitually recognise the five books, the Pentateuch, as having been written by Moses; and constantly refer to the most wonderful events, recorded by him, as to well-known and fully accredited "historical facts." So that it may be truly said, we have not only the testimony of the Son of God, but also of the prophets and the apostles, whom He inspired, in direct contradiction to Dr. Colenso's book.

And the contexts of Holy Scripture, thus appealed to, are so extensive that no theories as to the nature, or degree, of Scripture-Inspiration, can possibly shake the testimony they bring. Surely, if ever man were inspired, Ezekiel was so, in a mysterious degree; surely Stephen was so, when "full of the Holy Ghost," speaking before the Sanhedrim. But let Scripture-Inspiration be admitted, in

---

[1] Ps. lxviii.; cvi.; cxxxv.; cxxxvi.; Isa. xi. 11; Jer. ii. 6; xi. 4, 5; xxxi. 32; Ezek. xx. 5—26; Dan. ix. 10—15; Amos vi. 5; Mark xii. 19; John i. 45; Acts vii. 2—51; xv. 21; 1 Cor. x. 1—13; Heb. iii. to xi.

ever so faint a degree, it is conclusive for our present purpose. Let it, for instance, be acknowledged (and probably Dr. Colenso does not deny this) that the Epistle to the Hebrews is a part of canonical Scripture, and that its writer was inspired, in ever so general a sense, to write it, then it follows that his testimony to the Pentateuch, and indeed to the book of Joshua also, as to books narrating "historical fact," is conclusive. So, too, as regards Stephen's speech, and St. Paul's admonition to the Corinthians, in 1 Cor. x. 1—13. And such testimony becomes, in fact, the testimony of the Holy Ghost to the historical truth of the books in question.

§ IV. HEZRON AND HAMUL.

However, let me proceed to the refutation of those specific charges which Dr. Colenso has brought against the Pentateuch; and, in doing so, let me exhibit his unfitness to be a translator of, or a commentator on, these Hebrew books.

It is several times[1] affirmed in Holy Scripture, that all the souls, out of Jacob's loins, which went down into Egypt, were threescore and ten. St. Stephen, indeed, "full of the Holy Ghost," does, for some reason or other, prefer to quote from[2] the Septuagint, and gives them as threescore and fifteen. The Septuagint itself gives to Joseph nine sons, and not only two, Ephraim and Manasseh. This variation in number, acceded to by Stephen, under such extraordinary circumstances, suggests at once some important considerations concerning the increase of the Israelites in Egypt, and Dr. Colenso's assumptions thereon, to be noticed at a future page. It also suggests to us that the computation of seventy souls, as all that were to be reckoned to Jacob, when he went down into Egypt, is made upon some principle, and from some unexplained motive, which (as understood by the Jewish translators 300 years B.C.) did not require that literally *all* should be included; as to the biblical use of which word *all*, we shall have a few remarks to make presently.

I am aware that commentators have professed to consider inaccurate

---

[1] Gen. xlvi. 8, 26, 27; Exod. i. 1, 5; Deut. x. 22.
[2] Acts vii. 14; Septuagint, Gen. xlvi. 27; Exod. i. 5.

the place of the Septuagint thus referred to. But there is the fact that Stephen, at such a moment, was permitted so to quote, and that, to many minds, will be of more weight than the doubtful criticisms of certain commentators.

However, Bishop Colenso states his first objection thus:—

> "19. 'And the sons of Judah, Er, and Onan, and Shelah, and Pharez, and Zarah; but Er and Onan died in the land of Canaan; and the sons of Pharez, Hezron, and Hamul.' (Gen. xlvi. 12.) It appears to me to be certain that the writer here means to say that Hezron and Hamul were *born in the land of Canaan*, and were among the seventy persons (including Jacob himself and Joseph and his two sons) who came into Egypt with Jacob. He repeats the words again and again:—'These are the names of the children of Israel, which came into Egypt.' (Ver. 8.) 'All the souls *that came with Jacob into Egypt*, which came out of his loins, besides Jacob's sons' wives, were threescore and six' (ver. 26), which they would not be without Hezron and Hamul. 'And the sons of Joseph, which were born him in Egypt, were two souls; and all the souls of the house of Jacob, which *came into Egypt*, were threescore and ten.' (Ver. 27.) So, again, we read:—'These are the names of the children of Israel, which *came into Egypt;* every man and his household *came with Jacob.*' 'And all the souls, that came out of the loins of Jacob, were seventy souls; for Joseph was in Egypt already.' (Ex. i. 1, 5.) 'Thy fathers *went down into Egypt*, with threescore and ten persons; and now the Lord thy God hath made thee as the stars of heaven for multitude.' (Deut. x. 22.) I assume, then, that it is absolutely undeniable that the narrative of the Exodus distinctly involves the statement, that the sixty-six persons, 'out of the loins of Jacob,' mentioned in Gen. xlvi., and no others, went down with him into Egypt."—Pp. 17—19.

He then proceeds to show, what we are not concerned to deny, that since Judah was forty-two years old, when he went into Egypt, and was married when about twenty; since, also, he had three sons (Er, Onan, and Shelah), who each had grown to maturity before Pharez was born of Tamar, by Judah himself; therefore, the sons of Pharez, Hezron, and Hamul, *could not have been born in Canaan.* And he adds:—" Yet the statement that Hezron and Hamul were born in the "land of Canaan is vouched so positively by the many passages "above quoted, which sum up the seventy souls, that, to give up "this point, is to give up an essential point of the whole story."

The question is, Does the writer say that Hezron and Hamul were born in Canaan? He does not.

1. Dr. Colenso has misquoted in a most singular way. The verse, with its punctuation, in the English Bible, is:—" And the

sons of Judah; Er, and Onan, and Shelah, and Pharez, and Zarah: but Er and Onan died in the land of Canaan. And the sons of Pharez were Hezron and Hamul." The Bishop leaves out "were;" unintentionally, no doubt. And he seems quite innocent of knowing, that all depends upon that word "were," with its conjunction: *i.e.*, all depends upon the presence of ויהיו, in the Hebrew text. It is, also, remarkable that the Bishop's *punctuation* of the verse is accurate, according to the Hebrew; only, when copying that, he did not see the word ויהיו. The Bishop puts a *semicolon* after the word "Canaan," which is right; the Authorized Version has a *full-stop*, that is wrong.

2. If we take only the verse, Gen. xlvi. 12, the writer does not state that Hezron and Hamul were born in Canaan. He says that they were sons of Pharez, and intimates something else, which the Bishop could not perceive.

3. If we take the other passages, referred to by Dr. Colenso, it is plain that the expression, "out of Jacob's loins," includes Jacob's grandsons. It includes Ephraim and Manasseh, who were born in Egypt, and may, therefore, include Hezron and Hamul, even though they were born there.

4. Similarly the expressions, "went down into Egypt," "came into Egypt," give us no reason to suppose that Hezron and Hamul were born in Canaan, for the same expressions are (at Gen. xlvi. 27, and Exod. i. 1, 5) used also of Joseph's two sons, who were born in that land, and never "went" or "came" into it, literally speaking, any more than Hezron and Hamul, who were born there too.

5. Ephraim and Manasseh may be said, metaphorically, to have gone or come into Egypt, because they were "in the loins" of their father Joseph, who literally did so. In the same sense, Hezron and Hamul went, or came, down thither; being "in the loins" of Pharez, when he went down there. But, if so, asks[1] Dr. Colenso, "Why not also the great-great-grandsons, and so on, *ad infinitum?*" The reason is, that Hezron and Hamul were selected to be heads of families, as we see in Num. xxvi. 21; their names it was, therefore, necessary to specify, and especially because they were put in the place of Er and Onan; the names of other grandsons born in Egypt, it was not. Besides, the question itself is absurd, as the *ad infinitum* plainly shows.

[1] Page 22, Ans. (i.) (vi.).

6. The expression, "came with Jacob," gives us no reason to suppose that Hezron and Hamul were born in Canaan; for it is used of Joseph, in passages above referred to, and we are sure that he did not go down to Egypt "*with* Jacob." The Bishop seems unaware that the phrases, ליעקב, Gen. xlvi. 26, and את יעקב, Exod. i. 1, mean not necessarily, nor exactly, *with*, in the English sense. They would be as well, or better, translated, "as Jacob's," or "for Jacob," or "as to Jacob," or "in relation to Jacob;" in fact, "counted with Jacob," or "reckoned to him;" and, therefore, might include, not only Jacob himself, but also all souls to be reckoned to his house, as at that time.

The Bishop should be careful how he, who appears to know little, or nothing, of Hebrew, charges with inaccuracy (pp. 22, 23,) the writer of such a lucid book as the Pentateuch, who, to say the least, was a first-rate Hebrew scholar.

7. We cannot reasonably suppose the sacred writer to have been guilty of so gross an absurdity as to say that Hezron and Hamul were born to Pharez before the descent into Egypt, when that person would have been about four or five years old. Commentators suggest, as Dr. Colenso observes, that Hezron and Hamul are counted among the seventy souls, because they were placed in the stead of Er and Onan, sons of Judah who died in Canaan. In reply, the Bishop asks (p. 24) two questions: *First*, "How is it that Hezron and Hamul, the sons " of *Pharez*, are mentioned; and Zabdi, and the other sons of " *Zarah*, are not mentioned?" *Second*, "If Hezron and Hamul are " substituted for Er and Onan, for whom are Heber and Malchiel, " the sons of Beriah, Asher's son (ver. 17), supposed to be sub- " stituted?"

The reader can reply to the first of these questions by referring to Num. xxvi. 19—22, where he will find that Zarah reckons for one family, "of Zerah, the family of the Zarhites;" but that Pharez reckons for three, "of Pharez, the family of the Pharzites," "of Hezron, the family of the Hezronites; of Hamul, the family of the Hamulites." In fact, this passage plainly intimates the substitution of Hezron and Hamul for Er and Onan. I am afraid that Dr. Colenso included the Hezronites and Hamulites among the Pharzites; whereas the writer's meaning is to separate the Hezronites and Hamulites, as distinct families; and to leave other sons of Pharez, under the title of Pharzites. Two of Pharez' sons, Hezron and Hamul, are thus registered as heads of houses: no son of Zarah is. Probably this was done by Jacob's direction, to fill up the number of Judah's sons, to whom he had given the royalties of the firstborn, which he had taken from Reuben. (Gen. xlviii. 5, 22; xlix. 4.) That Jacob did exercise the power, under Divine direction, of bestowing peculiar family and (therefore) national privileges, upon certain sons, to the exclusion of others, we are sure. "And now thy two sons, Ephraim and Manasseh, which were born unto thee in the land of Egypt, before I came unto thee into Egypt, are mine; as Reuben and Simeon, they shall be mine." (Gen. xlviii. 5, 6.) The Bishop says, this is nothing to the purpose, because Ephraim and Manasseh were adopted as heads of tribes; Hezron and Hamul were not. True; Ephraim and Manasseh were, under Divine direction, taken as heads of tribes, for Joseph, and for Levi; Joseph thus having the property-rights of the firstborn, viz., a double portion, which Jacob had taken from Reuben. The royalties of the firstborn were, as I have said, taken from Reuben, because he foully sinned, and were given to Judah. And (is it unlikely?) to make up, in his posterity, that part of the birthright to Judah, Jacob did for him the same thing, in principle, as he did for Joseph. Two sons of Joseph he took as heads of tribes; two grandsons of Judah he took as heads of houses, to make up for the loss of Er and Onan. The principle of action is the same in each case. Reuben's birthright was shared between Judah and Joseph, and extraordinary means taken to secure to each his part.

Is it nothing that Hezron is that particular grandson of Judah, through whom the Son of God assumed the human nature? (Matt. i. 3; Luke iii. 33.) There is the royalty: Hezron progenited the true King of Israel.

By referring to Ruth iv. 12, Dr. Colenso will learn that the blessing of Pharez' family was proverbial in Judah: "Let thy house be like the house of Pharez," &c. See also Ruth iv. 18—22.

8. To answer Dr. Colenso's second question, "For whom are "Heber and Malchiel, Asher's grandsons, substituted?" brings us to the pith of the matter. For *no one:* and that makes all the difference. And if Dr. Colenso will take his Hebrew Bible, he will see, that the writer introduces the names of Hezron and Hamul, as

he does not introduce those of Heber and Malchiel; nor, indeed, any other names mentioned at Gen. xlvi. 8—27.

The following is a possible, and (I believe) is the correct translation of ver. 12 :—" And the sons of Judah, Er, and Onan, and Shelah, and Pharez, and Zarah: but Er and Onan died in the land of Canaan; therefore, there were the sons of Pharez, Hezron and Hamul."

Let me make this plain. The punctuation of the English version is certainly wrong. There should be only a *semicolon* after the word " Canaan." The one sentence, having two clauses, is as follows ; " but Er and Onan died in the land of Canaan; therefore there were Pharez' sons, Hezron and Hamul:" viz., to Judah for sons. The ellipsis is of לבנים ליודה. The use of the substantive verb, and its prefix, here fixes its sense. Any one can see, by looking at an English Bible, that it is not usual in Hebrew genealogies to use the words " was," " were,". &c., &c. Thus, Gen. xlvi. 8—24, it is written, " And the sons of Reuben," " And the sons of Levi," " And the sons of Asher," &c., &c. And in this particular genealogy the writer never once uses the substantive verb, in introducing the names, except those of Hezron and Hamul. Why does he there? Just criticism says he has a special object; and that object is expressed by the peculiar use of the prefix ו. It is to throw back the statement of Hezron and Hamul's birth, as consequent to the statement of Er and Onan's death:—Er and Onan died in Canaan; therefore there lived, as sons to Judah, Hezron and Hamul.

Let the reader examine all other genealogies in Genesis. There is no similar use of ויחיו in one of them. The seeming cases are Gen. xxxv. 22; xxxvi. 11, 22. But neither of these is really like the one before us, Gen. xlvi. 12. The forms ויהי, ויהיו, &c., are properly used to introduce a new fact or narrative, naturally suggested by what precedes, but not necessarily connected with it: *e.g.*, " Now it came to pass," &c., &c. " Now the sons of Jacob were twelve," &c. (Gen. xxxv. 22.) In Gen. xxxvi. 11, 22, the writer's purpose is formally to carry on the genealogy, of which he had just mentioned the root, " These are the names of the sons of Esau," &c. " Moreover the sons of Eliphaz were," &c., &c. " These are the dukes of the Horite," &c. " Moreover the children of Lotan were," &c., &c. He had introduced no fresh fact: in Gen.

xlvi. 12 he does introduce a fresh fact, viz., "Er and Onan died in the land of Canaan;" and to that fresh fact the ויהיו carries the statement of Hezron and Hamul's birth.

All depends upon the rendering of ו as the conjunction. *However, but, therefore,* &c., &c. I give abundant examples below,[1] out of the book of Genesis.

Should it be thought that this is a case of mere *pointing*, I beg to say it is not so. The situation alone of ויהיו determines its force. But if it were only a case of pointing, this is precisely a case of that kind in which the pointing should be held in serious regard. That the effect of the pointing, as it stands, will justify the rendering proposed may be seen from the authorities.[2] Dr. Colenso limps along, disregarding the text and the pointing equally.

"Er and Onan died in the land of Canaan; therefore there were the sons of Pharez, Hezron, and Hamul." If Dr. Colenso can prove this translation to be inadmissible, we shall be glad to see him do so. If he feels that it may be, even possibly, correct, all he has said about Hezron and Hamul comes to nothing.

§ V. THE WHOLE ASSEMBLY.

Dr. Colenso's next objection is so extraordinary that, were we not compelled to believe him serious, we should decline to notice it. One feels really ashamed to think so; but, with this fancied objection before us, it is difficult to suppose that the Bishop of Natal is competent to read critically, or to explain, the easiest chapter in the Hebrew Bible. If not, then he is one of the last men who should have ventured a hostile attack on the Pentateuch. It is really necessary to warn the laity not to be led away by the pretentious appearance of the Bishop's publication.

, Continually in the Pentateuch, as elsewhere, we read of "The Congregation," "The Assembly," "The whole Assembly," "All the Congregation," of the children of Israel. Dr. Colenso cites the

[1] Gen. iii. 23; vii. 21; viii. 9; xii. 10; xx. 9; xxix. 33; xxxix. 4, 6; xlviii. 17. See also Nold. Concord., Heb. Par., p. 289, 297, sub vocibus, *quare* and *ideo*.

[2] Glassius' Philolog. Sacra., i., p. 602; Gesen. Heb. Gram., p. 191, 231; Lee's Heb. Gram. p. 156.

places referred to below,[1] of which we take the following, as effectually raising the question to be answered:—" And Jehovah spake unto Moses. . . . Gather thou the Congregation together unto the door of the Tabernacle of the Congregation." . . . " And the assembly was gathered unto the door of the Tabernacle of the Congregation." (Lev. viii. 4.) And "There was not a word of all which Moses commanded, which Joshua read not before all the congregation of Israel, with the women, and the little ones, and the strangers that were conversant among them." (Josh. viii. 35.)

But, reasons Bishop Colenso, though some of the passages may well include, as Joshua viii. 35 does, the women and the children and the old men, suppose we take only the 603,550 warriors. (Num. ii. 32.) They were to assemble " at the door of the tabernacle of the congregation," and, therefore, must have come within the court.

" 34. This vast body of people, then, received on this occasion, and on other similar occasions, as we are told, an express command from Jehovah Himself, to assemble 'at the door of the Tabernacle of the Congregation.' We need not press the word ' all,' so as to include every individual man of this number. Still the expression, 'all the Congregation,' the 'whole Assembly,' must be surely understood to imply the *main body* of those who were able to attend, especially when summoned thus solemnly by the direct voice of Jehovah Himself. The *mass* of these 603,550 men *ought*, we must believe, to have obeyed such a command, and hastened to present themselves at the ' door of the Tabernacle of the Congregation.'

" 35. As the text says distinctly, 'at the door of the Tabernacle,' they must have come *within the Court*. And this, indeed, was necessary for the purpose for which they were summoned on this occasion, namely, to witness the ceremony of the consecration of Aaron and his sons to the priestly office. This was to be performed inside the Tabernacle itself, and could only, therefore, be seen by those standing at the door.

" 36. Now the whole width of the *Tabernacle* was ten cubits, or eighteen feet, reckoning the cubit at 1·824 feet (see *Bagster's Bible*), and its length was thirty cubits or fifty-four feet, as may be gathered from E. xxvi. (Horne's *Introd.*, iii. p. 232.) Allowing two feet in width for each full-grown man, nine men could just have stood in front of it. Supposing, then, that ' all the Congregation' of adult males in the prime of life had given due heed to the Divine summons, and had hastened to take their stand, side by side, as closely as possible, in front, not merely of the *door*, but of the whole *end* of the Tabernacle, in which the door was, they would have reached, allowing eighteen inches between each rank of nine men, for a distance of more than 100,000 feet,—in fact, nearly *twenty miles!*

---

[1] Lev. viii. 14; Exod. xii. 6; xvi. 2, 3; Num. i. 18; x. 3, 4; xiv. 5; xv. 36; xvi. 19, 25, 47; Josh. viii. 35.

"37. Further, the *Court* was one hundred cubits in length and fifty cubits in breadth (E. xxvii. 18); that is, it was about 180 feet long and ninety feet broad. And, since the length of the Tabernacle, as above, was fifty-four feet, we have, for the space left between the Tabernacle and the hangings of the Court, before and behind, 126 feet, that is, sixty-three feet in front and sixty-three feet behind, or, perhaps, we may say, eighty-four feet in front and forty-two feet behind. Thus, then, eighty-four feet would represent that portion of the men in the prime of life, who could by any possibility have been crowded inside the Court in front of the Tabernacle, while the whole body would be represented by 100,000 feet! Or, if we suppose them to fill the *whole width* of the Court, ninety feet, instead of merely the space directly in front of the Tabernacle, eighteen feet, still the whole body would extend to a distance of 6,706 yards, nearly *four miles;* whereas that portion of them who could find any room to stand in front of the Tabernacle, filling up the whole width of the Court, would be represented by eighty-four feet, or twenty-eight yards!

"38. But how many would the *whole Court* have contained? Its area (sixty yards by thirty yards) was 1,800 square yards, and the area of the Tabernacle itself (eighteen yards by six yards) was 108 square yards. Hence the area of the Court outside the Tabernacle was 1,692 square yards. But the 'whole Congregation' would have made a body of people, nearly twenty miles—or, more accurately, 33,530 yards—long, and eighteen feet or six yards wide; that is to say, packed closely together, they would have covered an area of 201,180 square yards. In fact, the Court, when thronged, could only have held 5,000 people; whereas the able-bodied men alone exceeded 600,000. Even the ministering Levites, 'from thirty to fifty years old,' were 8,580 in number (N. iv. 48); only 504 of these could have stood within the Court in front of the Tabernacle, and not two-thirds of them could have entered the Court, if they had filled it from one end to the other. It is inconceivable how, under such circumstances, 'all the Assembly,' 'the whole Congregation,' could have been summoned to attend 'at the door of the Tabernacle,' by the express command of Almighty God."

"We need not," says the Bishop, "press the word 'all' so as to "include every individual man of this number." A remark indicative of one of two bad things, either great ignorance of Holy Scripture, or a sad want of candour. The mode of speech employed is one of 'commonest occurrence in the Hebrew Bible; and the expressions, "all the congregation," "the whole assembly," &c., &c., may mean either certain selected persons representing *all*, or as many as could possibly be accommodated, or could conveniently attend. Take one of the Doctor's selected examples.[1] So "all the congregation" stoned the blasphemer. Does he suppose that the 603,549 remaining

[1] Lev. xxiv. 10—14; Deut. xvii. 6, 7; Acts vii. 58.

"warriors" were, each of them, engaged in stoning this poor wretch? The fourteenth verse might have given the Bishop a hint, "Let all that heard lay their hands upon his head"; the witnesses commenced the execution, which was completed by persons deputed for all the congregation. But since it was a public, judicial, and therefore national act, "all the congregation" are said to do it. So, as will be seen, on other public and national matters certain selected persons represented "all the congregation," who were on that account spoken of as summoned, and attending. So, again, the people were scattered "throughout all the land of Egypt" (Exod. v. 12) to gather stubble instead of straw. Does the Bishop suppose that the people wandered all over Egypt, from the waters of the Mediterranean to the Cataracts of Syene, to gather stubble? "All" is here put, generally, for a great distance. So, all the dust of Egypt became lice. (Exod. viii. 17.) Does the Bishop suppose that literally *all* the dusty surface of Egypt, every particle of it, one hundred and fifty leagues long and from three to seven wide ("Volney's Travels," vol. i., p. 11) became lice?

But there are passages which teach us plainly that "all the congregation," or "the whole assembly," &c., are spoken of as being summoned, and present, when only certain persons, representing them, *e.g.*, the elders, heads of tribes, priests, &c., were intended. Thus Moses is told to speak "unto all the congregation" about the Passover; and he, consequently, called "for all the elders of Israel, and said unto them." To instruct the elders was to instruct the people; and, on various public occasions, to summon the elders was to summon "all the congregation." So Moses said (Deut. xxxi. 28—30), "Gather unto me all the elders of your tribes, and your officers, that I may speak these words in their ears, and call heaven and earth to record against them." And yet it is added, "And Moses spake in the ears of all the congregation of Israel the words of this song, until they were ended." To speak "in the ears of the elders, and officers," was to speak "in the ears of all the congregation" whom they represented. Dr. Colenso, to be consistent, ought to require, in a passage like this, that Moses should speak all the song referred to close into the ear of every man, woman, and child of Israel. So, in later times, "David consulted with the captains of thousands and hundreds, and with every leader"; and then it is added, "And David said unto all the congregation of Israel." (1 Chron. xiii. 1, 2.) Again, the manslayer was to "stand before the congregation in judgment," *i.e.*, before the judges deputed, for that purpose, by " the congregation "; and "the congregation shall judge between the slayer and the revenger of blood," "and the congregation shall deliver the slayer out of the hand of the revenger of blood, and the congregation shall restore him," &c. (Num. xxxv. 12—25.) In which cases, " all the congregation " means certain persons, deputed to act for it.

Take one more example : " The children of Israel shall put their hands upon the Levites." (Num. viii. 10.) It means certain elders, or officers, representing the people for that occasion.

§ VI. MOSES, AND JOSHUA, ADDRESSING ALL ISRAEL.

It is true, as Dr. Colenso observes (p. 32) that, sometimes, " the " *elders* are plainly distinguished from *all the congregation*"; the elders, and other officers, were sometimes assembled, as distinct from the congregation. Thus, (Numb. x. 1), when one trumpet was blown, "the princes, heads of thousands, of Israel " were to assemble ; when two, " all the assembly shall assemble themselves together at the door of the tabernacle of the congregation." Also it is true that Joshua's language, (ch. viii. 35), is as inclusive as it can be. Yet common sense explains the passage, even were there no other means of doing so. Does the Bishop imagine that poor Joshua sat down, in the open, to write with a million or two of people about him ; to write, (ver. 32), " in the presence of the children of Israel," or to read, (ver. 35), " before all the congregation ? " To write " in the presence," or to read " before," are phrases which imply that the reading and writing, referred to, were carried on, and known, as public, national acts ; and that all the people were consenting parties to the law, so written and read by Joshua. His mode of speaking, on such matters, is sometimes peculiarly distinct. Thus " Joshua called for all Israel ; *and* for their elders, and for their heads, and for their judges, and for their officers, and said unto them." (Josh. xxiii. 2.) The first *and* ought to be omitted. Joshua called לכל־ישראל לזקניו " for all Israel ; for their elders, and " &c., the omission of ו *and* before " elders," and its careful insertion before *heads, judges*, and *officers*, decides his meaning. Joshua called for all Israel ; viz., for their elders, &c., &c. So again,[1] "Joshua gathered all the tribes of Israel to Shechem; and called for the elders of Israel, and for their heads," &c., &c., (as before). This explains how the business of the "whole assembly," when summoned, was conducted. All were welcome to come, but not all were obliged to come. Only their heads, and their judges, and their officers, went "before God" into the tabernacle, whether in Moses' time, or in Joshua's. Public business[2] was proclaimed, "Moses gave commandment, and they caused it to be proclaimed throughout the camp." And the persons so employed were the elders, the priests, and the Levites. "Moses with the priests, and Levites, spake unto all Israel;" and yet it is said, "Moses charged the people the same day." To charge the elders, and the priests, was to charge the people. And so,[3] lastly, "the children of Israel" repented for Benjamin, and asked, "How shall we do for wives for them?" when it is meant, and afterwards said, "Then the elders of the congregation said, How shall we do for wives for them?"

A lively picture of reading the law "in the ears of all the people" is found, at Neh. viii. 1—8. "Nehemiah the Tirshatha, and Ezra the priest, the scribe, and all the Levites that taught the people, said," &c. On this occasion, the reader was Ezra the scribe; on Dr. Colenso's, he was Joshua. Ezra stood "upon a pulpit of wood and read" assisted by "Jeshua, and Bani, and Sherebiah, Jamin, Akkub," and others.

We can now do without the Doctor's arithmetic, at least on this subject, and without the following remarks as well. See pp. 36, 37.

"How then is it conceivable that a man should do what Joshua is here said to have done, unless, indeed, the reading of every word of 'all that Moses commanded' 'with the blessings and cursings, according to all that is written in the book of the Law,' was a mere dumb show, without the least idea of those most solemn words being *heard* by those to whom they were addressed? For, surely, no human voice, unless strengthened by a miracle, of which the Scripture tells us nothing, could have reached the ears of a crowded mass of people, as large as the whole population of LONDON. The very crying of the 'little ones,' who are expressly stated to have been present, must have sufficed to drown the sounds at a few yards' distance.

"42. It may be said, indeed, that only a portion of this great host was

---

[1] Josh. xxiv. 1.   [2] Exod. xxxvi. 6; Deut. xxvii. 1—14.   [3] Judges xxi. 7—16.

really present, though 'all Israel' is spoken of. And this might have been allowed without derogating from the general historical value of the book, though, of course, not without impeaching the *literal* accuracy of the Scripture narrative, which by some is so strenuously maintained. But the words above quoted from Joshua are so comprehensive, that they will not allow of this. We must suppose that, at least, the great body of the Congregation was present, and not only present, but able to hear the words of awful moment which Joshua addressed to them. Nor can it be supposed that he read them first to one party, and then to another, &c., till 'all the Congregation' had heard them. The day would not have sufficed for reading in this way 'all the blessings and the cursings' in Deut. xxvii., xxviii.— much less 'all the words of the Law,'—many times over, especially after that he had been already engaged, as the story implies, on the very same day, in writing 'a copy of the Law of Moses' upon the stones set up in Mount Ebal (Josh. viii. 32, 33)."

§ VII. THE EXTENT OF THE CAMP—THE PRIEST'S DUTIES.

At Levit. iv. 11, 12, it is written, "And the skin of the bullock, and all his flesh, with his head, and with his legs, and his inwards, and his dung, even the whole bullock shall he carry forth, without the camp, unto a clean place, where the ashes are poured out, and burn him on the wood with fire." It pleases the Bishop to interpret literally of the priest the words " he shall carry forth." And immediately he falls on with his arithmetic. Indeed one is tempted to think that, so far as the Holy Bible is concerned, the Bishop knows nothing but arithmetic. He reckons the people Israel, fairly enough at about 2,000,000; and, very handsomely, proposes to allow each living person three times as much room as a dead man's coffin. Indeed, he is unpleasantly minute:—

"Let us allow, however, for each person on the average three times six feet by two feet, the size of a coffin for a full grown man." "Let us allow for each person thirty-six square feet, or four square yards. Then it follows that for 2,000,000 of people (without making any allowance for the tabernacle itself, and its court, and the 44,000 Levites,) male and female (Num. iii. 39), 'who pitched round about it' (Num. i. 53), the camp must have covered, the people being crowded as thickly as possible, an area of 8,000,000 square yards, or more than 1,652 acres of ground."

"Thus the refuse of these sacrifices would have had to be carried by the priest himself (Aaron, Eleazar, or Ithamar,—there were no others) a distance of three-quarters of a mile. From the outside of this great camp, wood and water would have had to be fetched for all purposes, if, indeed, such supplies of wood and water, for the wants of such a multitude as this, could have been found at all in the wilderness—under Sinai, for instance, where they are said to have encamped for nearly twelve months together. How much would remain in such a neighbourhood, after a month's consumption of the city of London, even at Midsummer? And the 'ashes' of the whole camp, with the rubbish and filth of every kind, for a population like that of London, would have had to be carried out in like manner, through the midst of the crowded mass of people. They could not surely all have gone outside the camp for the necessities of nature, as commanded in Deut. xxiii. 12—14. There were the aged and infirm, women in childbirth, sick persons, and young children, who could not have done this. And, indeed, the command itself supposes the person to have a 'paddle' upon his 'weapon,' and, therefore, must be understood to apply only to the *males*, or, rather, only to the 600,000 *warriors*. But the very fact, that this direction for ensuring cleanliness—' for Jehovah thy God walketh in the midst of thy camp; therefore shall thy camp be holy; that He see no unclean thing in thee, and turn away from thee'—would have been so limited in its application, is itself a very convincing proof of the unhistorical character of the whole narrative.

" 45. But how huge does this difficulty become, if, instead of taking the excessively cramped area of 1,652 acres, less than *three square miles*, for such a camp as this, we take the more reasonable allowance of Scott, who says, ' this encampment is computed to have formed a moveable city of *twelve miles square*,' that is, about the size of London itself—as it might well be, considering that the population was as large as that of London, and that in the Hebrew tents there were no first, second, third, and fourth stories, no crowded garrets and underground cellars. In that case, the offal of these sacrifices would have had to be carried by Aaron himself, or one of his sons, a distance of six miles; and the same difficulty would have attended each of the other transactions above mentioned. In fact, we have to imagine the priest having himself to carry, on his back on foot, from St. Paul's to the outskirts of the metropolis, the 'skin, and flesh, and head, and legs, and inwards, and dung, even the whole bullock,' and the people having to carry out their rubbish in like manner, and bring in their daily supplies of water and fuel, after first cutting down the latter where they could find it! Further, we have to imagine half a million of men going out daily—the 22,000 Levites for a distance of *six miles*—to the suburbs for the common necessities of nature! The supposition involves, of course, an absurdity. But it is our duty to look plain facts in the face."

It is, indeed, a frightful picture—a priest of any Church, whether in his robes or out of them, " having to carry, on his back on foot, " from St. Paul's to the outskirts of the metropolis, the skin, and " flesh, and head, and legs, and inwards, and dung," of a whole bullock. How much worse in the heats of the Arabian desert, where all gentlemen, but especially all priests, wore fine white linen breeches. Even at Natal it would be horrible. May we venture to hope that

Dr. Colenso did not, with all his judicious zeal, practically illustrate this difficulty before the Zulus?

It is a pity the Bishop could not have been personally acquainted with Ezra. That great man, and accomplished priest, resided a long time with those skilful calculators the Chaldeans, and was well prepared to sympathize with Dr. Colenso in the power of numbers. They might have passed an hour or two together, over the pages of the Pentateuch, with much profit to the Bishop of Natal. Ezra was inspired of God to explain the law of Moses, and to readjust the Levitical services, at a time when the Jews had fallen into comparative ignorance during seventy years' disuse of them in Babylon. In his book we have much valuable information as to the relative duties of the priests, and their attendant Levites. This is the particular information which, at the moment, we require.

What occupation does Dr. Colenso find for the 8,580 Levites, mentioned at Num. iv. 48? Might not the passage from Chronicles, which he has quoted, at p. 131, have suggested to him the explanation he requires, " the people killed the Passover, but the priests sprinkled the blood from their hands, and the Levites flayed them." (2 Chron. xxx. 16; xxxv. 11.) Those who might kill, and those who might flay—in short, who prepared the sacrifices for the priests —is it too much to suppose that they might also carry away the dung, &c.? Was it quite impossible for 8,580 men, trained to outdoor labour in the heat of Egypt, to organize a continuous service of hand-carriage, or of ambulances, in the sands of the desert? Dr. Colenso, who can think so exactly about coffins, and dead bodies— why has he not also thought about biers?

The duties of the Levites were clearly enjoined in the Pentateuch —viz., to do everything relating to the service of the Tabernacle, except the priestly duties of immediately sprinkling the blood, and offering up the sacrifices. Ezra tells us (ch. vi. 16—19) that, when the second temple was dedicated, under his superintendence, " they set the priests in their divisions, and the Levites in their courses, for the service of God, which is at Jerusalem; as it is written in the book of Moses." From which assertion two things follow :—1. That Ezra knew the duties of the Levites were defined in the book of Moses; and, 2. That these duties being spoken of in Exodus, Leviticus, and Numbers, we have the three chief parts of the Pentateuch spoken of as one book at the time of Ezra, and ascribed to Moses as its author.

The writer in the Chronicles is even more distinct. Says Hezekiah, when effecting the reformation at Jerusalem (2 Chron. xxix. 5, 16, 34), " Hear me, ye Levites, sanctify now yourselves, and sanctify the house of the Lord God of your fathers, and carry forth the filthiness out of the Holy Place." All impurities were carried out, whether from Temple or Tabernacle, not by the priests (as Dr. Colenso supposes), but by the Levites. Also it was part of their duty to help prepare the sacrifices, when the priests were too few; as Dr. Colenso says correctly they were in the wilderness. " But the priests were " too few, so that they could not flay all the burnt-offerings; where- " fore their brethren the Levites did help them, till the work " was ended." So, too, when Hezekiah celebrates the Passover (2 Chron. xxx. 13—27), " The priests and the Levites were ashamed, and sanctified themselves, and brought in the burnt offerings into the house of the Lord. And they stood in their place after their manner, according to the law of Moses the man of God: the priests sprinkled the blood, which they received at the hands of the Levites." The work of the Levites, of whom there were 8,580 at the Exodus, in assisting the priests, was to be learned out of the law of Moses, the man of God. Moreover, at the 17th verse, we learn a most important fact, easily to be gathered also from the books of Exodus and Leviticus; his Passover lamb, and other offerings, each man, who brought them, was expected to kill for himself—" For there were many in the congregation that were not sanctified; therefore the Levites had the charge of the killing of the Passovers for every one that was not clean, to sanctify them unto the Lord." Had they been clean, they would have killed for themselves.

Similarly, in reference to Josiah's great passover. (2 Chron. xxxv. 10—14.) Now where such abundant provision was made for the killing, we need feel no uneasiness about the removal of the refuse.

If we turn to the passages referred to below [1], we shall perceive to what effect the duties of the Levites were defined. Every one, not a Levite, was, in regard to all the duties of the Tabernacle, " a stranger;" and, if he " came near," should be put to death (Num. i. 51). And every Levite, not a Priest, was, in regard to " the charge of the sanctuary, and the charge of the altar," counted also as " a stranger," and if he " came near" was to be put to death. (Num. iii. 10 and xviii. 5.) But all other " service of the tabernacle " they

[1] Num. i. 49—51; iii. 6—9; viii. 13—26; and xviii. 1—7.

were competent to do "before Aaron and before his sons" (Num. iii. 7, 8, and viii. 22). They were given to Aaron and his sons, as servants, not only to set up and take down and carry the tabernacle in the wilderness; but also to do, and assist in, all duties of the tabernacle, save the priestly in the sanctuary and at the altar, as long as the Levitical dispensation lasted. Hence their title, נתונים נתונים *Nethunim, Nethunim,* "wholly given" as servants to the priests for the Lord. (Num. iii. 9, and viii. 16.)

Besides, it is important to remember, when considering the number of priests and their duties, at any time, that some of the offices connected with them were originally, and could still be, performed by laymen. The person who offered was continually required to kill his own sacrifice.[1] The "first-born," as we shall elsewhere explain, were originally told off to do this duty for their brethren. And, before the Levitical priesthood was established, Moses· "sent young men" (laymen first-born) "of the children of Israel, which offered burnt offerings, and sacrificed peace offerings of oxen unto the Lord." (Exod. xxiv. 5.) And, in far later times, if we refer to Ezra vii. 24 and viii. 17, 20; and to Neh. x. 28 and xi. 21; we shall see that some of the duties of the Levites, as Nethunim, probably those which did not involve immediate attendance on the priests, could be deputed to others, of whom it is by no means clear that they belonged to the tribe of Levi. In fact, Dr. Colenso continually loses sight of one great principle, affecting the law of Moses and sanctioned by the Saviour, viz., that in many particulars it admitted of variation and adjustment, according to local circumstances. (Matt. xii. 5. See also, 1 Chron. xxiv. 3, and Nehem. xii. 44—47.)

We may truly say of such writers as the Bishop of Natal, "Ye do err, not knowing the Scriptures." And I appeal to every layman, who reads this page, not to suffer his mind to be disturbed by Dr. Colenso's present exhibition of ignorance, nor by any other which he may publish after it. Far from being overburdened, as Dr. Colenso supposes, with the duties of the sacrifice, the priest was furnished with abundant means of assistance. (1 Chron. xxiii. 27—32.)

Every layman may trust his Bible, and look to that as its own best expositor. Hence I preferred replying from Scripture as above. But we may just add that, in the passage Lev. iv. 11, 12, referred to by the Bishop, "he shall carry forth"—it is by no means certain the

---

[1] Lev. i. 5; iii. 2; iv. 29.

he does mean the priest. It might better, perhaps, be rendered, as at Lev. xvi. 27 and elsewhere, "one shall carry forth." Dr. Colenso ought to have known this simple Hebrew idiom; that the third person of the verb is often thus used indefinitely, as of *some one, any one*, not specified in the contexts. The truth is, the Doctor did not know the meaning of הוציא, *he shall cause to go forth;* i.e., to be removed. Scholarly instinct will base this criticism entirely upon the *Hiphil*, or *causative*, form of the word used. But since, from frequent use, the word obtains the desired meaning; *carry forth*, i.e., personally, it may be as well to refer to a few examples to show how the context must determine its force. Joseph says, "Cause (הוציאו) every man to go out from me" (Gen. xlv. 1); does Dr. Colenso suppose that the attendants were lifted out bodily? "Moses said unto God, Who am I that I should go unto Pharoah, and that I should bring forth" (the same word) "the children of Israel out of Egypt?" Does the Bishop suppose that Moses thought he was to carry 2,000,000 of people in his pocket, or on his shoulders? This supposition would be about as reasonable, as that the priest was to carry the whole bullock, with his skin, and inwards, and dung, all through the camp to the ash-pit. It is useless to multiply examples.[1]

The Bishop's uneasiness at page 40, in reference to the "daily necessities" of the people, is explained by reference to Deut. xxiii. 12—24. This paddling difficulty has reference only to persons on war service. And as to its "limited application" proving the "unhistorical character of the whole narrative" (see p. 23, above), its application was just as wide as the camp. The injunction involved a general principle of cleanliness.

§ VIII. ON READING HOLY SCRIPTURE.

In reading any books, but especially those which claim to have been inspired, we are bound to give the authors credit for common-sense, at least; until they have been clearly proved devoid of it. Whenever we find statements in Holy Scripture, and in the books of Moses as a part of it, which seem to violate the principles of plain understanding, we may be sure that, in some way or other, we labour

[1] Exod. xiii. 9; xxix. 46; Lev. xxv. 42; Num. xx. 10.

under misapprehension. And a little more attention will, probably, discover the explanation we require. It is unreasonable to believe that any writers, whether original authors or mere compilers, have been guilty of the enormous and ridiculous mistakes, of the absurdities, inconsistencies, and contradictions, boldly charged against them by Bishop Colenso. Supposing he had proved anything, we should say he had fallen into the disastrous error of proving too much. When, *e.g.*, he supposes[1] that the Levitical law required " each priest " in the wilderness " to eat daily eighty-eight pigeons for his own portion, " ' in the most holy place,' " we cannot help reading on. Not that, after this, we expect to find any solid arguments against the Pentateuch; but only to see what other curious things he is going to tell us. More than four pigeons an hour, with just a little spare time! This is even worse than other difficulties already touched upon.

A careful study of God's Word will soon convince us that in most parts of it, but especially in the historical, a reader is expected to supply many necessary particulars from his own general knowledge, and sometimes from his imagination. Dr. Colenso has ostentatiously refused to admit this element of interpretation; and quotes an incorrect remark by Canon Stanley—" and if we have no warrant to take away, we have no warrant to add " (p. 70). True; we have no warrant to add to the doctrines of the Holy Bible, nor to its established text. But we are continually required to supply many rational particulars, which tend to explain, and to harmonize, the sacred writings. This warrant is found in the nature of all writings, especially of ancient history. And it is arbitrarily enjoined by commonsense. The particulars required may have reference to the characters, and lives, of persons; the climate, geographical features, and natural phenomena of countries; the times of the year, or seasons; solar and lunar considerations, &c., in reference to particular parts of any narrative; the social, and political, arrangements of States; the constitutional, and national, characteristics of their people; the mutual relations, and comparative strength, of co-existent governments; the extraction, descent, and even the physiological peculiarities, of different races of men; all these, and a multitude of other matters, appeal to the general information, or research, or even to the imagination, of the reader. In studying books, like the Pentateuch, these cannot be ignored. It is impossible to read, *e.g.*, the books of Samuel, or of

[1] See p. 128.

Kings, (to say nothing of some of the finest parts of the Prophets) without becoming unavoidably conscious that we have just described a fixed necessity of interpretation. Or, take another illustration. Dr. Colenso (p. 114) can see no signs in the Pentateuch that Jacob had a large " body of servants "—" If he had had so many at his com- " mand, it is hardly likely that he would have sent his darling Joseph, " at seventeen years of age, to go, all alone and unattended, wander- " ing about upon the veldt in search of his brethren ?" Yet Jacob, ad- dressing Joseph, incidentally asserts an important fact (Gen. xlviii. 22), " Moreover I have given to thee one portion above thy brethren, which I took out of the hand of the Amorite with my sword and with my bow." בחרבי ובקשתי. There is no mistake about it; this was a serious act of war. When did he this? and how, unless he had many trained servants, like Abraham's? (Gen. xiv. 14.) We are left to supply both the time, the agents, and other matters necessary to the truth of this statement. And, similarly, when (Gen. xxxiv. 25) Simeon and Levi " took each man his sword, and came upon the city boldly, and slew all the males." Did they do so single-handed?

§ IX. ISRAEL "ARMED," AND DWELLING "IN TENTS."

" The children of Israel went up harnessed out of the land of Egypt." (Exod. xiii. 18.)

Dr. Colenso observes that the word חמשים, here rendered *harnessed*, appears to mean " armed," or " in battle array," in all the other passages where it occurs. And he refers, in proof, to Josh. i. 14; iv. 12; and Judges vii. 11. And he then proceeds to argue as follows:—

> " It is, however, inconceivable that these down-trodden, oppressed people should have been allowed by Pharaoh to possess arms, so as to turn out, at a moment's notice, 600,000 armed men. If such a mighty host—nearly nine times as great as the whole of Wellington's army at Waterloo (69,686 men, Alison's *History of Europe*, xix., p. 401)—had had arms in their hands, would they not have risen long ago for their liberty, or, at all events, would there have been no danger of their rising? Besides, the warriors formed a distinct caste in Egypt, as Herodotus tells us (ii. 165), 'being in number, when they are most numerous, 160,000, none of whom learn any mechanical art, but apply themselves wholly to military affairs.' Are we to suppose, then, that the Israelites acquired their arms by 'borrowing,' on the night of the

Exodus? Nothing whatever is said of this, and the idea itself is an extravagant one. But, even if in this, or any other, way, they had come to be possessed of arms, is it conceivable that 600,000 armed men, in the pride of life, would have cried out in panic terror, 'sore afraid' (Ex. xiv. 10), when they saw that they were being pursued?"

"Besides, we must suppose that the *whole body* of 600,000 warriors were armed, when they were numbered (Num. i. 3), under Sinai. They possessed arms surely, at that time, according to the story. How did they get them, unless they took them out of Egypt?"

The Bishop is aware that several explanations of this seeming difficulty have been attempted; but he does not recount them fairly; and, probably, because he did not fully comprehend their force.

Let us first take that rendering, to which he, not quite justly, persists in adhering, as if no other could possibly be correct; and of which he strangely magnifies the difficulty. Let us suppose the word, חמשים, means *armed*. How could these 600,000 men have obtained the arms? Could they have obtained them, by any means, in Egypt? It is true, as explained above, at p. 19, that the language does not require us to believe that all the men who went out of Egypt were armed. When Moses says, "the children of Israel," inclusively, we may here, if we please, understand him to mean, a very large number, or even the greater part, of the 600,000 men, were armed. Nor is it correct, in the Bishop to say, that at the "numbering" under Sinai, "we must suppose" that all the men "numbered" were in actual possession of arms at that time.

Yet, even supposing we included every man of the 600,000, there is nothing impossible, nor perhaps improbable, in the assertion that they were literally *armed*. The Bishop assumes, but without authority, that, if they "borrowed" arms of the Egyptians, they must have done so "at a moment's notice." Whoever reads attentively the first chapters of Exodus, viz., all that narrate the plagues, and the interviews of Moses and Aaron with Pharaoh, will perceive that we cannot certainly determine what length of time intervened between Moses' first speaking to the elders of Israel (Exod. iv. 29), and the 14th of Abib, the night of the Passover, on which they left Egypt. We are sure that one week elapsed between the first and second plagues; that at least two days were occupied in the plague of the frogs; and that the darkness lasted three days. But no statement is made concerning the duration of, or the intervals between, the other plagues. Perhaps we should not be extravagant, if we concluded that the ten plagues occupied fully ten weeks.

It is also certain that, from Moses' first appearance to his brethren, a large number of them, and those the better informed, and more influential, of the people, would be convinced that the time of their deliverance was at hand. Whatever might be the case with the majority of the common people, who, at one moment (but before the plagues began), "hearkened not unto Moses, for anguish of spirit, and for cruel bondage" (Exod. vi. 9, 12), it is certain that some believed from the first (Exod. iv. 31); and we cannot doubt but that many would know that the end of the period of bondage, named by the Lord to Abraham (Gen. xv. 13), was close at hand. Many would retain their faith in Jacob's prophecy of their rescue (Gen. xlviii. 21); many more, it may be, in Joseph's (Gen. l. 24; Exod. xiii. 19). So that, from the first appearance of Moses and Aaron, with the announcement of their approaching liberty, a large part of the people would be convinced that their departure from Egypt could not be delayed much longer. However, we may conclude, with certainty conclude, that, from the *fourth* plague, viz., that of the flies, when Pharaoh first showed a disposition somewhat to yield (Exod. viii. 28), the people would be convinced of the ultimate success of Moses and Aaron. From the time the hail was threatened, we are sure they did; and that many of the Egyptians thought so too (Exod. ix. 20); and more particularly from the time the locusts were threatened, when "Pharaoh's servants" entreated him to "let the men go." Of the exact time which elapsed between the plague of the flies, and the night of the Exodus, we are not informed. But, there is no unfairness in asserting, that we may reasonably feel assured that for several weeks the Israelites felt certain they were about to quit Egypt. And it is important to observe that the hint for their "borrowing" would have been given from the first; for it pleased the Almighty to direct Moses to this object, when he was at Horeb, and, in fact, before he had consented to undertake the mission to Pharaoh. (Exod. iii. 22.) The words amount to a specific direction, given to Moses that they were to do so. It was part of his first business to tell them to do so. And, to this very end, there may have been a providence that "the people were scattered abroad throughout all the land of Egypt, to gather stubble instead of straw," so soon. One of the first thoughts of the men would be, arms! of which, too, they probably possessed some already. For, as to Dr. Colenso's question, If they had had arms, "would there "have been no danger of their rising?" it was that very thing which Pharaoh is said (Exod. i. 9, 10,) to have feared they would do.

Is it possible that when Dr. Colenso wrote this part of his wretched little book, he was thinking of Whitworths and Armstrongs, of the largest size, and most improved manufacture? But it is for us to observe that the Egyptians used, for war, spears and javelins, bows and arrows, daggers, slings, and the throw-stick, or (in Australia) the *boomerang*. These were the Egyptian arms.[1] All of them, light of carriage, and easy of concealment. And any old woman, sharp boy, or smiling girl, could both "borrow," and carry, and hide them. Who shall say how many thousands of these "small arms" were so obtained, and so concealed, by thousands of women and children, studiously set upon the task of getting them? We may accept Herodotus' statement, that the armed caste, *Anglicè*, standing army, of Egypt, was, at the highest, 160,000; but that does not contradict the fact, for which Wilkinson is authority, that the Egyptian people were naturally fond of field sports, and used in them bows and arrows, spears and javelins, slings and throw-sticks; and that, in fact, archery was a common pastime. The book of Genesis assures us (xiv. 5; xxvii. 3; xxxiv. 25; xlviii. 22), that the Hebrews were a martial people, fierce enough, and sometimes too fierce, and that their traditional weapons were the sword and the bow; and this character they retained, till Jerusalem was destroyed. Besides, we all know how easily arms can be extemporized by an earnest people, craving for their liberty. One stick of the *Calamus Magrostes*, of which I shall have to speak, which covered the banks of the Nile, and abounded in Goshen, would be long enough for three spears; and one of them, with a common Egyptian knife at the end of it, would make a weapon which Dr. Colenso would be anxious to avoid, like any other sensible man. As for his remarks, about the people crying out, in "panic fear," when they were caught in a trap at Pi-hahiroth, encumbered with their wives, their children, and their cattle; what men of mettle would not have done the same? Depend upon it, there was more trembling in the Khyber Pass, than the brave Englishmen who fought there cared to acknowledge. And

[1] Wilkinson's "Anc. Egypt," vol. iii., pp. 38, 60, 253.

there would have been much more, if all had had wives and children there to feel for. To fight at Pi-hahiroth, was death; to surrender, was life, without liberty; and that, the Greek proverb says, is worse.

I conclude, then, that it is extremely probable that a very large number of the 600,000 Israelites were literally *armed*, after the fashion of their day.

But Bishop Colenso knows very well that the word need not mean *armed*. It may mean "marshalled," or "arrayed," in any order, under any system. ("Kept in *hand*"—חמש, *five*.) Or, as he remarks, it may possibly be taken, and has been taken by some in this place, to mean "by fifties." And then he feebly adds, p. 49, "It will be seen, however, that these meanings of the word will not "suit the other passages quoted." And is Dr. Colenso so little acquainted with Hebrew (though he professes "critically" to examine the Pentateuch) as not to know that there is, perhaps, no other language in the world, which admits finer shades of meaning, in the use of the same word, in different passages; having regard to the sense of the root, from which it is derived? I have already referred to one instance in which the Bishop has manifested either great ignorance or sad want of candour. Here is a worse. He observes, p. 49, that the word חמשים has been thought by some to mean by "fives" (Dathe,[1] *in quinque partes divisum*) or by "fifties," because it "has a resemblance to חמש, *five*." Has a resemblance! Why, without the points, it is the very plural of the word itself; and has the same "resemblance" to it that *Cherubim* has to *Cherub:* and, with the points, it is that same plural, excepting two *dots*. From the Doctor's mode of speaking, a plain reader would suppose anything, but this, to be the case. We have no reason to believe that the Hebrew Bible contains every form of any particular word which correct idiom could bring into actual use. And they, who read Hebrew without the points, are perfectly justified in saying that חמשים may be a participial noun, meaning *fived*, *i.e.*, divided into five bodies, as Dathe, and others, have concluded. They would hardly, however, be justified in saying it means "by fifties," or "by fifty in a rank," as correct idiom would then demand a repetition of the word, which the verse does not supply. Besides, the division

[1] Pentateuch, vol. i., p. 269.

into thousands, and hundreds, and fifties, and tens, does not appear to have been made, until some time after, at Jethro's suggestion. (Exod. xviii. 21.)

Dr. Colenso's argument requires that we should take this word as a passive *armed*, and that makes all he says depend upon the *pointing;* had two *dots* been left out, the word could not have been taken in the sense he insists on. Now this is vicious reasoning on Dr. Colenso's part, supposing him, that is, to be acquainted with Hebrew. The word חמשים is one of those particular words in which the pointing ought *not* to be relied on. It is true the defective mode of writing passive participial plurals, *e.g.*, ִ for ִי, is found rather frequently in the earlier books of Scripture: but still it is defective pointing; and, moreover, it so happens that though the best Spanish copies read, as our Bible has it, חֲמֻשִׁים, other editions and MSS. read חֲמֻשִׁם, which is more strictly regular. All I wish to impress upon my readers is, that the Bishop's argument is vicious at the root; and shows either that he was ignorant of the bearing of the *points* on this part of the argument, or else, knowingly, passed it over, and made the groundless assumption, that the word חמשים *must* be a passive *participial* form.

However, supposing we admit it to be such a form, it then means not necessarily *armed*, but "kept in hand," drawn well together, marshalled skilfully, systematically, and cleverly, for their *exit;* not a "rabble rout," not a mob, but decently and in order, in system, ready at call, known in their divisions, under recognised "officers." But by no means "in battle array." Gesenius tells us, Gram., p. 179, that חמש, *five*, means, as a root, to *draw together*, to *contract;* and our word חמשים would, therefore, mean *kept well together*, not *straggling*. It seems to me that, in speaking of the Exodus, people have not taken account enough of the fact that the Israelites were חמשים, *organized*, long before they left Egypt. They did not labour on the public buildings of Egypt, as a mob. No doubt they worked in parties, and gangs. And, we know, they had their own officers. For the שטרים, or "officers of the children of Israel" mentioned, at Exod. v. 14, were evidently Hebrews. The men of these several gangs, appointed to make brick, &c., would probably reside near one another with their families, and their foremen or officers. It is even possible they might have been organized in gangs of fifties; but, casting that aside as not needed by my argument, I conceive that the word had been passed along that, whenever they left Egypt, they were to keep together in their gangs, under the same foremen, with their families, and their cattle, and travel by such and such a road, and in such and such an order. There was by no means the confusion on the night of the Exodus, which Dr. Colenso supposes. But, as we shall have to speak of the institution of the Passover, and the people's departure from Egypt, I shall content myself here with concluding—

1. That the people Israel may have been *armed;* and that Dr. Colenso's argument is not worth a handful of Egyptian stubble;

2. That the word חמשים means "kept in hand," or "organized;" and does not mean "by fifties," nor "in battle array."

§ X. THE ISRAELITES "BORROWED."

Much has been said sneeringly about the Israelites having "borrowed" of the Egyptians. (Exod. iii. 22; xi. 2; xii. 35, 36.) And Dr. Colenso cannot deny himself the pleasure of joining in the sneer (p. 25). It would be folly to undertake to convince the reader that one of the commonest words in the Hebrew Bible, שאל, which habitually stands for *pray*, means strictly *ask*, and not *borrow*. I cannot believe but that Dr. Colenso must have known this. Still, there is no doubt that, from the peculiar circumstances referred to in the context, and also from the force of נצל, *to draw out, to spoil,* which immediately follows, it has acquired, in the places referred to, the sense of "borrow;" and that most commentators have agreed in that. What then? Jews *borrowed*, Egyptians *lent*.

Does a commercial people, like ours, need to be informed that often enough, too often, sanguine persons borrow in perfectly good faith, and with clear consciences, what they intend and expect, but afterwards fail, to repay? Do people never lend in entire, yet too sanguine, confidence in the chances that the borrowers can, or will be able to, pay? In the affairs of life do lenders and borrowers never wittingly join in a doubtful transaction, believing that, upon the whole, there are probabilities of not losing in the end? Do people, who have the means, never at moments of anxiety, or pity, or generosity, lend others, what they ask for, hearing their asseverations that they will pay, but never expecting to see the money again? "Take it, and God be with you. If you can pay, I know you will, but if not ———." Is this feeling not likely to have moved the Egyptians, during the plagues? Lend as much as they could, might they not have thought they were getting rid of a Jewish nuisance, very cheaply? Might they not have even desired, and expected, to buy the goodwill of Israel, by lending with facility what they asked for?

As for the Israelites, why should they not have expected, and have intended to pay? Canaan was their land, and they knew it. It was but a short way from Egypt. They had no reason then to anticipate forty years of wandering in a desert. It was a land flowing with milk and honey, and they knew it. Had they no traditions of Abraham, Isaac, and Jacob? Had they never heard of Isaac's parental blessing upon their father Jacob? Or had they no confidence that the peculiar blessing of God would be with them? They might well expect to be able to pay; and, doubtless, designed to do so.

Does an act of war never cancel national debt? And did not the Egyptians wantonly levy war against Israel, by attacking them after they had consented to their departure? We will not ask, how the Egyptians would have acted under similar circumstances. But, at least, we may venture to hint, in the most delicate way, what might possibly be the opinion of Americans. Do objectors to the Pentateuch fancy that the Israelites must needs have been tied down to payment by the private bonds of an elaborate commercial system, which recognises the claims of stocks, and shares, and bills of exchange?

Did not the Israelites " borrow " by the express command of God? And could the foreknowledge of God, as to their ultimate incapacity to pay, impair the purity of conscience, with which they would borrow? If so, then—but we had better stop there.

And, lastly, is there any evidence that the Israelites did never pay? We are not aware that they pleaded any " Statute of Limitations."

§ XI. THE ISRAELITES IN TENTS.

Dr. Colenso's remarkable book had scarcely been published, when certain members of the daily press began to shout as if in triumph that Holy Scripture had been, as they imagined, successfully charged with unveracity. Among them a leading literary journal observed, with many other particulars equally correct, that Dr. Colenso "analyses grammar and style—traces the changes in languages and the variations in the sense of words," &c. And there is no doubt but that Dr. Colenso's book has attracted greater attention, even from the clergy, because he has, here and there, spangled his pages with Hebrew letters. But if our laity are thus to be deceived by journals, professing literature, it is time that somebody should tell them that Dr. Colenso does not analyse grammar and style, does not "trace the changes of languages, and variations in the sense of words"—because he cannot. Dr. Colenso knows nothing of Hebrew; and scarcely ever introduces a Hebrew word, but to make some mistake about it. He is utterly incompetent to examine the Pentateuch "critically."

Thus, at p. 45, he is shocked to find it said, " Take ye every man for them which are in his tents." (Exod. xvi. 16.) He cannot understand, nor believe, how the Israelites could have been so soon provided with tents—an inquiry to which we shall come presently. But, observing that, at Levit. xxiii. 42, 43, the Feast of Tabernacles was established, "that your generations may know that I made the children of Israel to dwell in *booths*, when I brought them out of the land of Egypt," Dr. Colenso reflects upon the strange conflict which, he supposes, lies between the two statements; and proceeds to give us the important information that the word סכה , *booth*, is not the word אהל, *tent*. But that is all he knows about it; and, venturing only one step further, he falls instantly into error.

Dr. Colenso is too hasty in charging the authors of Holy Scripture with not knowing their native language. Had a Zulu accused him of not understanding English, we can well imagine what amusement the anecdote would have created at Natal. What shall we say when the Bishop charges the writers in Genesis and Samuel with ignorance of Hebrew? At pp. 22, 23, the Bishop says that the author of Genesis writes "inaccurately;" at p. 45, that the author of the second book of Samuel uses the word סכה "improperly."

This is because, at 2 Sam. xi. 11, and, as the Bishop says, "one "or two other places," he uses סכות for *tents;* which, says the Bishop, can only mean *booths,* as a shelter made of boughs. Now, the actual plural, סכות, occurs in *four* places, viz., 2 Sam. xi. 11, and xxii. 12, and 1 Kings xx. 12, 16, for *tents;* but the singular, סכה, five times for a *tent,* for a *booth* three times, and once for a *covert;* while its kindred word, סך, never means *booth,* but always either tent, or covert; so that the general force of כך, סכה, סכות, is *covering,* whether by thicket, booth, or tent. This might be expected from its root, which means *to cover.* And, as a *covering,* סכה, is sometimes synonymous with אהל, a *tent,* and even with בית, a *house.* When Dr. Colenso says, that *booths* is the "proper meaning" of סכות, *Succoth,* he is probably following the commentators, who intimate as much, because "the feast of Tabernacles," when Israel dwelt in *booths,* is habitually termed,[1] חג הסכות, or "feast of Succoth;" all of which instances of the use of the word ought to be considered as one. The word is also used for *booths,* or rather *fences,* made for cattle. (Gen. xxxiii. 17.) Yet the Bishop should have known that one proper, and one of the earliest uses, of the word, is for *covert,* or *thicket.* Job says (ch. xxxviii. 40), speaking of the lions, "When they couch in their dens, and abide in the covert" (בסכה), "to lie in wait." And, hence, the word may mean, a *covert,* or *thicket,* of canes, or what not.

But the Bishop's great difficulty is, How could they have been so early provided with tents in the wilderness? And, "further, if they "had had these tents, how could they have carried them? They "could not have borne them on their shoulders, since these were "already occupied with other burdens. And these burdens them- "selves were by no means insignificant."

> "For, besides their 'kneading-troughs,' with the dough unleavened, 'bound up in their clothes upon their shoulders,' as well as all other necessaries for daily domestic use, for sleeping, cooking, &c., there were the infants and young children, who could scarcely have gone twenty miles a-day, as the story requires; there were the aged and infirm persons, who

---

[1] Levit. xxiii. 34; Deut. xvi. 13; Ezra iii. 4, &c., &c.

must have likewise needed assistance; they must have carried also those goods of various kinds, which they brought out of their treasures so plentifully for the making of the Tabernacle; and, above all this, *they must have taken with them grain or flour enough for at least a month's use,* since they had no manna given to them till they came into the wilderness of Sin, 'on the fifteenth day of the second month after their departing out of the land of Egypt.' (Exod. xvi. 1.)

"57. There were the *cattle,* certainly, which might have been turned to some account for this purpose, if trained to act as pack-oxen. But then, what a prodigious number of trained oxen would have been needed to carry these 200,000 tents! One ox will carry 120 lbs., and a *canvas* tent, 'that will hold *two* people and a fair quantity of luggage,' weighs from 25 lbs. to 40 lbs. (Galton's 'Art of Travel,' pp. 33, 177). Of such tents as the above, with poles, pegs, &c., a single ox might, possibly, carry *four,* and even this would require 50,000 oxen. But these would be of the lightest modern material, whereas the Hebrew tents, we must suppose, were made of *skins,* and were, therefore much heavier. Besides this, these latter were *family* tents, not made merely for soldiers or travellers, and required to be very much larger for purposes of common decency and convenience One ox, perhaps, might have carried one such tent, large enough to accommodate ten persons, with its apparatus of poles and cords; and thus they would have needed for this purpose 200,000 oxen. But oxen are not usually trained to carry goods upon their backs as pack-oxen, and will by no means do so, if untrained."

It might be very fairly questioned whether the language at Exod. xvi. 16, "for them which are in his tents," does require us to believe that they were literally furnished with tents. Long after this, when the people dwelt in towns of houses, the phrase was, "To your tents, O Israel." (1 Kings xii. 16.) "So all Israel went to their tents" (2 Chron. x. 16); *i.e.,* every man to his *home.* But, letting that pass, nothing can be clearer than the way in which Israel at the Exodus may have been supplied with *tents.* When "they journeyed from Rameses to *Succoth*" (Exod. xii. 13), they probably arrived at a place where they made themselves *booths,* and at a place remarkably *wooded.* Not necessarily with trees, for few sorts of trees grow, or ever grew,[1] in Egypt and its neighbourhood; and yet groves of palms, and of acacias, and of sycamores, abounded. *Thickets* of cane, of various kinds, but especially of one kind, crowded the banks of the Nile, and the marshes of the Delta, and were especially abundant on

[1] Wilkinson's Anc. Egypt, vol. iii., p. 167.

the route which the Israelites took. Let us assume,[1] as we may with safety, that Robinson's view of that route is probably correct. "Goshen lay along the Pelusiac arm of the Nile, " on the east of the Delta, and was the part of Egypt nearest " to Palestine." The Israelites broke up from Rameses, and proceeded by Succoth and Etham to the Red Sea; from Etham they turned more to the right and " marched down the western side of the " arm of the gulf to the vicinity of Suez." The word *Succoth* properly means, as I have said, not only booths, but thickets. At Succoth they tarried, we know not exactly how long. For, although Dr. Colenso observes (p. 63), in reply to Kurtz, that " nothing whatever is said, or " implied, about these 'days of rest,' in the Scripture;" and that "there " would surely have been some reference made to them, if they really " occurred," we must observe that, at Succoth, they are implied, and reference is made to them ; for at Succoth " they baked unleavened cakes of the dough which they brought forth out of Egypt." (Exod. xii. 39). In short, they halted, camped, made booths, and cooked ; how long they stopped, we are not told. I shall speak about this again ; meanwhile, *Succoth* may mean, *thickets;* and the reed, or cane,[2] " grows in immense numbers on the banks, and in the " streams, of the Nile. Extensive woods " (*Succoth*) " of the canes " *Phragmit* and *Calamus Magrostes,* which rise to the height of " twelve yards, cover the marshes in the neighbourhood of Suez. " The stems are conveyed all over Egypt and Arabia, and are " employed by the Orientals in constructing the flat terraces of their " habitations," &c., &c. Here, then, are the materials for supporting tents, or making *spear and javelin* handles, of which they probably had (as I have shown) a large number already. Is it unreasonable to think that *Succoth* was a town, in a wooded country, and in the neighbourhood of these thickets, where the canes were prepared for export into Arabia, whither the Israelites were going (though they knew not by what road), and that here they were furnished with facilities for supporting tents, and for carrying burdens? In fact, that as Pi-hahiroth, *the mouth of Hiroth*, is descriptive of the physical aspect of one spot, on which Israel encamped; so Succoth is, of another?

---

[1] Robinson's Bib. Res., vol. i., pp. 77—80.
[2] Paxton's Illus. Scr. Nat. Hist., p. 16.

As for Dr. Colenso's questions, Of what the tents could be made? and how would they carry them?—is he quite ignorant of the abundant manufacture[1] of cotton, and linen, and woollen cloths in Egypt? And of woollen stuff the Egyptian tents were made, like those of some Arabs at the present day. Is he quite unaware of the large, loose, flowing robes, in which the Egyptians, like other Orientals, delighted? Does he not know that the Israelites entered the desert in the height of spring-time; in the "month of flowers, when first most welcome spring appears;"[2] on April 9, B.C. 1560?[3] Does he not know that people might safely sleep, even as early as the end of March, in the open air, as no doubt many of the Israelites did? Does he not know that it very rarely rains in summer,[4] in Egypt, or in the desert of Arabia; and that, therefore, very light tents would have done for the time? Two or three of the external robes of the men or women, supported on spears, or sticks of cane, would have done for a family. Does he not know that the Arabs, to this day, weave excellent tents of goats' and camels' hair, and that Egyptian women were excellent weavers with small hand-looms? And so were the women of Israel. (Exod. xxxv. 25, 26.) Does he not know that each of such tents, stretched upon pickets only three or four feet high, and divided into two compartments, one for the men, the other for the women, accommodates a whole family, even in the severity of winter, of which Dr. Colenso says so much (p. 79), in reference to Israel's residence at Sinai. In short, is it, or is it not, a fact, that thousands of Arabs do make such tents, and keep alive in them also, during summer and winter, in the desert?

Now as to the means of carriage, the Israelites had plenty. There were asses in Egypt, as elsewhere. There were camels. And, to Dr. Colenso's especial purpose, the Egyptian oxen were[5] trained to draught. Is Dr. Colenso not aware that Egyptian women, and why not Jewish, were wont to be carried in small waggons, each of them drawn by two trained oxen? These were such waggons as Joseph sent for Jacob and his family. (Gen. xlv. 19.) Or is he prepared to show that the sons of Israel, when they left Egypt, did not possess

---

[1] Wilkinson's Anc. Egypt, vol. ii., p. 59; vol. iii., pp. 113—145; and Lane's Mod. Egypt, vol. i., pp. 34—56.
[2] Bochart's Hieroz., p. 556.   [3] Gresswell's Three Witnesses, p. 84.
[4] Volney's Travels, vol. i., pp. 313, 368.
[5] Wilkinson's Anc. Egypt, vol. iii., p. 178.

camels, and oxen, and asses, as well as sheep and goats? Abraham's herds consisted of sheep and oxen, and goats, and camels and asses (Gen. xxiv. 35); so doubtless did Isaac's; so Jacob's, before he left Padan-Aram (Gen. xxx. 43); and afterwards (Gen. xxxii. 14, 15); so when he went down to Egypt, for he took "their goods, which they had gotten in the land of Canaan" (Gen. xlvi. 6); and when the people came out of Egypt, they took "their flocks and herds, even very much cattle" (Exod. xii. 38)—מקנה כבד מאד, where, though sheep and oxen alone seem specified, it is scarcely reasonable to exclude camels and asses. Job's *substance* (מקנהו) was sheep, camels, oxen, and asses. (Job i. 3.) It is more correct to suppose that sheep and oxen having been mentioned as the chief of their wealth, the possession of the rest is implied.

The means of carriage were plentiful; and the means of making tents more so. But we may have occasion to say more on this subject, when speaking of the actual departure from Egypt.

§ XII. THE ISRAELITES POLLED.

There is, however, a difficulty suggested by Dr. Colenso, to which I now invite special attention. The Israelites are supposed to have been polled, and taxed, at Exod. xxxviii. 25; they were certainly polled at Num. i. 1, 2, about six months afterwards. Two strange, but perhaps imagined, difficulties are started: viz., 1. That the number of men, above twenty years old, polled is the same on both occasions; 2. That, in each tribe, the number comes out *neatly* in tens; *Anglicè*, in round numbers.

But, perhaps, the Bishop had better state the matter in his own words:—

> "46. '*And Jehovah spake unto Moses, saying, When thou takest the sum of the children of Israel, after their number, then shall they give every man a ransom for his soul unto Jehovah, when thou numberest them, that there be no plague among them when thou numberest them. This they shall give, every one that passeth among them that are numbered, half a shekel after the shekel of the Sanctuary; an half shekel shall be the offering of Jehovah.*' (Ex. xxx. 11—13.)
>
> "We may first notice, in passing, that the expression, 'shekel of the Sanctuary,' in the above passage, could hardly have been used in this way,

until there *was* a Sanctuary in existence, or, rather, until the Sanctuary had been *some time* in existence, and such a phrase had become *familiar* in the mouths of the people. Whereas here it is put into the mouth of Jehovah, speaking to Moses on Mount Sinai, six or seven months before the Tabernacle was made. And in Ex. xxxviii. 24, 25, 26, we have the same phrase used again, of the actual contributions of the people *towards the building of the Sanctuary.*

"The LXX, indeed, render the Hebrew phrase by τὸ δίδραχμον τὸ ἅγιον, 'the sacred shekel.' But this can hardly be the true meaning of the original, נשקל הקדש; and, if it were, the difficulty would still remain, to explain what the 'sacred shekel' could mean, before any sacred system was established.

"47. But these words direct that, whenever a numbering of the people shall take place, each one that is numbered shall pay a 'ransom for his soul,' of half a shekel. Now, in Ex. xxxviii. 26, we read of such a tribute being paid, 'a bekah for every man, that is, half a shekel after the shekel of the Sanctuary, for every one that went to be numbered, from twenty years old and upward,' that is, the *atonement-money* is collected; but nothing is there said of any *census* being taken. On the other hand, in Num. i. 1—46, more than six months after the date of the former occasion, we have an account of a very formal numbering of the people; the result being given for each particular tribe, and the total number summed up at the end; here the *census* is made, but there is no indication of any *atonement-money* being paid. The omission, in each case, might be considered, of course, as accidental; it being supposed that, in the first instance, the numbering really took place, and in the second the tribute was paid, though neither circumstance is mentioned.

"But then it is surprising that the number of adult males should have been *identically the same* (603,550) *on the first occasion as it was half a year afterwards.*"

I crave the reader's serious attention, because the answer now maintained will be: 1. That there was neither polling nor taxing at Exod. xxxviii. 25; 2. That the Commentators have fallen into the error of making the number of men polled determine the silver used about the tabernacle, whereas the silver used determined the number of men; 3. That the Commentators have incorrectly assumed that all the men, above twenty years old, in each tribe, were polled; whereas they only were polled who were in fighting condition. It will be seen that the observations, 2 and 3, instantly strike away the supposed difficulty about the round numbers.

Now I feel delicacy in entering upon this matter; and must really crave the reader's patience and pardon. Dr. Colenso would shut us out by quoting such dreadful names as Michaelis, Hengstenberg, Kurtz, Hävernick, Kalisch, &c., &c. (Pp. 42—44; and all through his book.) Such names are, indeed, enough to frighten any plain English curate. Why are Englishmen always going down to Egypt, *i.e.*, Germany? Is there no *corn* (as Buxtorff calls *religious instruction*) in England? One great scholar overwhelms us with the exegesis of the Greek Testament, and plenty of references to German, but no Hebrew. Another sends out an awful volume on " The Inspiration of Scripture "—about two-thirds of it being made up of references to Germans. What will the Germans say of Dr. Colenso? I see he has " reserved the right of translation," and hope, for the honour of the country, that he will never part with it. But who is to speak in the face of such authorities as these?

However, just one word. The places which concern the question before us are Exod. xxx. 11—16; xxxviii. 25—28; and Num. i. 1—46. Let the reader carefully examine the first: he will find that Moses is told, *When*—no time is there fixed—When he takes the sum of the people, from twenty years old and above, each man is to give half-a-shekel for the service of the tabernacle, as atonement money. It is not said *when* they are to be numbered; nor for *what purpose:* but it is intimated in the expression " every one that passeth " כל־העבר, that not every male would be numbered, even though he were above twenty years old. Now at Exod. xxxviii. 21—31, the sum is given of all the gold, silver, and brazen work, about the tabernacle. And the reader will observe that, at v. 25—28, all the silver, and its particular application, is carefully mentioned. It is described as the contributions of half-a-shekel each (about fifteenpence) from the men who were numbered. The numbering is spoken of as a thing past. And the fact is that the book of Exodus was written some time after the numbering carefully recorded at Num. i. 1. Hence the writer speaks of it as an event well known to have occurred, not at the time to which he is referring at Exod. xxxviii. 21, &c., when the tabernacle had just been completed, but at a time to which he would afterwards refer, and did refer, and when the tabernacle had been set up. . The tabernacle was set up on the first day of the first month of the second year in the wilderness: the first numbering took place just one month afterwards. (Exod. xl. 2; Num. i. 1.) The book of Exodus was written after both events; though before the entrance into Canaan.

Now I said that the amount of silver used fixed the number of the men to be polled. A general order was given Moses that, whenever he polled the men, he should tax them half-a-shekel each. (Exod. xxx. 12.) The next thing done was to give general directions to all to contribute what they pleased. And the people poured in their gifts every morning (Exod. xxxv. 5; xxi.; xxix.), until Bezaleel asked Moses to stop them, for they had more than they wanted. (Exod. xxxvi. 3, 5.) In this general contribution the poorest man knew he need not bring more than half-a-shekel; it is even conceivable that some had it not to give; but all might bring as much as they pleased: gold, or silver, or precious stones, &c., &c. (Exod. xxxv. 22—29.) The work was done out of hand; and when the *silver* parts (Exod. xxxviii. 25) were finished, Bezaleel knew that he had used 100 talents, and 1,775 shekels of silver; and Moses knew that he would have to enrol 603,550 men, in fighting condition, above twenty years of age. About six months after, viz., when ordered, he did that very thing. (Num. i. 1—46.) No wonder the numbers came out "neat." Moses and the elders took very good care they should. And Dr. Colenso, knowing (as we all are proud to admit) so thoroughly the power of numbers, would have done the same. Moses had 603,550 men to apportion among twelve tribes, and he did so in round *tens;* the distribution being made according to the size of the tribes, the number in each, incapacitate for war, and other considerations easily to be conceived as affecting the selection of men for such a purpose. One might be fit for war at sixty, another not at fifty. At that numbering, the individual taxation was adjusted. All paid half-a-shekel each. And, if any were too poor, doubtless, their richer brethren paid for them.

Some one may ask, Why do you levy the tax of the *militia* upon the silver, and not upon the gold, or even upon the brass? The answer is, because the half-shekel, or bekah, was the smallest coin used, and it was silver. The twenty *gerahs*, which made the shekel, were weights; probably *beans*.[1] So that a silver *bekah* was silver weighing ten beans, and the silver shekel, twenty.

Moreover, that the men numbered paid in silver; and, therefore, whether they first paid, or were first numbered, were *told* according to the silver, and no other metal, is clear from Exod. xxxviii. 25, "And the silver of them that were numbered was," &c., &c. To

---
[1] Gesen. Thesaur., pp. 305, 1475.

show which arrangement also, the directions about taxing are put between the golden work and the brazen work, in Exod. xxx. 11—16.

Now, Dr. Colenso says, in his innocence,—" The expression, " 'shekel of the Sanctuary,' could hardly have been used in this " way, until there was a Sanctuary in existence, or rather, until " the Sanctuary had been some time in existence, and such a phrase " had become familiar in the mouths of the people." Of course not; and this is one place that proves the Book of Exodus was written some time after the putting up of the Sanctuary, &c., &c.; and Moses uses the expression, בשקל הקדש, as expressive of the measure by which he had been previously told in the Mount to make all the estimations of the Sanctuary (Levit. xxvii. 25); and, among others, the war-ransom of the militia. The silver shekel was the standard.

I say—the amount of silver required for the tabernacle fixed the number of fighting men to be enrolled in the wilderness; and not the number of such men, the amount of the silver.

The prevalent idea is that the number of men, given to each tribe, in the first chapter of Numbers, represents *all* the men, in each tribe, above twenty years of age. But nothing of the sort is said in the context. They were all those, of whom each was יצא צבא, ready, as a mode of *living*, to go into war; *i.e.*, fit for war, as a *habit* of life. That is the force of the participle used. And the English version has caught the idea; " all that are able to go forth to war." (Num. i. 3.) A similar idea is expressed at Exod. xxx. 14, when the intended numbering was first mentioned to Moses; " every one that passeth among them that are numbered " כל העבר, every one that " passes muster." The inner limit of age, viz., twenty years, is fixed; but the outer, I believe, nowhere; and for manifest reasons. But Josephus tells us that, in subsequent times, none were expected to pay the war-ransom after fifty years of age. This hints that the Jews knew that *all* men, above twenty years, were not included in the numbering. I do not suppose that any outside limit of age was fixed in the wilderness. But it is certain that many men above twenty years of age would be unfit for war at the first numbering by Moses. It is true that none were so frail at the Exodus as not to be able successfully to undertake the journey; which (we shall have to see) was not over hurried. But there must have been many old men, the contemporaries of Moses and of Aaron, unfit for war. Probably many accidentally maimed by labour in Egypt. Probably some, though in health, naturally deformed; and many, who though living in comparative strength and likely to live, were nevertheless the subjects of chronic disease, which would unfit them for active service.

I conclude, then, 1. That the numbers in Num. i. 1—46, are indices to the size of the tribes; but do not include *all* the men above twenty years of age. 2. That no numbering took place at Exod. xxxviii. 25 where the amount is given of silver used in certain parts of the tabernacle. 3. That the amount of that silver, at half-a-shekel a man, fixed the number of men to be enrolled; and not the men enrolled the amount of the silver. And that, thus, the round numbers are accounted for.

Also, note this—Even if the last suggestion be wrong, the mere fact that Moses was to enrol only men, who were fit for habitual war, would of itself account for the round numbers. For, when we consider the various duties of active service, nothing could be easier than for Moses and the elders to arrange for round numbers, as mere matter of convenience, by taking in each case a few men, more or less, capable of sundry military duties, though not for the crash of close battle. An English Colonel who had to reduce his regiment from any odd number, say 1,187, to a peace standard, would have no difficulty in closing with a round number, say 850; yet, perhaps, he would get rid of some sturdy rogues, and prefer retaining old and tried respectable privates, though not in such robust condition.

As for Dr. Colenso's introduction, at p. 44, of the odd number, 22,273, of the first-born, that has nothing to do with the present business. We shall touch upon that subject by-and-by.

§ XIII. THE INSTITUTION OF THE PASSOVER.

" 65. '*Then Moses called for all the elders of Israel, and said unto them, Draw out now, and take you a lamb according to your families, and kill the Passover. And ye shall take a bunch of hyssop, and dip it in the blood that is in the basin, and strike the lintel and the two side-posts with the blood that is in the basin; and none of you shall go out at the door of his house till the morning. . . . And the children of Israel went away, and did as Jehovah had commanded Moses and Aaron; so did they.*' (Exod. xii. 21—28.)"

"That is to say, in *one single day*, the whole immense population of Israel, as large as that of London, was instructed to keep the Passover, and actually did keep it. I have said, 'in one single day;' for the first notice of any such feast to be kept is given in this very chapter, where we find it written (ver. 12), 'I will pass through the land of Egypt *this night*, and will smite all the firstborn in the land of Egypt, both man and beast.'

"It cannot be said that they had notice several days beforehand, for they were to '*take*' the lamb on the tenth day of the month, and '*kill*' it on the fourteenth (vers. 3, 6), and so ver. 12 only means to say, 'On *that* night—the night of the fourteenth—I will pass through the land of Egypt.' For the expression in ver. 12 is distinctly הזה, '*this*,' not ההוא, 'that,' as in xiii. 8; and so (ver. 14), '*This* day shall be unto you for a memorial;' and, besides, in the chapter preceding (xi. 4), we read, 'And Moses said [to Pharaoh], Thus saith Jehovah, *about midnight* will I go out into the midst of Egypt, and all the firstborn in the land of Egypt shall die,' where there can be no doubt that the 'midnight' then next at hand is intended. It is true that the story, as it now stands, with the directions about 'taking' the lamb on the tenth day, and 'keeping' it till the fourteenth, are perplexing and contradictory. But this is only one of many similar phenomena, which will have to be considered more closely hereafter.'

It is really difficult to gather together, in any moderate space, the wonderful mistakes, and miscalculations, into which Bishop Colenso has fallen. To do him justice, one feels almost compelled to copy the very words he uses. Yet his errors are so numerous, and so wrought into the entire book, that if one were to do so, he must copy nearly the whole of it, as well as write one of his own in reply.

The Bishop's first difficulty is how "in one single day the whole "immense population of Israel, as large as that of London, was "instructed to keep the Passover, and actually did keep it." "And "how could the order, to keep the Passover, have been conveyed, "with its minutest particulars, to *each individual household* in this "vast community, in one day—rather, *in twelve hours*—since Moses "received the command on the very same day, on which they were "to kill the Passover *at even*. (Exod. xii. 6.)?"

There is a verse in the Holy Bible to which I will not allude particularly; but it is very apposite to this inquiry. Suppose we answered Dr. Colenso, "They used carrier-pigeons." For they *did* use carrier-pigeons. And as the Bishop has had occasion to speak of pigeons further on in his book, I shall, in the proper place, give him some information about those interesting birds. However, at present, assuming the Bishop to be right, and that the information had to be conveyed throughout a populous place, as large as London, in twelve hours—were there no horses in Egypt? no *Nile-streams* in Egypt, bearing " swift messengers," in the shape of light boats? Was there not in¹ Egypt, the " swift dromedary, traversing her ways"? All these means of rapid communication existed in the land of Goshen, where Israel dwelt. The *Tawara*, or Arabs of Tor,² viz., the Arabs of the desert close by Goshen, " on the eastern side of the branch of Suez," rear a particular sort of camel, now called *Hedjina;* in shape like the common camel, but more slender, and much fleeter. " He is made use of by couriers," and " if he has once got the start by four hours, the swiftest Arabian mare can never overtake him." For, he will trot easily six miles an hour, for thirty or forty hours successively. The " swift dromedary " is peculiarly a native of the desert El Tih, close by Goshen where Israel dwelt. But no matter, how long would a twopenny post-boy take to worm his way through London, with the promise of roast lamb (and a holiday) at the end of it? How long would a light-dragoon orderly take to dash, from the Horse-guards, a distance of six miles with the intelligence that the French had landed at Dover? How long would all London take to learn it? The departure from Egypt was of equal moment to the sons of Israel.

But here too, as usual, Bishop Colenso is wrong, because he will dabble in criticism. He says that " in one single day," " rather in " *twelve* hours," Moses received the command to keep the Passover, transmitted it to the people, and that it was kept; in this short time, " For the expression in ver. 12 is distinctly הזה *this*, not ההוא *that*, " as in xiii. 8; and so (ver. 14) ' *this* day shall be unto you for a " ' memorial;' and, besides, in the chapter preceding (xi. 4), we read, " ' And Moses said, Thus saith Jehovah, *about midnight* will I go out " ' into the midst of Egypt,' " &c., &c.

There is not a word in the narrative to justify the Bishop's conclusion; there is not a word to warrant our thinking that the directions for the Passover were given to Moses on the 14th Abib, at the *second* evening of which it was to be kept; there is not a word to forbid our thinking they were given on the 10th, or 9th, or, indeed, any other day of that month. The first mention of the subject is at Exod. xii. 1, 2. " And the Lord spake unto Moses and

¹ Jer. ii. 23.   ² Volney's Travels, vol. ii., p. 293.

Aaron in the land of Egypt, saying, This month shall be unto you the beginning of months," &c. And, as there is no previous allusion to the month, the word זה, as here used, must mean this "month *in* which I am speaking;" and the communication may have been made on the first day of it. Bishop Colenso has fallen into the error of supposing that זה must mean *this*, day or time, *at* or *on* which one is speaking; and cannot mean *this*, day or time, *of* which one is speaking. That is his mistake exactly. But it often means the time, thing, or circumstance, *of* which one is speaking. I give examples[1] from the Pentateuch, Gen. vii. 11; xix. 21; Exod. iii. 15; xxx. 31; and Levit. xi. 4; *i.e.*, this day, this name, this oil, these animals, of which I am, or have been, speaking; or am about to speak. So the Lord, at Exod. xii., this month, in which I am speaking, shall be unto you the beginning of months, (ver. 1); thus, having introduced the month, "In the tenth of this month, of which I speak, they shall take to them every man a lamb," (ver. 3) "and the whole assembly shall kill it in the evening" (ver. 6); and, having thus introduced "the evening" as the commencement of night, "For I will pass through the land of Egypt this night," *of* which I am speaking, (ver. 12). God spake nothing *on*, or *during*, the night of Passover; He only slew the firstborn. "And this day," *of* which I am speaking, not *on* which, "shall be unto you for a memorial." (Ver. 14.) Is the Bishop's mistake clear? The 12th verse proves it. And what will he say when we inform him that *this* זה sometimes means *that*? (Deut. iii. 25, and Judges v. 5.) "I pray thee let me go over, and see the good land that is beyond Jordan, that goodly mountain, even Lebanon," החר הטוב הזה; Moses had not ascended Pisgah, when he uttered this prayer, of which I am speaking. (Deut. iii. 27.) "The mountains melted from before the Lord, that Sinai from before the Lord God of Israel," זה סיני מפני יהוה; when Deborah sang that song, she was far away from Sinai, near Megiddo in the valley of Jezreel.[2]

I trust this error, of which we are speaking, in reply to the Bishop, has been clearly exposed.

· The Bishop is altogether wrong in supposing that the directions about the Passover must have been given on Passover-day, the 14th of Abib. They may have been given, and probably were, before the 10th.

Another great error, into which Dr. Colenso has fallen, is that of

[1] Nolden's Concord., Heb. Part, p. 332.   [2] Glassius' Philolog. Sacr., vol. i., p. 160.

supposing that, because the Israelites were "thrust out" of Egypt, and left "in haste," on the morning of the 15th Abib (Exod. xii. 31—33, 39; Num. xxxiii. 3), they, therefore, left unprepared. They had not, indeed, "prepared for themselves any victual"—though they had made their "dough" (Exod. xii. 34, 39), and the word "prepared" must be interpreted accordingly. They had not prepared any sufficient or proper quantity of victual, with especial regard to their journey. They knew not the exact moment they would be allowed to start, and reckoned upon a short time for baking—which short time was not allowed them, until they arrived at Succoth (ver. 37). It was ordered providentially so, that they might not be tempted to leaven their dough. In other respects they had had abundant time to get ready. To start in a great hurry implies no lack of preparation; every dilatory traveller, whose carpet-bag his cheerful wife has packed for a month, knows what it is to be all but too late for the train. The Israelites left in a hurry, but were well prepared. Let us remember that the plague of three days' "darkness over the land of Egypt, even darkness which may be felt," was the ninth; and immediately preceded the smiting of the firstborn. (Exod. x. 22.) What were the Israelites doing during these three days? At this time they were perfectly sure their departure was at hand. (Exod. x. 29, and xi. 8.) And the reasonable answer to such a question is that, during these three days, when the Egyptians could not see an inch before them, "neither rose any from his place for three days" (Exod. x. 23), all the children of Israel who "had light in their dwellings," were busily engaged in preparing for their journey. During those three days they, doubtless, concentrated their flocks; prepared their camels and their asses; made comfortable arrangements for the little children, and the women with child, for whom Dr. Colenso is so properly concerned, at p. 62; passed the necessary commands through their שטרים, or officers, to the several sections into which they had been divided, for purposes of labour, and became החמשים, *i.e.*, organized for the route. The very direction, "none of you shall go out of his door until the morning" (Exod. xii. 22), and the warning of Moses contained, in ver. 23, indeed the plain assurances of immediate rescue, given in ver. 11—17, must have kept the Israelites in earnest expectation all the Passover night, with the conviction that they would be permitted to leave in the morning. And yet Dr. Colenso can write thus:—" Not one was 'to go out at the "'door of his house until the morning.' (Exod. xii. 22.) Conse-"quently, they could not have known anything of what had happened "in Pharaoh's house and city, as also among his people throughout "the 'whole land of Egypt' (Exod. xii. 22), until the summons from "Moses, or at least, the news of the event, reached each individual "house." (P. 60.) Could not have known! Why were they told to keep in doors so, except to avoid being smitten in their firstborn? And had they not been clearly told what was to happen to the Egyptians on that dreadful night? (Exod. xi. 5; xii. 12, 23, 27.) In fact, what did the whole business of the slaughtered lamb, in every house, portend? But such are Dr. Colenso's extraordinary errors in the presence of the plainest assertions of Holy Scripture. And here is another:—" And this appears to be confirmed by the statement, " (Exod. xii. 35, 36,) that, when suddenly summoned to depart, they "hastened, at a moment's notice, to 'borrow' in all directions "from the Egyptians, and collected such a vast amount of treasure, "in a very short space of time, that they spoiled the Egyptians." (P. 56.) Whereas, we before explained, at p. 31, that the signal to borrow had been given long before (Exod. xi. 2, and iii. 22); for the reader must carefully observe that we are not informed what time elapsed between the Lord's having spoken to Moses at Exod. xi. 2, and Moses addressing Pharaoh so terribly at ver. 8 of the same chapter: nor between his having done so, and the Lord's again speaking to him, at Exod. xii. 1. Moses, when threatening Pharaoh, merely said, as to time, " about midnight," without specifying the midnight of what day. While if, as is more than probable, the Lord's speaking to Moses (Exod. xii. 1, 2) was on the first day of Abib, there were twelve clear days during which the " borrowing " could be proceeded with.

§ XIV. BISHOP COLENSO AS CHIEF PASTOR OF A FLOCK.

These remarks about the borrowing, viz., that it had been going on some twelve days, and probably as many weeks (Exod. iii. 22), p. 31, above, will show how unreasonable are the observations quoted below from Dr. Colenso's book. And let us now consider, somewhat attentively, what he says about the flocks of Israel.

"69. But the supposition of their borrowing in this way, even if they lived in such a city, involves prodigious difficulties. For the city, in that case, could have been no other than Rameses itself, from which they started, (Exod. xii. 37,) a 'treasure-city,' which they had 'built for Pharaoh,' (Exod. i. 11)—doubtless, therefore, a well-built city, not a mere collection of mud-hovels. And so the story, in Exod. ii. 5, of the daughter of Pharaoh going down to bathe in the Nile, in the immediate proximity of the place where Moses was born, implies that his parents, at all events, lived not far from the royal residence. But, if the Israelites lived in such a city together with the Egyptians, it must have been even larger than London, and the difficulty of communication would have been thereby greatly increased. For we cannot suppose that the humble dwellings of these despised slaves were in closest contiguity with the mansions of their masters. And, in fact, several of the miracles, especially that of the 'thick darkness,' imply that the abodes of the Hebrews were wholly apart from those of the Egyptians, however difficult it may be to conceive how, under such circumstances, each woman could have borrowed from her that 'sojourned in her house.' Thus we shall have now to imagine the time that would be required for the poorer half of London going hurriedly to borrow from the richer half, in addition to their other anxieties in starting upon such a sudden and momentous expedition.

"70. The story, however, will not allow us to suppose that they were living in any such city at all. Having so large flocks and herds, 'even very much cattle' (Exod. xii. 38), many of them must have lived scattered over the large extent of grazing ground required under their circumstances; and, accordingly, they are represented as still living in 'the land of Goshen.' (Exod. ix. 26.) But how large must have been the extent of this land? We can form some judgment on this point by considering the number of lambs, which (according to the story) must have been killed for the Passover. The command was, 'They shall take to them every man a lamb, according to the house of their fathers, a lamb for an house: and, if the household be too little for the lamb, let him and his neighbour, next unto his house, take it according to the number of the souls; every man, according to his eating, shall make your count for the lamb.' (Exod. xii. 3, 4.) Josephus (*de Bell. Jud.* vi. 9, 3) reckons *ten* persons on an average for each lamb; but, he says, 'many of us are twenty in a company.' Kurtz allows *fifteen* or *twenty*. Taking *ten* as the average number, two millions of people would require about 200,000 lambs; taking *twenty*, they would require 100,000. Let us take the mean of these, and suppose that they required 150,000. And these were to be all '*male* lambs of the first year.' (Exod. xii. 5.) We may assume that there were as many *female* lambs of the first year, making 300,000 lambs of the first year altogether.

"71. But these were not all. For, if the 150,000 lambs that were killed for the Passover comprised *all* the males of that year, there would have been no rams or wethers left of that year for the increase of the flock. And, as the same thing would take place in each successive year, there would never be any rams or wethers, but ewe-sheep innumerable. Instead, then, of 150,000, we may suppose 200,000 male lambs of the first year, and 200,000 female lambs, making 400,000 lambs of the first year altogether. Now a sheepmaster, experienced in Australia and Natal, informs me that the total number of sheep, in an average flock of all ages, will be about *five times* that of the increase in one season of lambing. So that 400,000 lambs of the first year implies a flock of 2,000,000 sheep and lambs of all ages. Taking, then, into account the fact that they had also large herds, 'even very much cattle,' we may fairly reckon that the Hebrews, though so much oppressed, must have possessed at this time, according to the story, more than two millions of sheep and oxen."

It is dangerous to approach Dr. Colenso on matters of arithmetic; but, on the present occasion, I hope we shall be safe. There is not the least error in the Bishop's arithmetic, only he is about 1,000,000 out in his calculation; because he starts with a false assumption.

This is a summary of what he says, as to the number of the flocks of Israel:

Male lambs, of the first year 200,000
Female do. do. 200,000
Remaining flock, of all ages 1,600,000

Total 2,000,000

Apparently the Bishop is not aware that the ewes of Egypt lambed twice a year;[1] "Their sheep were twice shorn, and twice brought forth lambs in the course of one year." So that 400,000 lambs, of the first year, imply only 200,000 ewes. Moreover, Buffon tells us[2] (we must really be plain on this matter) "that one ram will serve 25 or 30 ewes"—let us say 25—so that 200,000 ewes required only 8,000 rams. Therefore the Israelitish flocks, when they left Egypt, need not have been more than

Rams 8,000
Ewes 200,000
First year lambs . . . 400,000

that is to say, they needed only 608,000 sheep of all ages to enable them to keep the Passover; even accepting Dr. Colenso's allowance for stock. Now, suppose we still add 392,000, for the sake of

---
[1] Wilk. Anc. Egypt, vol. ii., p. 17. Diodorus, Sic. i. 36.
[2] Buffon's Nat. Hist., vol. v., pp. 251—254, &c., &c.

stock, we shall then have 1,000,000 for the whole flocks of Israel, instead of 2,000,000 as Bishop Colenso supposes. So that he is more than 100 per cent. wrong (aye! far more than that) as a sheep-master.

For, we need not such addition for stock. Let us go more into particulars. Buffon tells us that sheep begin to procreate at about eighteen months; but should not be allowed to do so until the ram is three years old, and the ewe two. He also says that ewes, "if they are well taken care of," will continue to produce "through life," viz., for ten or twelve years; though they commonly begin to grow old at "seven or eight." The rams, he adds, continue to propagate until they are eight years old; and prefer the older ewes. Moreover he adds, that though ewes commonly produce but one lamb, they often have two at a birth. Now Jacob, and his sons, were clever sheepmasters (Gen. xxx. 37—43); and I think, therefore, that considering ewes would lamb, as Buffon says, in October or November or December or January or February, we may venture to say that there is no absolute necessity so to enlarge the number of the flock for the sake of stock. In fact, there were five lambing months, between the first 14th Abib (April—May), when Israel left Egypt, and the second 14th Abib, when they kept the next Passover at Sinai. (Num. ix. 1.) And we may notice, from the age above given during which sheep are prolific, that we are allowed a period of at least five years for stock, from the same rams and ewes.

It appears, then, to be certain that the flocks of Israel, at the Exodus, need not have counted more than 608,000 head; but, for sake of stock, let us say 1,000,000; and then the Bishop is 1,000,000 wrong in his calculation. Dr. Colenso may be a good Bishop; but he is certainly a bad Pastor. Moreover his calculation is made entirely for *sheep;* but the word צאן, for *flocks* (Exod. xii. 38), would include also *goats*. Of which it is important to observe (again taking Buffon for authority), that, in breeding, the ratio of he-goats to their consorts is as 1 to 150; while of sheep it is as 1 to 25. This again diminishes, for goats, the amount of stock necessary for propagation.

Now, the Bishop being thus wrong in his estimation of stock, it follows that he is also wrong in his calculation of room for them. For he proceeds to ask (p. 59), "What extent of land, then, " would all these have required for pasturage?" and "having made

" enquiries on the subject from experienced sheepmasters "—viz., of Natal, New Zealand, and Australia—he comes to the following conclusion,—

> " Let us allow *five* sheep to an acre. Then the sheep alone of the Israelites would have required 400,000 acres of grazing land—an extent of country considerably larger than the whole county of Hertfordshire or Bedfordshire, and more than twice the size of Middlesex—besides that which would have been required for the oxen. We must, then, abandon altogether the idea of the people living together in one city, and must suppose a great body of them to have been scattered about in towns and villages, throughout the whole land of Goshen, in a district of 400,000 acres, that is twenty-five miles square, larger than Hertfordshire (391,141 acres)."

I fear that when Dr. Colenso consulted the sheepmasters of Australia, and other colonies, he forgot that those gentlemen trade extensively in wool, and keep up their stocks accordingly. We are not informed that the Israelites did so. However, being wrong as he is, in assuming that the flocks of Israel must have been 2,000,000, when they may have been less than 1,000,000, he is also wrong in concluding that they would require 400,000 acres of grazing land, when half the quantity, 200,000, would have done for them. But this question of room is of no importance whatever; we are content to allow Dr. Colenso the utmost he requires; nor have we the slightest wish to reduce his estimate of the extent of the Israelitish flocks. Our object was, merely, to show that his calculation is based upon unjustifiable assumptions.

§ XV. THE MARCH OUT OF EGYPT.

Attention has been already called to the error of supposing that, because the Israelites left Rameses on the morning of the 15th Abib in haste, were "thrust out," they could not have made preparation for the journey. On the contrary, there is good reason to believe they had been warned to hold themselves in readiness many weeks before; and that especially during the three days of Egyptian darkness, which immediately preceded the last plague, and during which all Israelites had light in their dwellings, they were engaged in concentrating their flocks and herds, in arranging the order of their march, and, in short, in making all necessary preparations.

Hence all that Dr. Colenso has said, in his Chapter XI., about " this vast body of people of all ages, summoned to start, according " to the story, at a moment's notice, and actually started, not one " being left behind," (p. 61) &c., &c., is really nothing to the purpose. Neither is there the slightest reason to suppose that " they then " came in from all parts of the land of Goshen to Rameses, bringing " with them the sick and infirm, the young and the aged ; further, " that, since receiving the summons, they had sent out to gather in " all their flocks and herds, spread over so wide a district, and had " driven them also to Rameses." (P. 62.) The fact being that we have cause to believe that, during the Egyptian persecution, the Israelites were confined to two cities with their suburbs, viz., to Rameses and Pythom (Exod. i. 11). And the fact also being that, as we have observed, the three days of darkness on Egypt had given them ample time to collect their flocks together.

That they possessed great flocks there is small reason to doubt ; although Dr. Colenso's estimate of 2,000,000 of sheep, and goats, was based upon incorrect assumptions. The Egyptians themselves, sometimes, possessed immense flocks. Wilkinson mentions the tomb of one who appears to have had no fewer than 974 rams, implying, as he observes, " an equal number of ewes, independent of lambs, which in the benign climate of Egypt were twice produced within the space of one year." They, probably, kept them chiefly for their wool, inasmuch as the Egyptians (at least in the Thebaid) did not eat mutton ; but modestly contented themselves with roast beef, and goose and onions.[1] Now if we remember that the Israelites were sheep-masters of the highest skill ; that the Egyptians regarded shepherds in much the same light as slaves ; that the Israelites were slaves, and had originally been intrusted with Pharaoh's flocks (Gen. xlvii. 6) ; that, in Egypt, the social, or rather unsocial, system of "caste" prevailed ; and trades and other occupations of life descended from father to son ; that the land of Goshen, where Israel dwelt, was peculiarly fitted for the maintenance of flocks and herds ; that the hair of the goats, and the wool of the sheep, had an instant money-value to the Egyptian Government ; if we consider these things, there can be no doubt that the Israelites were permitted to possess, and did possess, very large flocks indeed.

If you draw a line, due north, from Grand Cairo, to the Mediter-

[1] Wilkinson, vol. ii., p. 368.

ranean Sea; and another line, due east, from the same place to the Red Sea; you have the land Goshen, cut off by these two lines from the rest of Egypt, on the west and on the south. There have been many disputes as to the exact spot, on which the Israelites dwelt, but all the disputants are agreed that Goshen was the district north and east from Memphis; and Memphis stood near the place where now stands Cairo. This part of Egypt was the richest of all; "the land of Egypt is before thee; in the best of the land make thy father and thy brethren to dwell." (Gen. xlvii. 6.) And Israel did dwell in Goshen. (Gen. xlvi. 28; xxxiv.; xlvii. 4, 6, 27.) Moreover, this land of Goshen was anciently filled with great, and teeming, cities.[1] Where Damietta now stands, there once stood Sin, the key of Egypt on the side of Palestine, 130 miles only from Jerusalem, on the Pelusiac branch of the Nile. On the same branch of the Nile, a little south of Pelusium, was Bubastis; and near it Pythom, one of those two cities, to which the Israelites were assigned. There, too, was On, or Aven, of which Potiphar, Joseph's father-in-law was priest, and prince; which, also, was the chief residence of the priests, and other wise men, of Egypt. There, again, was Taphanes, or Taphne, sixteen miles south of Pelusium, the emporium of commerce with the Mediterranean and Red seas; in which town stood, so Jeremiah tells us, one of the Egyptian king's palaces. (Jer. xliii. 9.) There, also, was Zoan, on one of the eastern branches of the Nile; perhaps the oldest city in Egypt, but, certainly, one of the royal residences of Pharaoh, and the place in which, the Psalmist tells us, Moses wrought his miracles. (Ps. lxxviii. 12.)

And the existence, within the land of Goshen, of these large, rich, and influential, cities, implies a corresponding richness in the population, cultivation, and resources, of all the neighbouring territory. In fact, Goshen, from the Pelusiac branch of the Nile, to the desert, and Red Sea, was formerly the richest, best cultivated, and best watered, territory of Egypt.

Through this territory the Israelites marched. Hence to suppose them, as Dr. Colenso does, "to have travelled through the open desert," (p. 63), is at once a fatal mistake. But I must not anticipate. There is no reason to suppose that they all started from Rameses. The head-quarters were there; the elders and other principal people; there, too, no doubt Moses and Aaron met, and

[1] Paxton's Sacr. Geog, p. 203, &c.

consulted with, the chiefs of the people; from that place necessary directions for the march were issued. And when the elders, and other chief men, led the way from Rameses towards Succoth, and all the people tended from Pythom, and the suburbs of both towns, in the same direction, it could be said with truth, and is said, "the children of Israel journeyed from Rameses to Succoth, about 600,000 on foot that were men, besides children." (Exod. xii. 37, 38.)

"And now," says Bishop Colenso, "let us see them on the march itself. If we imagine the *people* to have travelled through the open desert, in a wide body, fifty men abreast, as some suppose to have been the practice in the Hebrew armies, then allowing an interval of a yard between each rank, the able-bodied warriors alone would have filled up the road for about *seven miles*, and the whole multitude would have formed a dense column more than *twenty-two miles* long, so that the last of the body could not have been started till the front had advanced that distance, more than two days' journey for such a mixed company as this."

But, why make this absurd supposition at all? Elsewhere, viz., at pp. 47, 48, Dr. Colenso will not admit, on any account, that the people went out in this way fifty-abreast, or abreast at all; חמשים, when it suits him, means *armed* and nothing else. And now it suits him to conceive of the *people*, fifty-abreast, and to make a ridiculous tail, twenty-two miles long. But it will not suit me. As explained, (see above p. 34), חמשים means "kept in hand" in pre-arranged order, under recognised leaders. They did not walk abreast; nor did they all follow along the same road. Though they did all move in one direction, viz., that towards Palestine, from their different localities. A clever writer has said it seems that "after the immemorial arrangement of caravans in the east," the march was "consigned to the management of five presiding officers," thus giving a certain meaning to חמשים; but, as he gives no authorities for this "immemorial arrangement," we need not depend upon him. Let us understand that the people went out of Egypt, not by fifty in a rank, nor under five leaders, in five divisions, but simply kept well in hand, under many leaders, with a pre-arranged order of march.

Now, if Dr. Colenso's book had any value at all, that value would be found in its calculations. But others have brought this subject to the test of arithmetical calculation, as well as Dr. Colenso, and have proved, not only from arithmetic, but also from personal

measurement and observation on the spot, that the "march out of Egypt" was quite practicable. Three routes have been selected, and disputed over. Sicard takes the people, from Memphis (Cairo), a little south, then east by south, through the plains of Gendeli, to a point about seventy miles south of Suez, where (according to him) Pi-hahiroth lay, half a mile from the shore of the Red Sea. Niebuhr and Burckhardt, first-class travellers, fix the passage at a point about twenty miles south of Suez; having taken the people first almost due east from Memphis (Cairo), through a country similar to the plains of Gendeli. And, lastly, Robinson has taken the people from Rameses, south-east, to Suez; and maintains, probably with truth, that the people crossed the Red Sea there. All agree that the "march out" was practicable, so far as the physical characteristics of either route were concerned. Let us hear Sicard, a man after Dr. Colenso's own heart:—" I have myself made the calculation on the spot" (this, I fear, Dr. Colenso has not done), "and the following is the result of
" my observations:—From Mount Diouchi to the Nile, the plain is
" 6,000 common paces wide, and 12,011 long. Now, if a rank of
" 2,000 men were drawn up in a space of this length, there would be
" precisely six clear paces between man and man; and if, in its width,
" there were 1,200 files, each of which consisted of 2,000 men,
" having five paces from file to file, it is evident that 2,500,000, at
" least, could be commodiously encamped; and each man being
" distant six paces one way, and five the other, from his neighbour,
" the intervening space would be amply sufficient for their flocks and
" camels. . . . From Rameses, the route of the Hebrews was
" directly east, through the spacious valley formed by the continuous
" range of Diouchi and Jorah, which join their extremities at the
" western shore of the Red Sea, opposite Sinai. The valley is
" so wide that, even in the narrowest part of it, *several thousand*
" persons could walk abreast; and, with regard to forage, the whole
" length of the valley, although, like the vast, grassy steppes, which
" are not inhabited by a fixed population, it is called, in the Hebrew
" idiom, a wilderness, abounding with tamarisk, clover, and sanfoin,
" of which camels are passionately fond, as well as with a variety of
" brushwood, for kindling fires."

This is very pretty figuring; and we may venture to say that Abbé Sicard would have made a better Quartermaster-General than Bishop Colenso.

However, let us hear Robinson (*Biblical Researches*, vol. i., p. 84):—

" As the Israelites numbered more than two millions of persons, besides flocks and herds, they would, of course, be able to pass but slowly. If the part left dry were broad enough to enable them to cross in a body one thousand abreast, which would require a space of more than half-a-mile in breadth (and is, perhaps, the largest supposition admissible), still the column would be more than two thousand persons in depth; and, in all probability, could not have extended less than two miles."

I merely give these extracts to show that painstaking enquirers, in modern times, have, like Dr. Colenso, reduced the question of "the March out of Egypt" to figures; and have concluded, unlike him, that, so far as the physical conformation of the country is concerned, that march-out was possible for more than two millions of people, with their flocks and with their herds.

But what did these last do for provender? Now, 'tis ten thousand pities to see how Christian commentators, following, one behind another, some bad leader, will mar, will daub, a grand, sublime, majestic picture! Says one, "There were two routes to Canaan; the one northward by the coast of the Mediterranean, which was the nearest and most common; the other along the western arm of the Red Sea, through the wild and inhospitable desert that divides Egypt from Arabia Petra." And Kitto (to whom Dr. Colenso betakes himself):—"The journey to this point," viz., where they encamped by the sea, " had been, for the most part, over a desert, the surface of which is composed of hard gravel, often strewed with pebbles." (*Hist. of Jews*, p. 177.) Is Kitto a safe compiler for an earnest, spiritually-minded Bishop? However, in what way has Kitto learned that? From personal observation, *how?* Alas! alas! Egypt has become "the basest of kingdoms," under the curse of God. (Ezek. xxix. 15.) And it is never safe, from its appearance now, to draw adverse conclusions as to aspect or capabilities then, when Israel left Rameses. Listen to an Infidel. Volney[1] says, speaking of the neighbourhood of Suez (not far from which Israel crossed the Red Sea):—" Formerly these districts were covered with towns, which have disappeared with the waters of the Nile. The

[1] Volney's Travels, vol. i., pp. 196—200.

"canals which conveyed them are destroyed; for in this shifting soil, "they are presently filled up, both by the sands driven by the winds, "and by the cavalry of the Bedouin Arabs." Volney has just been speaking of the impossibility, "amid these shifting sands," of successfully making and keeping open a canal through the Isthmus of Suez; and takes note that the only safe route, for this purpose, to Suez, is that which the ancients selected for their canal, viz., from Memphis (Cairo), through "a continued plain from the banks of the Nile" to the Red Sea. This is the route by which Dr. Robinson supposes the Israelites to have gone; "the direct and only route was along the "valley of the ancient canal," in which valley, imagination not very strong may picture water and provender to have abounded before the canal was formed, by Sesostris as is supposed. All this region was formerly well irrigated, and studded, as we mentioned, with cities, of which scarcely a trace remains. Of Memphis, Lord Lindsay says (*Travels*, vol. i., p. 189):—" We rode for miles through groves of "palms and acacias, cultivated fields, and wastes of sand, over what "we knew must be the site of Memphis, but Noph is indeed waste "and desolate." And Dr. Robinson (*Researches*, vol. i. p. 40), that two large " mounds of rubbish, a colossal statue sunk deep in the "ground, and a few fragments of granite, are all that remain to attest "the existence of this renowned capital." Zoan, the mighty Zoan, is now Zaan, " a small fishing village in the neighbourhood of the "ruins of this ancient place of renown, all of which, with a few "fragments of obelisks, are nearly invisible, from the mounds of "rubbish in which they are buried. But, among those that are open "to observation, many large blocks present a vitrified appearance; "thus affording clear and strong evidence that 'the Lord hath set "' fire in Zoan' (Ezek. xxx. 14)."—*Paxton's Sacr. Geog.*, p. 203. Taphanes is no more; but, "like the baseless fabric of a vision, leaves not a wrack behind." On, that proud City of the Sun, the great college of the priests of Egypt, to which Herodotus, Plato, and others, repaired to investigate her science and institutions, has perished. "Its site," says Robinson, "is still marked by low mounds, " inclosing a space about three quarters of a mile in length, by half "a mile in breadth; which was once occupied, partly by houses, and "partly by a celebrated temple of the sun. This area is now a "ploughed field, and the solitary obelisk of red granite, covered

"with hieroglyphics, which still rises in the midst, is the sole
"remnant of the ancient worshippers of that luminary." While
Volney, standing on the terraces of Suez, says, "From the tops of
"the terraces the eye, surveying the sandy plain to the north-west,
"the white rocks of Arabia to the east, or the sea and the mountain
"Mokattam to the south, cannot discern even a single tree, or the
"smallest spot of verdure." (*Travels*, vol. i., p. 201.) Mokattam,
or the Brown Mountain, is the range that terminates close by Cairo,
so that Volney at Suez looked right across Goshen. Yet it is
from the present state of a country thus cursed of God that Bishop
Colenso, backed up by poor Kitto, would draw a most fallacious
conclusion concerning Israel's " march out of Egypt."

Still, the present state of some parts of Goshen, or Lower Egypt,
may give us some faint idea what it was when in high prosperity.
"No flat region," says Dr. Duff, "can be more beautiful. The
"waters of the annual inundation had not wholly withdrawn from
"the land, but half subsided on the channel of the river. Vast level
"plains spread out on all sides, having their carefully-cultivated soil
"clad in the living green which distinguishes the first fresh blades of
"vegetation in the month of May in the British climes; and their
"borders fringed with rows, and their points of junction garnished
"with clumps and groves, of date trees, palmyras, sycamores, and
"other evergreens. Thus, for miles together, it presented the aspect
"of a well-dressed garden. The numberless branches and canals for
"distributing the redundant waters of the river, and the many
"pieces of mechanism in busy play to supply the deficiencies, or
"perpetuate the effects of the inundation, were conspicuous objects
"in the landscape." And Jablonsky, speaking of Rameses, whence
Israel commenced their march, says the name "signifies the land of
"shepherds. On the low and marshy meadows with which that
"district abounded, pasturage was so abundant that Maillet describes
"the grass as equal to the stature of a man, and so luxuriant that an
"ox may browse a whole day lying on the ground." In short, the
Bible intimates distinctly that the Israelites saw nothing of
wilderness until the end of their second day's march, when
"they encamped in Etham, in the edge of the wilderness." (Exod.
xiii. 20.) The site of Succoth is not known; Etham lay on the
edge of the eastern desert, probably not far from the head of the

gulf; and "the position of Migdol, Pi-hahiroth, and Baal Zephon, "cannot be determined, except that they probably were on or near "the great plain back of Suez." (Robinson, vol. i., p. 81.)

I know not wherefore, but most commentators have thought proper to conclude that the Israelites spent only three days between Rameses and Pi-hahiroth. The Bible says nothing of the sort; but intimates a very different fact indeed. It is true they occupied three days in the journey; or rather made three marches of it. And even in late days, as Volney testifies (*Travels*, vol. i., p. 200), the caravan which left Cairo (Memphis) on the 27th of July did not reach Suez until the 29th. But there is much to lead us to think that the Israelites spent more, and probably a great many more, than three days between their leaving Rameses and crossing the bed of the Red Sea. They encamped at Succoth, baked, and spent we know not what time there; they encamped at Etham, how long they stopped we know not; they encamped at Pi-hahiroth, and the very command, given them to do so, seems to imply that the onslaught of Pharaoh and his army did not take place immediately.

The Israelites broke up from Rameses about half-past three o'clock on the morning of April 9, in the year [1] B.C. 1560; and they occupied exactly one month in reaching the wilderness of Sin (Exod. xvi. 1); and more than two months before they came to Sinai (Exod. xix. 1, 2.) But the journey from Suez to Sinai is a journey of only eight days, at an easy rate of travel. Robinson occupied in it just that time, viz., from March 16 to March 24, 1838, having rested on the intervening Sabbath day. (*Researches*, vol. i., pp. 87, 135.) Robinson gives, as the camel's pace, 2·019 miles to the hour (vol. i., p. 545); and all the host of Israel may fairly be supposed, with their flocks and herds, to have travelled at least at so slow a rate. Be that as it may, the Israelites did occupy just ten journeys in travelling from Shur, where they landed, after passing through the Red Sea (Exod. xv. 22) to Sinai (Numb. xxxiii. 8—15). It is evident, therefore, that they travelled at a most leisurely pace, and that of the more than two months' time consumed, between Rameses and Sinai, a very small portion of it was taken up with actual travelling; for the rest, they remained stationary at the places of their several encampments. The Egyptians were accustomed to mourn for their

[1] Gresswell's Three Witnesses, ch. i., sec. 10, p. 84. 1862. Parker, Oxford.

kings seventy-two days.¹ Is it unreasonable to believe that several
days were passed in the grief and consternation caused by the
slaughter of the firstborn, of whom Pharaoh's eldest son was one?
Suppose we allow ten days to transpire for this purpose, before
Pharaoh's grief and fear subsided, and rage and revenge occupied
their places, and prompted him and his people to follow after Israel?
Then the three days' journey, between Rameses and Pi-hahiroth,
must be stretched over a period of ten, and allow an encampment of
three days each to two of the three stations, Succoth, Etham, and
Pi-hahiroth; with an encampment of four days for the remaining
one. Here was ample time for a gentle passage, between station and
station, for all the people, old and young, and women with child;
with abundant leisure for attention to casualties. And I should
think that all the multitude, with their flocks, and with their herds,
did concentrate, not at Rameses, but from Rameses and Pythom,
their suburbs, and the intervening country, first towards Succoth,
and next towards Etham, the recognised common route to Palestine
and Syria, by various roads well known to lead thereto. So that
they browsed as they passed along; and without now waiting to
speak of the dates, and the *drees* (or prepared dried food) with
which the Egyptians fed their cattle, there was no such danger as the
Bishop supposes, that "such grass as there was, if not eaten down
" by the first ranks, must have been trodden under foot at once and
" destroyed, by those that followed them mile after mile" (p. 64).
One would think that the Doctor was thinking of the croppy growth
on the Southdowns; he certainly could not have had in view such
grass as Jablonsky describes, which grew as high as a man's head, and
would provender an ox from one spot, if he chose to lie in it, all day.
(See above, p. 63.) With such facts before us, the question
becomes idle, " What, then, did those 2,000,000 of sheep and
" oxen live upon during the journey from Rameses to Succoth,
" and from Succoth to Etham, and from Etham to the Red Sea?"
(P. 61.)

But Dr. Colenso is uneasy about " the sick and infirm, or the women
" in recent or imminent childbirth, in a population like that of London,
" where the births are 264 a-day, or *about one every five minutes.*"
(P. 62.) But why so? At p. 38 above, we have seen him assume
that the Israelites must have travelled " twenty miles a-day." I know

¹ Wilkinson's Anc. Egypt, vol. ii., p. 69.

not by what route he takes them. But the distance "from Rameses "to the head of the Gulf, according to the preceding *data*,[1] would be "a distance of some thirty or thirty-five miles; which might easily "have been passed over by the Israelites in three days," *i.e.*, at the rate of, at the most, twelve miles a-day. A camel's average pace is, as we have said, little more than two miles an hour. The Israelites, therefore, travelled about six hours each day; that is to say, they were halted three-fourths of each day, or about eighteen hours, to say nothing of the intervening days, which, I believe, they passed at Succoth, Etham, and Pi-hahiroth. Now, these family affairs, I am told, usually come off at night; but, at any rate, six hours is no very lengthy period to be passed between a mother's "imminent "childbirth," and the actual encampment of a little stranger. As for the allusion to London, and one birth about "every five minutes," I am surprised that Dr. Colenso, who is so good a ready reckoner, did not tell us fairly the ratio of these births, at night, and various other periods of the day; that was necessary to his argument. For, assuming that the Israelites set out every morning about six o'clock, and travelled until noon, Dr. Colenso ought to have told us how many of the births, at one every five minutes, would have taken place during the six hours while they travelled, and how many during the eighteen hours they were halted. I will dare to say that, in due course of nature, nearly all of them took place between the hours of twelve at noon and six A.M. of the following day; and that few, very few of them, occurred between the hours, six A.M. and twelve at noon, during which they were travelling. Even according to the Doctor's own showing, there would be but seventy-two births in the six hours; and what are these among so many? Now, the Egyptians used palanquins, waggons, litters, and other modes of gentle carriage; and, we may be sure, that men inured to making bricks, in the burning clime of Egypt, were at no loss for wit how to carry a tender woman, great with child.

Once upon a time, a friend of mine was out of a ship that foundered at sea. He had scarcely stepped into the boat, when the ship went to the bottom. Not many hours elapsed before the captain's wife took to the "stern-sheets" of the boat, and there, attended by one other lady, and covered by my friend's top-coat, brought forth a splendid boy. After beating about on the open

---

[1] Robinson's Bibl. Research., vol. i., p. 80.

sea, for twenty-eight days, they reached land; both mother and baby doing well.

These twenty-eight days' pitching up and down, in a jolly-boat at sea, could hardly have been as snug, nor as warm, as three days' journeying in Egypt, at the rate of two miles an hour, for six hours a-day. But Dr. Colenso will understand very well that what took place in an English boat at sea, might be better managed in an Egyptian waggon on land. And much better by an Egyptian roadside, such as Jablonsky describes. See p. 65, above.

I conclude, then, that the Israelites, though "thrust out" of Egypt, and leaving hurriedly, at a moment's notice, did travel at the rate of about two miles an hour, for six hours, during three days, between Rameses, Succoth, Etham, and Pi-hahiroth; that they encamped at each of the three last-mentioned places, probably for several days; that they had abundant means of providing for the aged, and sick, and women with child; that they journeyed through a rich country, by various routes, along known roads, tending to the well-known wilderness between Egypt and Palestine, and that this route of three days was through a country which was *then* fertile, and abounded with water and with pasture, though *now* it is desert. And, indeed, for this last conclusion—viz., that the country, now desert, was once fertile—Robinson affords us direct authority:—

" On another day we rode out to the site of ancient Heliopolis,
" about two hours N.N.E. from Cairo. The way thither passes
" along the edge of the desert, which is continually making its
" encroachments, so soon as there ceases to be a supply of water
" for the surface of the ground. The water of the Nile soaks
" through the earth, for some distance, under this sandy tract; and
" is everywhere found on digging wells, eighteen, or twenty, feet
" deep. Such wells are very frequent in parts where the inundation
" does not reach. The water is raised from them by wheels turned
" by oxen, and applied to the irrigation of the fields. Wherever
" this takes place, the desert is quickly converted into a fruitful
" field. In passing to Heliopolis, we saw several such fields, in the
" different stages of being reclaimed from the desert; some just laid
" out, others already fertile. In returning by another way, *more*
" *eastward*, we passed a succession of beautiful plantations, wholly
" dependent on this mode of irrigation. The site of Heliopolis is
" marked by low mounds, inclosing a space about three quarters of a

"mile in length, by half a mile in breadth, which was once occupied
"partly by houses, and partly by the celebrated Temple of the Sun.
"This area is now a ploughed field, a garden of herbs; and the
"solitary obelisk, which still rises in the midst, is the sole remnant
"of the former splendours of the place. This was the On of the
"Egyptians, where the father of Joseph's wife was Priest. (Gen.
"xli. 45.)"—*Bib. Research.*, vol. i. p. 36.

Nor let the reader suppose that Exod. xiv. 3, "The wilderness hath shut them in," is opposed to this conclusion. It is probable the "wilderness" here has reference to the eastern desert, which commenced at Etham (Exod. xiii. 20), and from which Israel "turned southward, and encamped at Pi-hahiroth." Pharaoh would naturally suppose that the sight of that wilderness had caused them to do so. But, even if we suppose that the country immediately round Pi-hahiroth, close on the shores of the Red Sea, was thus called a wilderness, Abbé Sicard has hinted to us in what sense it was so; the Hebrew word, מדבר, meaning, not only a stony desert, but any uninhabited tract of country, as a steppe, or moor, or down; though found, nevertheless, with pasture; or, as Abbé Sicard would say, even abounding with "tamarisk, clover, and sanfoin." For מדבר, means properly, a sterile, even sandy, region, unfit for tillage, through which nomad tribes fed their sheep (Exod. iii. 1; 1 Sam. xvii. 28, &c., &c.; Simonis, Heb. Lex., p. 370); and by no means a country unfit for pasture. This I perceive Dr. Colenso, 'by reference' to Gesenius, knows. See p. 88, below.

§ XVI. BETWEEN THE TWO EVENINGS.

Among other subjects connected with the narrative of the Exodus, Dr. Colenso has striven to throw doubt and ridicule over the account (found in Num. ix. 5) of the celebration of the second Passover at Mount Sinai. He exclaims, at p. 131:—

> "Again,—How did these priests manage at the celebration of the Passover?
>
> "We are told (2 Chron. xxx. 16; xxxv. 11), that the people killed the Passover, but '*the priests sprinkled the blood from their hands*, and the Levites flayed them.' Hence, when they kept the second Passover, under Sinai (Num. ix. 5), where we must suppose that 150,000 lambs were killed

at one time 'between the two evenings' (Exod. xii. 6), for the two millions of people, each priest must have had to sprinkle the blood of 50,000 lambs, in about two hours; that is, at the rate of about *four hundred lambs every minute, for two hours together.*

"Besides which, in the time of Hezekiah and Josiah, when it was desired to keep the Passover, strictly in such sort as it was written, 2 Chron. xxx. 5, the lambs were manifestly killed *in the court of the Temple.* We must suppose, then, that the Paschal lambs, in the wilderness, were killed *in the court of the Tabernacle;* in accordance, in fact, with the strict injunctions of the Levitical law."

So also, at p. 132, " How, in fact, could the priests have sprinkled " the blood at all, if this were not the case, that the animals were " killed in the court of the Tabernacle?

" But the area of that court contained, as we have seen, only " 1,692 square yards, and could only have held, when thronged, " about 5,000 people. How, then, are we to conceive of 150,000 " lambs being killed within it, by at least 150,000 people, in the " space of two hours—that is, *at the rate of* 1,250 *lambs a minute?*"

Such are Dr. Colenso's objections. Let the reader note that the following points are essential to his argument:—1. That the time meant by the phrase "between the two evenings" must be a period of only *two hours.* 2. That the Passover at Sinai must have been kept exactly as it was afterwards kept at Jerusalem both by Hezekiah and Josiah. 3. That 150,000 lambs had to be killed by 150,000 people. 4. That they had to be killed within "the court of the Tabernacle." 5. That the priests had literally to. *sprinkle* the blood in the same two hours. An error in any one of these five positions, but especially in either of the first three, may be fatal to his whole argument. He ought, indeed, to have been sure of the ground he was moving on; but he is as innocent as a baby new-born on the road from Rameses.

His first error proceeds from his not fairly treating, or not understanding the meaning of, the phrase, בֵּין הָעַרְבַּיִם, *between the two evenings.* The original command, respecting the Paschal lamb, was, " And the whole assembly shall kill it in the evening;" where the expression, rightly translated "in the evening," or "at even," may be literally rendered " between the two evenings," as the margin of the English Bible shows. The Bishop hazards no remarks of his own respecting this most singular Hebrew phrase. Why? Other matters he minutely examines for himself, and ventures (often rashly) to treat them on his own authority. Why not this? He does, however, at p. 133, refer, in a note, to the opinion of Kurtz, that " the Caraites and Samaritans are right " in their explanation of the phrase ; and proceeds to reason upon Kurtz' admission, as if it must needs be sound. Indeed, we may here remark that this English Bishop's mode of mixing up the commentaries, sometimes sound, sometimes otherwise, of German divines with his own objections is extremely undignified, and equally unsatisfactory. Why has the Bishop no original views of his own respecting these nice points of Hebrew criticism and construction? If he really knows Hebrew, he ought to have them; and, if he do not know Hebrew, why has he so ostentatiously sprinkled his pages with Hebrew letters? It is to the deep discredit of the English Church that her authors are perpetually referring to dreamy Germans; and books are published, in the present day, full of references to such foreign writers, which young clergymen are expected to receive almost as they would the Gospel.

I have to complain,—1. That Dr. Colenso has ventured to bring the solemn institution of the Passover, which typified the atoning death of Christ, into doubt and ridicule; and that by basing his argument upon a most disputed, and disputable, Hebrew phrase,— a phrase which even ancient Jews themselves could hardly be certain they correctly understood. 2. That Dr. Colenso has done this apparently, without being himself personally acquainted with the various authorities on the subject. In fact, it would seem, without really knowing anything of the matter. The reader will judge for himself. But, I submit, that, if Dr. Colenso had knowledge of the facts I am about to explain, he would never have been so unfair, or so irrational, as to base his argument upon the notion that " between the two evenings " could only be a space of *two hours* at even.

The various opinions entertained on this curious question may be learned from the authorities referred to below.[1] The best of which authorities is Bochart. And the following is a brief summary of the

---

[1] The Targum of Onkelos, or the Rabbinical Comments, of Jarchi, and Kimchi, and Aben Ezra, or as referred to by Fagius in "Critici Sacri," on Exod. xii. 6; Bochart's " Hierozoicon," De Agno Paschali, pp. 631—636 ; R. Moses ben Maimon., De Sacrificio Paschali, chap. i.; Simonis' Heb. Lex., p. 1243; Gesenius' Thesaur., p. 1065; and Lee's Heb. Lex., p. 476, b.

various opinions entertained as to the meaning of this peculiar phrase, בין הערבים, *between the two evenings.*

1. That of Aben Ezra, to which Dr. Colenso (quoting Kurtz) alludes, but not correctly. Aben Ezra's words may be thus translated :—" We have two evenings. One, the evening of the sun, *i.e.*, the time at which he sets and disappears under the earth. The second is that light, or irradiation, which still appears on the clouds after his setting. This time, which is included in the setting of the sun, and his irradiation on the clouds, lasts one hour and the *third part* of an hour." The language is itself indistinct and incorrect, for such a time is, in no sense, between two evenings, but is between sunset and actual night. This seems at once a fatal objection.

2. Accordingly, the Jerusalem Talmud says, *Berachoth*, cap. i. :— " All that time, when the face of the sun shines bright, is called day; when he begins to pale, it is called 'between the suns;' when it becomes dark, then is night." The Talmuds and the Targum say " between the suns," as their explanation of " between the two evenings." And the Babylonian Talmud, *De Sabbatho*, cap. ii., fol. 34, " The two suns are two times, in which the sun shines from the *meridian*, of which one is near to noon, the other to sunset." This introduces an important difference of opinion, for it makes " the two evenings " to be the whole afternoon from midday to sunset. And these Talmuds are among the highest Hebrew authorities.

3. Similarly, Jârchi and Kimchi, than whom, on such subjects, two higher authorities can scarcely be quoted, say :—" *Between the two evenings*, *i.e.*, the time in which the sun goes down to set. For there are two evenings. One is[1] when the sun begins to go down; and the other is when he sets. And the two evenings include the time between." Or, as Bochart gives *Jarchi, Kimchi, and Pomerius*, " they understand ' between the two evenings ' to be the whole afternoon, with the first part of night, as if the sun divided two evenings." Now if we take, according to Aben Ezra, the time between sunset and night to be *one hour and twenty* minutes, and remember that on the 14th of Abib, or April 9th (according to Gresswell, see p. 64, above), the sun would set about 6.20, then the opinion

---

[1] So the Greeks. " Hesychio emin δείλη πρωία, ἡ μετ' ἄριστον ὥρα, vespera matina tempus est a prandio (proximum); et δείλη ὀψιά ἡ περὶ δυσίν ἡλίου, vespera sera, quæ circa solis occasum."

of the Talmuds, and of Jarchi and Kimchi, comes to this: that the time between the two evenings on the 14th Abib was the whole time from 12 o'clock at noon to 7.40 in the evening, viz., a period of nearly eight hours instead of two; that unfair assumption upon which Dr. Colenso has thought proper to reason.

4. Bochart alludes to the opinion of some (*sunt, qui*) who think "between the two evenings" to mean both evenings of the 14th Abib, viz., the first evening, when it begins at about 6.20 p.m. (after the 13th Abib); and the second evening, when it ended, viz., about 6.20 p.m. (immediately preceding the 15th Abib). Bochart himself calls this "most absurd." But wherefore? If the Passover could be killed only at the end of the 14th Abib, how could it have been roasted, and eaten too, on the 14th? That some good Hebraists may think this opinion not absurd, the following extract from Professor Lee will prove:—"*The evening*, a term apparently as indefinite as among ourselves. According to the Samaritan and Caraite Jews, its duration was of two parts; first, beginning with the setting sun; the second at the end of the twilight. But, according to the Rabbins, first, when the sun began to decline towards the west; the second, when it had set,—which has been had recourse to purely for the purpose, in each case, of attaching a favourite interpretation to the dual form, viz., ערבים. Others have, for the same reason, had recourse to the Greek δείλη πρωία, and δείλη ὀψία. See Bochart, Hieroz., i., p. 559, and Rosenmüller, on Exod. xvi. 12, &c.; all of which, according to my notions, is groundless and wrong. See my sermon on the Sabbath, with the notes; where it is shown that the phrase, בין הערבים, *between the two evenings*, means between the period termed evening, ערב, on one day, and the same period of the next, including one whole day; so that the Paschal lamb was to be eaten some time between six o'clock on the 14th of Nisan (or Abib) and six o'clock on the next day, comprehending the whole day, viz., the 14th of Nisan, the day commencing with the Hebrews about six o'clock in the afternoon. Our blessed Lord, according to this, both ate the Paschal lamb at the due time appointed for that rite, and also suffered on that day so appointed. And hence also it is that we read of some who would not enter the Judgment-hall of Pilate, about daybreak on the same day, because they had not yet eaten the Passover. (John xviii. 18.)" This opinion, which Bochart calls "most absurd," is nevertheless probable.

5. I shall mention the interpretation which some have put upon the Targum's expression "between the suns," as equivalent to the phrase "between the two evenings." "Onkelos calls it שמשיא, which some interpret *suns*, others *evenings*. Between 'the suns, viz., the setting and the rising. A double evening, that of the day, and of the morning. The first is termed, *Hebraically*, 'the evening of the day,' ערב יום, but the second 'the evening of morn,' ערב בקר, and is a space of *twenty hours*, as if you should say ὀψιπρωῖον, or 'the commencement of the civil day,' being reckoned from the time next to sunset. The Greeks call it νυκθήμερον." (*Drusius on Num.* ix. 3, *in Critici Sacri.*)

6. I shall give the opinion of Maimonides, with whom I imagine we may understand Abarbanel to agree,[1] seeing that he so habitually refers to him, and lauds him as that "most learned Maimonides," "a man of the highest authority," "Maimonides most skilful in the sacred writings,"—let us hear the opinion of Maimonides: "The " Passover is slain at any time after noon (אחר חצות *à meridie*); for " to slay it before noon is profane. Nor is it slain except after the " evening continual sacrifice, which ought to be offered 'between " the two evenings,' after the burning of incense." Maimonides' exact words may be seen in *Bochart's Hieroz.*, p. 634; or in his *Treatise on the Passover*, cap. 1, §§ 1—20: he also says,—which Bochart does not quote,—that the slaying of the Passover, thus commenced " after the slaying of the evening continual sacrifice," "is " carried on, without ceasing, through the whole remaining portion " of the day. But if the Paschal Lamb were slain after the noon, " and *before the evening sacrifice*, it was well: for then one of the " priests carried the blood taken from the Paschal victim within, " while the blood of the evening continual sacrifice was sprinkled " on the altar; although if the altar were sprinkled with the blood " of the Paschal Lamb, *before that of the continual evening sacrifice*, " it was well." These last words of Maimonides are of great importance, as we shall see.

7. There is, lastly, the statement of Josephus, quoted by Dr. Colenso at p. 133, "They slay their sacrifices from the " ninth hour to the eleventh," *Wars*, vi., ix. 3; upon which it is important to remark that Josephus intends to give no critical explanation of the phrase בין הערבים; but merely to assert, as an

---

[1] Abarbanel's Exodium, Comment. Levit. cap. 4.

historical fact, that at that time, viz., when Cestius took the census of Jerusalem for Nero, they found it practicable to kill the passover within those two hours, the ninth and the eleventh, which were undoubtedly a part of the afternoon, viz., from three to five o'clock; and not the part of time chosen by the Samaritans, Caraites, and Aben Ezra, which was from about 6 p.m. to about 7.20 p.m. Still, if Dr. Colenso is willing to receive Josephus as convincing evidence of the fact that the time of killing the passover was *two hours* only, he must also receive his evidence, as to the historical fact, that it certainly could be, and was actually, killed in that space of time; at the period he mentions, viz., when 256,500 lambs had, he says, to be killed for all the people of Jerusalem.

Thus have I collated six different opinions (Josephus gives no opinion) as to the meaning of the phrase "between the two evenings." First, Aben Ezra's, who makes it to be *one hour and twenty minutes*, from 6 p.m. to 7.20 p.m.; and not one hour and a-half, as Dr. Colenso incorrectly states: second, the Talmudists, which say it means *six hours and twenty minutes*, from 12 o'clock at noon to 6.20 p.m.: third, that of Jarchi and Kimchi, who understand it to be about *seven hours and forty minutes*, viz., all the afternoon and the first part of the night, *i.e.*, from 12 o'clock at noon to about 7.40 p.m.; allowing, according to Aben Ezra, one hour and twenty minutes between sunset and night: fourth, that of some who took it to be the whole time between the rising and the setting sun, explaining it (see p. 73) as, in their sense, a space of about twenty hours: fifth, some in Bochart's time,—also represented by Professor Lee in these,—who understand the phrase to include all the *twenty-four hours* of the 14th Abib, one whole day: and, sixth, that of Maimonides, who says it means all the afternoon, from the meridian to the end of the day, viz., *six whole hours* and twenty minutes, from 12 o'clock at noon to 6.20 p.m., which ended the 14th Abib, or Passover-day. The Talmudists and Maimonides, in fact, agreeing.

Now I appeal to every candid reader to say whether with these diverse, these widely different, opinions as to the meaning of the phrase, "between the two evenings," Dr. Colenso can possibly be justified in taking it for granted it must mean a period of only *two hours*, and on that account in throwing ridicule over the account of the Passover mentioned in the book of Numbers?

Having thus exposed Dr. Colenso's unfairness, if he was acquainted with these opinions; his ignorance, if he was not; I proceed to make a remark or two more upon the meaning of this phrase בין הערבים *between the two evenings*. One may venture to say that Aben Ezra, and the Caraites and Samaritans, are manifestly wrong. He may venture to say so because he is supported by the Talmuds, by Jarchi, by Kimchi, and Maimonides; in short, by the great mass of the very highest authority. And he may also venture to say so for this simple reason, viz., that the Passover must be killed on the 14th Abib; but if Aben Ezra's opinion be taken, we could never be sure that it was not killed on the 15th. The natural visible termination of the 14th Abib would be *sunset;* but Aben Ezra's opinion carries us on into black night, viz., into the 15th Abib. Secondly, if force is really to be given to the *dual* form, ערבים, two evenings; one evening, or limit of the time intended, must have some sort of resemblance to the other; the word must mean two *phases*, or powers, of the sun; but Aben Ezra's limits are *sunset* on the one hand, and *black night* on the other; and it is hard to see in what sense black night represents any *phase* of the sun, *i.e.*, daylight, to those who had to be guided by it in slaying the Paschal Lamb.

Further, I would observe that, in regard to time, the Hebrews used three beautiful, but singular, duals: שחרים means *full morning;* צהרים means *full noon;* and ערבים means (I say) *full sunset*. So that as צהרים meant the noon, or middle point between dawn and sunset, when the sun is in his meridian, so שחרים meant the time when the full disc of the sun is first visible, in rising, above the horizon; and ערבים means the time when his full disc is last visible, in setting, above the horizon. The force of the dual must, at the very least, be to separate the two spaces of time, as to the morning between dawn and noon, and as to the evening between noon and night. So that taking Aben Ezra as a fair judge, if one hour and twenty minutes must elapse before sunset becomes night, then to give the force of ערבים we must take another hour and twenty minutes before afternoon becomes sunset. I maintain that, whatever time would elapse between sunset and night on the 14th Abib, at least double that time must be allowed to the phrase "between the evenings." This, even according to Aben Ezra, would make the period to be two hours and forty minutes; and not two hours, as Dr. Colenso supposes.

I conclude, therefore, 1. That Dr. Colenso has misrepresented Aben Ezra; 2. That Aben Ezra is plainly wrong; 3. That all probabilities are that the Talmudists, and Rs. Jarchi, Kimchi, and Maimonides (who, in effect, agree) are right; 4. That it is possible that the Passover might have been lawfully killed at any time of the day of the 14th Abib, provided the feast was not kept until the *second* evening, which terminated that day, and immediately preceded the 15th Abib; and that, consequently, all that Dr. Colenso has said is worth nothing so far as it depends, and it does entirely depend, upon his limitation of the sacrifice and sprinkling of the blood of the Passover in the wilderness to the period of *two hours.*

This proof that Dr. Colenso has no good authority for limiting the slaying of the Passover to the short space of *two hours* is utterly fatal to all he has said as to the impossibility of the three priests' sacrificing 150,000 lambs, for all the congregation, in the court of the tabernacle, during that brief time. Instead of having only two hours, they probably had all the time from earliest dawn to latest evening—about twenty hours; but I believe we may say, with confidence, they had at least half that time, viz., all that intervened between noon and latest evening. And if we grant to Dr. Colenso that 150,000 lambs had to be killed, then taking the first space of time, viz., twenty hours, and admitting the people into the court only 2,000 at a time (it would hold 5,000), then 150,000 lambs could be comfortably killed in seventy-five lots, at sixteen minutes to a lot. Taking the second space of time, viz., ten hours, then, admitting the people 3,000 at a time, the same could be done in fifty lots, at twelve minutes to a lot; easily enough, too, if each man killed his own. But this was not necessary. Levite, and lay, butchers, could be deputed for the purpose; and the business be so done more quickly. The killing, so Maimonides tells us, was managed by passing a bright, sharp knife once through the jugular, and back; this would kill any lamb in the world in a far less space of time than twelve minutes. But supposing we took the shortest space of time allowed by the Talmudists and Rabbins, say even six hours, which is less than they allowed, then admitting the people at the same rate, each man, in each lot, would have to kill his lamb in *three-fifths* of twelve minutes, viz., in seven minutes and twelve seconds. And it could be done.

But, says Dr. Colenso, there were only three priests, and they had to sprinkle the blood of all the 150,000 lambs in *two hours.* Of course, as we have showed, he is wrong as to the *two hours;* but he is wrong also in two other respects. The (so-called) sprinkling was part of the sacrificial service; and, even if the lambs had to be killed in *two hours*, the sprinkling (so called) might continue all night until the morning, a period not of two hours, but of *twelve*, allowing full sunrise to be about four a.m. And, as I remarked, Maimonides' observation about this "sprinkling" of the blood is most important. It might be collected in bowls, carried within, and left until, bowl after bowl, the priest *dashed* it, not sprinkled it, at the foot of the altar. And three priests thus engaged for twenty, or ten, hours could pour out the blood of 150,000 lambs with ease, being 50,000 each, at the rate of 2,500 an hour if in twenty hours, or twice the number if in ten. Ten hours would be the shortest time by which to limit them, seeing that the (so-called) sprinkling would go on all night until sunrise on the 15th Abib, *i.e.*, from about 6 p.m. on the 14th to about 4 a.m. on the 15th. And, indeed, it may be questioned, whether they would be limited to *any* time, seeing that Passover was only the commencement of the feast of "unleavened bread" which lasted seven days.

Maimonides' description of killing the Passover, at subsequent times, is as follows:—"Each man killed his own lamb, in the court of the temple." "Here the priests were arranged, in many rows, some holding silver, some golden, bowls." "A priest received the blood in a bowl, gave it to the next, he to the next, that as many as possible might be engaged in the holy work, until that priest was reached who stood next the altar. He poured it out at the foot of the altar."

Dashed it, or spilled it, or poured it, not sprinkled, in the English sense. Maimonides says, again and again, that the proper way was to pour it out all at once, "receiving the bowl full, and returning it empty." And the word זרק will bear this sense, viz., to throw out of the bowl loosely, widely. Dr. Colenso says, at p. 134, that "the "sprinkling of the blood is enjoined in the case of any sacrifice of any "kind (Lev. xvii. 6);" and so it is in this sense. But when more cautious sprinkling was required, it seems to have been expressly enjoined. (Lev. iv. 6, 17, 20, 35, &c.) In the case of the Passover, to dash the blood on the doorposts was the first directed mode— נתן, to place it there, in any way; and to throw it loosely at the altar will meet the force of זרק for subsequent times. For which sprinkling, a peculiar vessel מזרק was provided. Of which each Priest might take *two*, one in either hand, and thus *double* the rate of sprinkling.

I trust it has become very evident that Dr. Colenso is quite wrong, as to the time he has assumed for the sacrificing of the Passover; also wrong, as to the time to which he has limited the three priests, for the sprinkling; and even wrong, in the arbitrary sense which he has assumed for the word *sprinkling*. A man does, in one sense, sprinkle when he casts water, or blood, loosely from a bowl. He does also sprinkle when he takes a bit of broom, or hyssop, or even his five fingers, and dips them, or either of them, into the liquid first, and then scatters it.

However, we have granted Dr. Colenso that, for the sake of argument, to which he is in no way entitled. He has assumed that the Passover at Sinai was kept like subsequent Passovers, *e.g.*, those by Hezekiah and Josiah (2 Chron. xxx. 16, and xxxv. 11), but if the reader will refer to Num. ix. 1—5, he will see that there is no manner of reason for this assumption. The places referred to by the chronicler, as above, have regard to directions contained at Exod. xxiii. 17, and Deut. xvi. 2, 5; and there is the best reason for denying that those places had been written when the Passover was kept at Sinai. So that the "rites and ceremonies" of it, spoken of at Num. ix. 3, are those which had been delivered to Moses and the Israelites in Egypt. Moreover, if Dr. Colenso will take it for granted that the Passover at Sinai must have been a rehearsal, or model, Passover for subsequent times, he gets into another difficulty. For, at such Passovers, only the males had to appear (Exod. xxiii. 14—17; Deut. xvi. 16); and it would almost seem as if, to be consistent, Dr. Colenso ought to limit the number of those who would thus have to keep the Passover at Sinai, in a manner to correspond: and, if so, the number of lambs to be killed would be very seriously diminished, and all difficulty is, consequently, removed.

If, on the other hand, they kept the Passover at Sinai, in the same way as that in Egypt (which seems probable), then, again, all difficulty is swept out of the way; each man killed for his own party, and dashed the blood above, and on either side of, the entrance to the tent. For I cannot believe that the Bishop is serious when, at p. 136, he intimates that, because the people had no door-posts in the desert, the injunction of smearing the blood on the entrances to their dwellings could not be observed. Must there needs be *door-posts?* Had all the people door-ways when in Egypt? Or has Dr. Colenso any authentic pattern to exhibit? To dash the blood above, and on either side of, any entrance to any kind of residence, kept the spirit of the command.

I do not doubt myself but that all the Israelites kept the Passover at Sinai, and therefore I have replied to Dr. Colenso on that assumption. Whether they killed the lambs in the court of the Tabernacle may be questioned. But if they did, Dr. Colenso's error about the times for *killing* and for *sprinkling*, is fatal to his argument.

After all, the observance of the Passover, whether in the desert, or in Canaan, is matter for historical evidence rather than for arithmetical calculation. Was the Passover ever kept by the Jews? Did the Lord Jesus ever keep it? Is Josephus to be believed when he says that Cestius took the census of Jerusalem for Nero, at the time of Passover, and that then 256,500 lambs had to be killed, in the court of the temple, within two hours? Is there any truth in the accounts, contained in the Chronicles, of the Passovers kept by Josiah and by Hezekiah? Is there any truth in Ezra's account of the Passover kept, and sacrifices offered, at the rebuilding of the temple? In one word, when Israel numbered many, many millions, and "all their males" went up to Jerusalem to keep the Passover, was or was not that Passover ever killed in sufficient quantities, and at proper times, and with the necessary rites, so as to be accepted of the Lord? It may be hard for us, in these days, to realize the process; but there can be no doubt of the matter as mere subject of history. And if we are forced to admit that the Passover was wont to be kept acceptably for many millions of people after the temple was built, and before, when the Tabernacle was at Shiloh, we may as well admit it could be, and was, kept acceptably for 2,000,000 of people when the Tabernacle was at Sinai, although the exact process may be beyond our powers to ascertain.

§ XVII. THE NUMBER OF PRIESTS, AND THEIR PERQUISITES.

· The Bishop proceeds, in his chap. xx., to discourse upon "the " number of priests at the Exodus compared with their duties, and " with the provision made for them." He finds the priests far too few for the duties, and the perquisites far too many for the priests; and he states his objection thus:—

> "146. The book of Leviticus is chiefly occupied in giving directions to the priests for the proper discharge of the different duties of their office, and further directions are given in the book of Numbers.
> "(i.) In the case of 'every *burnt-offering*, which any man shall offer,'

whether bullock, or sheep, or goat, or turtle-dove, 'the *Priests, Aaron's sons,* shall sprinkle the blood upon the altar, and put fire upon the altar, and lay the wood in order on the fire, and lay the parts, the head and the fat, in order upon the wood;' and 'the *Priest* shall burn all on the altar, to be a burnt-sacrifice.' (Lev. i.)

" (ii.). So in the case of a *meat-offering* (Lev. ii.), *peace-offering* (Lev. iii.), *sin-offering* (Lev. iv.), or *trespass-offering* (Lev. v., vi.), the *Priest* has special duties assigned to him, as before.

" (iii.) Every woman after childbirth is to bring a lamb for a burnt-offering, and a pigeon or turtle-dove for a sin-offering, or two young pigeons for the two offerings, and the *Priest* is to officiate, as before. (Lev. xii.)

" (iv.) Every case of leprosy is to be brought again and again to the *Priest*, and carefully inspected by him till it is cured. (Lev. xiii.)

" (v.) Any one, cured of leprosy, is to bring a burnt-offering and a sin-offering, and the *Priest* is to officiate, as before. (Lev. xiv.)

" (vi.) For certain ceremonial pollutions, which are specified, the *Priest* is to offer sacrifice. (Lev. xv. 15, 30.)

" (vii.) For a male or female Nazarite, when the days of separation are fulfilled, the *Priest* is to offer a burnt-offering, a sin-offering, and a peace-offering. (Num. vi.)

" (viii.) Every day, morning and evening, the *Priest* is to offer a lamb for a continual burnt-offering, besides additional sacrifices on the Sabbath, the New Moon, at the Feast of Unleavened Bread, and at the Feast of the First-fruits. (Num. xxviii.)

" (ix.) In the seventh month, for several days together, besides the daily sacrifice, there were to be extraordinary additional sacrifices, so that on the fifteenth day of the month the *Priest* was to offer thirteen bullocks, two rams, and fourteen lambs, and in the seven days, from the fifteenth to the twenty-first, seventy bullocks, fourteen rams, and ninety-eight lambs. (Num. xxix.)

" (x.) Lastly, if it should be thought that the above sacrificial system was not meant to be in full operation in the wilderness, we may call attention to the frequent references made, in the enunciation of these laws, to the Camp, (Lev. iv. 12, 21 ; vi. 11 ; xiii. 46 ; xiv. 3, 8,) as well as to the words of the prophet Amos, (ver. 25,)—' Have ye offered unto me sacrifices and offerings in the wilderness forty years, O House of Israel ? '—which show that, in the Prophet's view, at all events, such sacrifices were required and expected of them.

" 147. And now let us ask, for all these multifarious duties, during the forty years' sojourn in the wilderness,—for all the burnt-offerings, meat-offerings, peace-offerings, sin-offerings, trespass-offerings, thank-offerings, &c., of a population like that of the city of London, besides the daily and extraordinary sacrifices,—how many Priests were there ?

" The answer is very simple. There were only *three*,—Aaron, (till his death,) and his two sons, Eleazar and Ithamar.

" And it is laid down very solemnly in Num. iii. 10, 'Thou shalt appoint Aaron and his sons, and they shall wait in the Priest's office ; and *the stranger that cometh nigh shall be put to death.'* So again, (ver. 38,) 'Aaron and his sons, keeping the charge of the Sanctuary, for the charge of the children of Israel; and *the stranger that cometh nigh shall be put to death.'* "

Before we reply particularly to these objections, it may be observed,—First, that if, at any time during the forty years' wandering in the wilderness, the Israelites found themselves, from local circumstances, literally unable to observe the Levitical rites, they would be unquestionably absolved from the duty of doing so. For instance, if (as Dr. Colenso maintains at p. 124) the poor women after childbirth could not possibly obtain the pigeons required for their offering, because there were none in the wilderness, then beyond doubt they were held guiltless for not offering them. A Christian man is expected to avail himself of the use of the sacraments for himself, and his children; but if, in a distant colony, it so happens that he cannot obtain them, he is not guilty before God of neglecting them. This remark, when applied to Dr. Colenso's difficulty about the pigeons (to be noticed more particularly) at once destroys all his arguments on that head; for if, as he says, the pigeons could not have been had " at all under Sinai;" why, then, of course there were none offered; nor had the unhappy priests to eat eighty-eight pigeons, each, every day, " in the most holy place," as he supposes. Second, that it is important for us to distinguish between *public* sacrifices which, (the conditions of their wandering life permitting,) were to be offered by the priests, as a necessary part of their public, daily, duty; and those sacrifices which were private, and optional. For it would be the case, with the Israelites, as with other nations, that the really devout persons among them were few; and such persons alone would attend strictly to their private religious obligations; the offering of certain sacrifices included. As matter of fact, we know that the sacrifices were so neglected in the wilderness, and that is the sin of which Amos indignantly reminds the people, in the passage quoted by Dr. Colenso. For instance, the Passover (that chief of sacrifices) was kept in the wilderness but once; and, as it has been said, "the Israelites were forty years in the wilderness, and kept the Passover only once, viz., at Sinai. This Amos indicates when he says, 'Have ye offered,' &c., &c. For that which was done only once, is held as if not done at all. 'One swallow does not make spring.' The Hebrews assign as the reason for this neglect that in the desert none of their sons were circumcised." (*Drusius on Num.* ix. 2, *in Critici Sacri.*) It is no argument against either the wisdom, or the holiness, of the Levitical institutions, or of its priesthood, if they were arranged in the foreknowledge of this neglect on the part of the people, or with a regard to this inaptness of local circumstances. While we have a perfect right to conclude that the completest provision would have been made at any subsequent time to meet the necessities of the people; if, indeed, those which were first arranged, had proved insufficient.

Dr. Colenso makes an unwarrantable assumption, viz., that "during the forty years' sojourn in the wilderness" there were but three priests. It is true there were but three priests at the first—Aaron, as the high priest; and his two sons as the chief priests, upon one of whom his high office would devolve. But it may be questioned how far this gives us a right to assume, as Dr. Colenso does, that no other priests were afterwards consecrated, and did not actually officiate in the desert. When Aaron came out of Egypt he was eighty-three years old. The narrative tells us nothing of the ages of Nadab, Abihu, Eleazar, and Ithamar, his four sons. They may have been near fifty years of age, or even older, at the Exodus; and may have had, each of them, sons nearly thirty years old at the time of the consecration under Sinai. These things may have been, and Dr. Colenso has no right to assume they were not. But he has so assumed, and bases a great deal of his argument upon the assumption, that there were but three priests during the forty years' sojourn in the wilderness. The account given of Aaron's family at Exod. vi. 23—26, makes nothing against these observations; for the book of Exodus having been written shortly before the entry into Canaan, its author is only desirous, in that passage, to give the genealogy of Phinehas, upon whom the high-priesthood was destined to descend. There may have been, therefore, during part, a great part, of the forty years' sojourning in the wilderness, many more than three priests. It is useless to say none are mentioned. Many Israelites must have played important parts among their people, at that time, whose names are not mentioned. Moses' two sons are never mentioned; except in the briefest way, at Exod. xviii. 3—5. And probably Phinehas, the son of Eleazar, the son of Aaron, would never have been mentioned but for his distinguished conduct at Shittim (Num. xxv. 7); in acknowledgment of which he inherited the high-priesthood. It is also evident that, in the numbering in the plains of Moab (Num. xxvi. 57—62), the family of Kohath or Aaron is studiously included among the whole number of Levites, the object of that numbering having been only to take the sum-total of the males of the tribe.

If, however, there were, or could possibly have been during a great part of the forty years in the wilderness, more and many more than three priests, a large division of Dr. Colenso's objections, on the score of the priestly services, is struck away.

Further, in his ostentatious exhibition of the onerous duties entailed upon the priests, Dr. Colenso has omitted, scarcely with fairness, to observe how many important offices, connected with attendance upon the priests, might legally be discharged for them by the Levites, who numbered 8,560, from thirty years old to fifty, at Sinai. (Num. iv. 48.) On this subject I have spoken above at p. 26. They might kill, they might flay, they might receive into bowls, and pass, the blood, they might and did cleanse away the traces of sacrifice—in short, a multitude of duties, and those the most laborious, were left to the Levites; all, indeed, but actual service at the altar. The priest's office was "for everything of the altar, and within the vail." (Num. xviii. 7.)

Now a great difficulty with Bishop Colenso is as to the disposal of the sacrifices. There were some, of which parts had to be eaten by the priests in the most holy place; some were given as food to the priests and their entire families; and, we may add, to the whole tribe of Levites also, as servants of the priests; and some were given as property to the priests, though of such a character, *e.g.*, the *skin* of the burnt-offerings, that they could not be eaten. And Dr. Colenso states the matter thus, pp. 126—128:—

> "Again we have in Numbers xviii. 9—11, the following commands addressed to Aaron by Jehovah himself :—'Every oblation of their's, every meat offering of their's, and every sin offering of their's, and every trespass offering of their's, which they shall render unto me, shall be most holy for thee and for thy sons. In the most holy place shalt thou eat it; it shall be holy unto thee.
>
> "'This also is thine; the heave offering of their gift, with all the wave offerings of the children of Israel: I have given them unto thee, and to thy sons and to thy daughters with thee, by a statute for ever: every one that is clean in thy house shall eat of it.'
>
> "Then follow other directions, by which it is provided that the priest

should have also 'the best of the oil, and all the best of the wine, and of the wheat, the first-fruits of them, which they shall offer unto Jehovah,' and 'whatsoever is first ripe in the land;' which laws we may suppose were intended only to be applied, when the people had become settled on their farms in the land of Canaan, as also the law, ver. 25—29, for their receiving also a tenth of the tithes of corn and wine and oil, which were to be given for the support of the Levites.

"But in ver. 14—18 we have again these provisions:—

"'Every thing devoted in Israel shall be thine. Every thing that openeth the matrix in all flesh, which they bring unto Jehovah, whether it be of men or beasts, shall be thine: nevertheless, the firstborn of man shalt thou surely redeem, and the firstling of unclean beasts shalt thou redeem.

"'But the firstling of a cow, or the firstling of a sheep, or the firstling of a goat, thou shalt not redeem: they are holy; thou shalt sprinkle their blood upon the altar, and shalt burn their fat for an offering made by fire, for a sweet savour unto Jehovah.

"'*And the flesh of them shall be thine, as the wave-breast and as the right shoulder are thine.*'

"Similar directions are also laid down in Lev. vii.:—

"'As the *sin*-offering is, so is the *trespass*-offering; there is one law for them: the priest, that maketh atonement therewith, shall have it. And the priest, which offereth any man's burnt-offering, even the priest shall have to himself the skin of the *burnt*-offering, which he hath offered. And all the *meat*-offering that is baked in the oven, and all that is dressed in the frying-pan and in the pan, shall be the priest's that offereth it. And every *meat*-offering, mingled with oil, and dry, shall all the sons of Aaron have, one as much as another.' Ver. 7—10.

"'For the wave-breast and the heave-shoulder have I taken of the children of Israel from off the sacrifices of their *peace*-offerings, and have given them unto Aaron the Priest and unto his sons, by a statute for ever, from among the children of Israel.' Ver. 34.

"155. These last directions are given in the story before Aaron and his sons were consecrated. Hence they must be considered as intended to apply to them, while the camp was in the wilderness, as well as to the 'sons of Aaron' in future generations. But what an enormous provision was this for Aaron and his four, afterwards two, sons, and their families! They were to have the skins of the *burnt*-offerings, and the shoulder and breast (that is, double-breast) of the *peace*-offerings, of a congregation of two millions of people, for the general use of their three families!. But, besides these, they were to have the whole of the *sin*-offerings and *trespass*-offerings, except the suet, which was to be burnt upon the altar (Lev. iv. 31, 35; v. 6), and the whole of the *meat*-offerings, except a handful, to be burnt as a memorial (Lev. ii. 2); and all this was to be eaten *only by the three males, in the most holy place!* (Num. xviii. 10.)

"156. And it would seem that they were not at liberty to *burn* the sin-offerings, or consume them in some other way than by eating: they must be 'eaten in the holy place.' At all events, we find it recorded that Moses, on one occasion, 'diligently sought the goat of the sin-offering, and, behold, it was burnt! and he was angry with Eleazar and Ithamar, the sons of Aaron, saying, Wherefore have ye not eaten the sin-offering in the holy place, seeing it is most holy, and God hath given it you to bear the iniquity of the congregation, to make atonement for them before Jehovah ? *Ye should indeed have eaten it in the holy place*, as I commanded.' (Lev. x. 16—20.)

"The very pigeons, to be brought as *sin*-offerings for the birth of children, would have averaged, according to the story, 264 a-day ; and each priest would have had to eat daily eighty-eight for his own portion, 'in the most holy place'!"

But there are several important considerations, under the effect of which the supposed difficulties vanish away. This grouping together of very different matters must not be allowed to deceive the reader. It becomes important to notice what portion of the sacrifices must necessarily be eaten, in the holy place, by the priests; what might be given out generally to the families of the priests, and to the Levites, their servants; and what offerings might be, if they chose, turned into money for their benefit. It is also even desirable to notice the extremely early age, viz., eight days (Lev. xxii. 27), at which the animals might be sacrificed, as materially affecting the size of them. And, lastly, there was one great principle, causing frequent exception to the prescribed duty of eating the sacrifice in the holy place; it was this—" no sin-offering, whereof any of the blood is brought into the tabernacle of the congregation to reconcile withal in the holy place, shall be eaten; it shall be burnt in the fire." (Lev. vi. 30.) I am at a loss to account for it; but it is, indeed, a very important, and extraordinary fact, that Dr. Colenso has omitted to quote a statement to this effect, in the passage he cites (at p. 128), from Lev. x. 16—20. He gives it thus—" Wherefore have ye not eaten the sin-offering in the holy place, seeing it is most holy, and God hath given it you to bear the iniquity of the congregation, to make atonement for them before Jehovah ? *Ye should indeed have eaten it in the holy place*, as I commanded." Whereas the passage is, "*Behold the blood of it was not brought in within the holy place:* ye should indeed have eaten it in the holy place, as I commanded." How came the Bishop to omit these most important words? They indicate a general principle affecting the sin-offerings. Whenever the atoning blood was *brought into the holy place*, the sacrifice had not to be eaten; but to be burned outside the camp ! Says Abarbanel—

"There are two sorts of sin-offering in public sacrifices; one, that which is *all* burned with fire; and another, that of which the greatest part was given to the priests to be eaten." (*Exod. Comm. in Lev.*, cap. 3.)

Yet, even as regards what the priests had to eat, there was one important principle, affecting all such sacrifices, clearly enjoined —what the priests could not eat they were to burn. Thus, at the Passover, "Ye shall let nothing of it remain until the morning; and that which remaineth of it until the morning ye shall burn with fire." (Exod. xii. 10.) This principle is distinctly laid down, for Aaron and his sons, at Exod. xxix. 34, and Lev. viii. 31, 32, " That which remaineth of the flesh, and of the head, shall ye burn with fire;" and for the people's peace-offerings generally, at Lev. vii. 15, 17.

It seems to me that the difficulty, suggested by Dr. Colenso, as to the disposal of the sacrifices, is done away with if we bear these several principles in mind. 1. That the great mass of the sacrifices alluded to were optional, not compulsory (Lev. i. to iv., &c., &c.), and, as matter of fact, were much neglected in the wilderness. " These offerings," says Maimonides, " were, nevertheless, all volun-" tary; for it is observed, respecting them, that, although they should " not be offered, no guilt should be incurred; as it is said (Deut. " xxiii. 22), ' If thou shalt forbear to vow, it shall be no[1] sin in thee.'" 2. That only of two sorts, viz., the sin-offering, and the trespass-offerings, was the priest bound to eat in the holy place. For the burnt-offerings were *holocausts*, and the peace-offerings (certain parts having been burned) were carried away by the master of the sacrifice. 3. No sin-offering was to be eaten, whose blood had been brought into the holy place for atonement; it was to be burned. 4. Boiled or roast, whatever the priest could not eat, he was to burn. 5. By far the largest part of the sacrifices were given, not only to the priests, but to their families, and attendant Levites (Num. xviii. 11—19). 6. The compulsory duties of the priests (as national officers), were comparatively small, viz., the continual sacrifice of a lamb, morning and evening; with those for the Sabbath, the new month, and the feast of first-fruits. Of the duties of the Passover we have spoken before.

[1] Maimon. Mor. Nev. " Reasons of the Law of Moses," ch. xxii. of precepts of the eleventh class.

Abarbanel sums up the matter as follows, (*Exod. Comment. in Levit.*, cap. 2, *de formis sacrificiorum*):—" From which it appears that these sacrifices differed in mode, thus:—The burnt offering was all consumed by fire; the sin-offering was partly burned by fire, partly eaten by the priests alone; and similarly, as regards the trespass-offering; but of the peace-offering some was burned, viz., the intestines; it was tasted by the priest, and then handed back to its owner. In these forms, you have the partition and disposal of victims to be burned on the altars."

There is one part of Dr. Colenso's objections so good that we have kept it to the last. I refer to his difficulty about the turtle-doves or young pigeons, to be offered in the desert; and have already noticed that, if, as Dr. Colenso *erroneously* asserts, they could not have possibly been obtained in the wilderness, then the poor women, and others, were absolved from offering them. And we may now add, that if they proved scarce, and their cost was great in proportion, then only those who could pay for them, need offer them; and the number of such offerings would be diminished accordingly. But let us have the Bishop's own words:—

"In fact, we have one of these commands, manifestly referring to their life in the wilderness (Lev. xiv.), where, after it has been ordered that the priest shall go out of the camp to look at the leper (ver. 3), and that the leper duly cleansed shall 'after that come into the *camp*, and shall tarry abroad out of his *tent* seven days' (ver. 8), and on the eighth day shall offer 'two he-lambs and one ewe-lamb,' &c. (ver. 10), it is added (ver. 21), 'And if he be *poor*, and cannot get so much, then he shall take one lamb, &c., and *two turtle-doves* or *two young pigeons*, such as he is able to get.' Here the 'turtle-doves or young pigeons' are prescribed as a lighter and easier offering for the poor to bring; they are spoken of, therefore, as being *in abundance*, as being within the reach of every one, in the wilderness, under Sinai! It would seem to follow that such laws as these could not have been written by Moses, but must have been composed at a later age, when the people were already settled in Canaan, and the poor, who could not afford a lamb, could easily provide themselves with pigeons. In the desert, it would have been equally impossible for rich or poor to procure them.

"152. It may be said, indeed, that the בני יונה, 'young pigeons,' were birds of the wilderness. Thus, we read, in Ps. lv. 6, 7, 'And I said, Oh that I had wings like a *dove* (יונה); for then would I fly away, and be at rest. Lo, then would I wander far off, and remain in the *wilderness* (מדבר); so Jer. xlviii. 28, 'O ye, that dwell in Moab, leave the cities, and dwell in the rock, and be like the *dove*, that maketh her nest *in the sides of the hole's mouth;*' and Ez. vii. 16, 'They that escape of them shall escape, and shall be on the mountains like *doves* of the *valleys*, all of them mourning, every one for his iniquity.' Yet the Psalmist, in Ps. lv. 6, 7, was hardly thinking of the 'great and dreadful' desert of Sinai. He had, probably, in view the wilderness of Judah, or some other wide extent of 'uncultivated, and comparatively barren, country, into which cattle are driven to feed' (*Ges. Lex.*, מדבר), far from the common haunts of men; and the יונה might be found dwelling in the rocks or valleys of such a solitude as this.

"153. The desert of Sinai, indeed, is also called מדבר, as in Num. xx. 4; Deut. viii. 15; xxxii. 10; Jer. ii. 6. But, in each of the above passages, some expression is added to show the terrific character of the Sinaitic waste; thus, in Num. xx. 4, 'Why have ye brought up the Congregation of Jehovah into this wilderness, that we and our *cattle* should die there? . . . neither is there any water to drink;' in Deut. viii. 15, 'that great and terrible wilderness, wherein were fiery serpents, and scorpions, and drought; where there was no water;' in Deut. xxxii. 10, 'He found him in a desert land (בארץ מדבר), in the waste, howling wilderness (ישמן);' in Jer. ii. 6, 'Where is Jehovah, that led us through the wilderness, through a land of deserts and of pits, through a land of drought and of the shadow of death?' It can scarcely be believed that the בני יונה, even if they could have been found here at all, would have been so numerous, that they could be spoken of as common birds, within the reach of the poorest of the Congregation, and be offered at the rate of 90,000 a-year."

Why this trifling with Hebrew words? The question is simply, Could or could not the Israelites get pigeons in Arabia Petræa? If they could, they were to offer them, on certain occasions, to the extent to which they were procurable. If pigeons were not procurable, then the people were absolved.

Dr. Colenso ought to have known that pigeons could be procured at Sinai; and that they are birds of the wilderness, even of such a wilderness as Arabia Petræa. Does he not know that one particular breed of pigeon is called "Mahomet," and is a native of the Arabian Peninsula? Is he not aware that "the Laugher" is a native of Palestine, not very far from Sinai; that "the Runt" is a native of Smyrna; and that "the Carrier" was originally bred at Bassora, and propagated throughout Syria, Palestine, Egypt, and the East? Is he not aware that the Assyrians worshipped pigeons, and that the people of Ascalon, in Philistia, would not kill or eat them, lest they should eat their gods? Does he not know that pigeons "are very fond of heat, and prefer the burning climates of the tropics to the temperate countries"? Is he not aware that "pigeons delight in open, mountainous, and sandy countries," like Arabia Petræa? Does he not know that the stock-dove, the parent of all the breeds, breeds in the holes of rocks, as well as in the hollows of trees; and that long before the captivity in Egypt, Abraham offered his two גזלים, probably stock-doves, but certainly pigeons of some kind? Is the Bishop unaware that the stock-dove is easily induced to breed in artificial cavities, and loves the society of man; so that some Israelites may have kept, and trained, and carried them, even in the desert?

At p. 54, I had occasion to remark that Bishop Colenso knew very little about sheep: I now regret to observe that he knows less about pigeons.

Is the Bishop not aware that pigeons are wonderfully prolific, and that Stillingfleet (not the prelate of that name) says that 14,760 were produced from *a single pair,* in the course of four years? Dr. Colenso himself can reckon how many birds could have been produced from one pair, in forty years. It is perfectly conceivable that, even in the desert of Arabia, tame pigeons were plentiful among the Israelites, and could have been procured easily by the poor women.

Does the Bishop not know that "tam in Syria, quam in Græcia, columbas ab omni ævo nidificasse"? Is he not aware that Bochart says of the יונה, or domestic pigeon (which the Israelites had to offer), that they had their *habitat* in places desert and rocky? And that the Arabs tell us the name *Semiramis* was compounded of two words, which mean either dove of the wood, or dove of the mountain, or *dove of the desert?*

There is[1] no difficulty in conceiving how these pigeons were caught, or bred, or kept (at least, to some extent), by the Israelites in the desert.

§ XVIII. THE CLERGY RESERVES.

Dr. Colenso's next objection I really cannot understand; nor am I able to answer it seriously.

> "158. Further, in Josh. xxi., we have an account of the forty-eight Levitical cities; and we read (ver. 19), 'All the cities of the children of Aaron, the priests, were thirteen cities, with their suburbs.'

[1] See Buffon's Nat. Hist., vol. xii., p. 197, &c., &c.; also Bochart's Hieroz., vol. ii., pp. 530, 545, &c., &c.

"At this time, according to the story, there was certainly *one* son of Aaron, Eleazar, and one grandson, Phinehas, and his family. Ithamar, Aaron's other son, *may* have been alive; but no mention whatever is made of him. We may suppose, however, that he had sons and daughters. For this small number of persons, then, there are provided here *thirteen* cities and their suburbs, and all, let it be observed, *in the immediate neighbourhood of Jerusalem*, where the *Temple* was built, and where the presence of the priests was especially required, but *in a later age*. Scott notes as follows:—

"'The family of Aaron could not at this time have been *very* numerous (!), though it had increased considerably (!) since his appointment to the priesthood. Yet thirteen cities were allotted to it as a patrimony, in the Divine knowledge of its future enlargement. For we have reason to think that no other family increased so much in proportion, after Israel's departure from Egypt, as that of Aaron.'

"The only conceivable reason for so thinking is the fact now before us, viz., that thirteen cities were assigned to them. We do not find the sons of Aaron numerous in the time of the Judges, or in Eli's time, or Samuel's, or David's, or Solomon's (except, indeed, in the record of the Chronicler). Aaron himself had at most only *two* sons living, and one of these had only *one* son."

I should have thought that any Bishop alive knew how to let a good and tenantable estate, until required for the exigencies of his own family. Besides, to support Dr. Colenso's objection, or indeed to reply to it, we need a Surveyor's Report of the number of houses in these thirteen cities, their state of repair when the Canaanites received, and were forced to comply with, their notice to quit; also, the extent and condition of the suburbs; also, the exact number of those Levites, and their families, who were in personal attendance on the priests. Also, we need to be informed, whether it was not lawful for other Levites to be put in possession, for a time, on behalf of the priests. When Dr. Colenso has obtained for us these few particulars, we will reply to him more seriously.

§ XIX. THE EXODUS IN THE FOURTH GENERATION.

When Bishop Colenso proceeds to dispute about the number of the Israelites at the Exodus, and the number of the Levites and the Danites at the same time, as he does in chapters xvii. and xviii., pp. 102—112, two positions are necessary to the soundness of his argument. One of these has reference to the time during which the Israelites were actually captive in Egypt; the other, to the meaning of the promise made to Abraham (Gen. xv. 13), that they should leave Egypt in the fourth generation, after their going down there.

To the first of these subjects, viz., the time during which Israel really lived in Egypt, he devotes chap. xv., pp. 91—95, and arrives at the conclusion that the whole time passed by the Israelites under the rule of the Egyptians was 215 years. It is quite unnecessary to trouble ourselves with any remarks upon that particular chapter. It professes to prove what most persons, in these days, are prepared to admit, viz., that St. Paul stated, under inspiration, that the covenant made at Sinai was 430 years after the promise first made to Abraham (Gen. xv. 9; Gal. iii. 17); and that, therefore, the whole period of time elapsing between Jacob's going down to Egypt and Moses bringing Israel out, on the 15th Abib, B.C. 1560, was about 215 years.

Be it granted, then, that the Sons of Israel sojourned in Egypt only 215 years.

The Bishop's object in thus clearly limiting, and fixing, the shortest possible time for Israel's sojourning in Egypt, is to show that the people could not have multiplied, in so short a period, to the extent in which Holy Scripture says they did. Of course, such an argument boldly, and entirely, rejects the claim of Scripture to any *miraculous* increase of the people. The writer, in Exod. i. 7, dwells peculiarly upon the wonderful increase of the people, and plainly asserts that God's special power and providence were exercised to promote it. This Dr. Colenso's argument altogether ignores; but that is nothing extraordinary for him; since all his book professes to bring down the Pentateuchal narratives to the test of mere arithmetic, and implies throughout it a denial of all miraculous intervention, or agency. This reflection will certainly be fatal to Dr. Colenso's book in the opinion of every serious Christian; and, besides that, we proceed to prove that all his calculations about the numbers of Israel fall to pieces, because he has entirely mistaken the meaning of the expression, "the fourth generation."

The Bishop takes the word דור, (Gen. xv. 13) in the sense of *natural, individual, generation;* and that is, certainly, one of its meanings in the Hebrew Bible, but that is not its meaning in the place before us. The word has several correct meanings as used in various places, and it will be my duty to show what its meaning is in the passage referred to. When Dr. Colenso divides 215 years into only four natural, individual generations, it is plain that he allows fifty-three years and three-fourths to each generation. And, if he should be wrong in doing so,—if, for instance, a natural generation should be twenty or thirty years, instead of fifty-three and three-fourths,—it will be manifest that, instead of four natural, individual generations in 215 years, we may have seven, or even ten, with some few years to spare. If the case should be so, it must necessarily prove the Bishop to be wrong to some considerable extent, and it may prove him to be so to an extent utterly destructive of his views concerning the number of the Israelites, Danites, and Levites at the Exodus.

Let us state Dr. Colenso's argument in his own words:—

"108. Again, when it is said, Gen. xv.16, 'in the *fourth* generation they shall come hither again,' this can only mean 'in the fourth generation' reckoning from the time when they should leave the land of Canaan, and go down into Egypt. Thus we find Moses and Aaron in the fourth generation from the time of the migration, viz., Jacob—Levi—Kohath—Amram—Aaron. Or, as Jacob was so aged, and Moses and Aaron also were advanced in life beyond the military age, we may reckon from those, as Levi, who went down into Egypt in the prime of life, and then the generation of Joshua, Eleazar, &c., in the prime of life, will be the fourth generation.

"109. Accordingly, if we examine the different genealogies of remarkable men, which are given in various places of the Pentateuch, we shall find that, as a rule, the contemporaries of Moses and Aaron are descendants in the *third*, and those of Joshua and Eleazar in the *fourth* generation, from some one of the *sons*, or *adult grandsons*, of Jacob, who went down with him into Egypt. Thus we have:—

	1st Gen.	2nd Gen.	3rd Gen.	4th Gen.	5th Gen.	
Levi	Kohath	Amram	Moses	...	...	E. vi. 16, 18, 20.
Levi	Kohath	Amram	Aaron	...	...	E. vi. 16, 18, 20.
Levi	Kohath	Uzziel	Mishael	...	...	L. x. 4.
Levi	Kohath	Uzziel	Elzaphan	...	...	L. x. 4.
Levi	Kohath	Izhar	Korah	...	...	N. xvi. 1.
Reuben	Pallu	Eliab	Dathan	...	...	N. xxvi. 7—9.
Reuben	Pallu	Eliab	Abiram	...	...	N. xxvi. 7—9.
Zarah	Zabdi	Carmi	Achan	...	...	Jo. vii. 1.
Pharez	Hezron	Ram	Amminadab	Nahshon	...	Ruth iv. 18, 19.
Pharez	Hezron	Segub	Jair	...	...	1 Ch. ii. 21, 22.
Pharez	Hezron	Caleb	Hur	Uri	Bezaleel	1 Ch. ii. 18—20.

"In the last instance, Bezaleel is in the *fifth* generation from Pharez. Perhaps he was a young man, and was reckoned in the generation next to that of Joshua: and, in fact, Josephus, *Ant.* iii. 6. 1, calls him the 'grandson of Miriam,' who is regarded by Jewish tradition as the wife of Hur. Thus he would have been a contemporary of *Phinehas*, the *grandson* of Aaron,— not of his son, Eleazar. Besides, Hezron, as well as his father, Pharez, was born, according to the story, in the land of Canaan; so that Bezaleel was actually still in the fourth generation from one who went down into Egypt.

"114. We conclude, then, that it is an indisputable fact, that the story, as told in the Pentateuch, intends it to be understood—(i.) that the children of Israel came out of Egypt about 215 years after they went down thither in the time of Jacob,—(ii.) that they came out in the *fourth* generation from the adults in the prime of life, who went down with Jacob.

"And it should be observed that *the second of these conclusions does not in any way depend upon the correctness of the former.*

"Upon this point Josephus writes, *Ant.* ii. 9. 1 :—

"'Four hundred years did they spend under these afflictions; for they strove one against the other which should get the mastery, the Egyptians desiring to destroy the Israelites by their labours, and the Israelites desiring to hold out to the end under them.'

"But of course, the last words of the above can only refer to the *last* portion of their sojourn in *Egypt*, since they were not struggling with the Egyptians till after Joseph's death, at all events. And so writes Josephus again, *Ant.* ii. 15. 2 :—

"'They left Egypt four hundred and thirty years after our forefather Abraham came into Canaan, but two hundred and fifteen years only after Jacob removed into Egypt.'

"And he writes of Moses, *Ant.* ii. 9. 6 :—

"'Abraham was his ancestor of the *seventh* generation.'

"And so he says of Joseph, *Against Apion*, i. 33 :—

"'He died four generations before Moses, which four generations make almost 170 years.'

"And Archd. Pratt observes, 'Science and Scripture,' p. 78 :—

"'It was to be in the *fourth* generation that his seed were to return to Canaan. But 430, or even 400, years is very much longer than four generations, and therefore must include something besides the bondage in Egypt, viz., the sojourning in Canaan. His prediction regarding the "fourth generation" was literally fulfilled. Moses and Aaron were sons of Jochebed, who was the daughter of Levi (Num. xxvi. 59), a text which incidentally confirms the correctness of our general outline. Eleazar, the Priest, the son of Aaron, was, therefore, of the fourth generation from Jacob [? Levi]. He returned to Canaan and died there, his father, Aaron, and that generation, having died in the wilderness.'

"115. From this it can be shown, beyond a doubt, that it is quite impossible that there should have been such a number of the people of Israel in Egypt, at the time of the Exodus, as to have furnished 600,000 warriors in the prime of life, representing, at least, two millions of persons, of all ages and sexes,—that is to say, it is impossible, *if we will take the data to be derived from the Pentateuch itself.*"

The Bishop has entangled the question with two whole pages of little print upon the pedigree of Joshua, the son of Nun, as given at 1 Chron. viii. 22, 27; his object being to show that the account in Chronicles cannot be relied on. On this point, it is sufficient to observe that we have nothing, at present, to do with the book of Chronicles. But, as to the question before us, we admit that it is said distinctly by the Almighty to Abraham, at Gen. xv. 13, "Know of a surety that thy seed shall be a stranger in a land that is not theirs, and shall serve them; and they shall afflict them four hundred years; and also that nation, whom they shall serve, will I judge; and afterward shall they come out with great substance. And thou shalt go to thy fathers in peace; thou shalt be buried in a good old age. But in the fourth generation they shall come hither again; for the iniquity of the Amorites is not yet full." But the Bishop is mistaken in thinking that the word "generation" here means a natural generation or begetment; and in so giving, to each of the four "generations" spoken of, the long and irrational period of fifty-three years and three-fourths.

Common sense says at once, the Bishop must, in this case, be wrong. Who will believe that, among a people whose males married at twenty years, in a country—Egypt—where girls were married at sixteen years, the proper time to assign to one natural generation is fifty-three years and three-quarters? It would, perhaps, be correct to set apart only twenty years to one generation; and to say that 215 years' sojourning in Egypt ought to count for ten natural generations, with fifteen years to spare.

This, too, is a subject upon which Holy Scripture has not left us without information for this particular occasion. We have an example suggested, by which to reckon natural, individual generations in Egypt, at the very time in question. Dr. Colenso has, for a purpose of his own, noted, at p. 97, that "we are told that the "children of Machir, the son of Manasseh, were brought up upon "Joseph's knees." But he has forgotten to say, also, that in the very same verses (Gen. l. 22, 23), it is added, that "Joseph saw Ephraim's children of the third generation." Now Joseph was "thirty years old, when he stood before Pharaoh, King of Egypt" (Gen. xli. 46), and he married soon after (Gen. xli. 50, 51); also he lived 110 years (Gen. l. 22). So that, taking thirty-two years as the age at which Joseph married, it follows that in seventy-eight years he had seen four generations of his own children, viz., Ephraim, his sons, grand, and great-grand sons. Leaving out the last of these as being, probably, but infants when Joseph died, and taking only married, or marriageable children, to mark a natural, individual generation, we have then seventy-eight years to divide into three such generations; *i.e.*, we have exactly twenty-six years to one natural generation. The Bishop has not the same right, when questioning the space which ought to be allotted to one natural generation, to reason upon the case of Machir, or others, who married later, or had fewer children, as we have to reason upon a case like Ephraim's. If we show, as we do, that seventy-eight years may fairly be reckoned as three natural generations, and 215 years, therefore, fairly as more than eight, we have shown that Dr. Colenso's presumption that 215 years counts only for four generations is on no account to be permitted; and all his reasoning built upon that presumption becomes untrustworthy. More than this, we have on our side the natural probability, we may say, indeed, the natural certainty, that twenty-six years is time enough, and to spare, for one natural, individual generation.

This, the Bishop's false assumption, viz., that 215 years counts only for four natural generations, lies at the root of all his calculations respecting the numbers of the people at the Exodus; and, in effect, destroys all that part of his book, which withers away like Jonah's gourd.

Again, it is certain, not only that Jacob's eldest sons were in the very prime of life, when they went down into Egypt (the age of all was, as we shall see, about forty years), but that some of them might be considered even young. Benjamin was only twenty-two years old. Also some of the grandsons were fully at marriageable age, one of them, at least, viz., Beriah, was already married. There can be no doubt that the work of procreation went actively on, from the time of their arrival in Egypt. But, according to Dr. Colenso, we are to wait, in the burning clime of Egypt, for fifty-three years and three-fourths, before we can count on a *second* generation. Is that reasonable?

I beg the reader to be here especially on his guard against a misapprehension, so easily fallen into, through two, very different, meanings of the word *generation*. The first meaning is that of a period to be determined by the average life of men in any country;

the second is that to be measured by their procreating powers. For this second I use the word *begetment*. We might say with truth that, in one point of view a generation of the first kind is seventy years; a generation of the second, viz., power of begetment, as few as twenty. It is with the *power of begetment* that we have to do.

Any reader may convince himself, by examining the English Bible, that the word "generation" is used in Holy Scripture in several different senses:—1. It means the "headship" of a whole family, or people; 2. Closely allied to this, it stands for a "nation;" 3. It stands for the whole mass of any people at particular, successive periods in their existence; 4. In a similar sense, it seems to be often equivalent with "history;" 5. It means a natural, individual procreation, or begetment; and, 6. It sometimes stands for a *seculum*, or age. Dr. Colenso's fatal error, as to the *numbers* of Israel, has been in assuming arbitrarily the fifth of these senses for the word "generation" in Gen. xv. 16, when it will not bear it there. For when the Almighty says to Abraham, "In the fourth generation they shall come hither again," He is speaking of the whole family, or seed, as one people under one head or patriarchate, and uses no word which will justify Dr. Colenso's limitation of it to a natural, individual begetment; it is as if it had been said, "In the fourth generation of the patriarchate, after they go down, without limiting the multiplication of thy seed."

For, of the two words used in Hebrew Scripture to express "generation," we have to do with דור, which means properly an undefined cycle of time, and is, accordingly, used for various periods in different places of Scripture. Nothing could be more opposite to the character of this word than to use it, as Dr. Colenso does, to express four equal periods of time, as for natural generations, in a space of a given number of years. Even when used in express reference to individual generations, it is employed, for varying periods of time, and for periods varying for different individuals, under precisely the same condition. Thus, of Job it is said (chap. xlii. 16), "After this Job lived a hundred and forty years, and saw his sons and his sons' sons, even four generations." In this case one natural generation would be about thirty-five years. This is one of the earliest uses of the word. So in Ephraim's case (Gen. l. 23), Joseph in eighty years (Gen. xli. 45, 46, and Gen. l. 23), saw four generations of his children; *i.e.*, the same number of genera-

tions as Job, in not much more than half the time. Yet, during the same eighty years, there were but two generations of Machir, the son of Joseph's firstborn, Manasses, or one generation in about twenty-six years and eight months. These two are, also among the earliest use of the word. So that no fixed limit, even according to a Hebrew average, can be given to the word דור, when used, as Dr. Colenso supposes it to be used, at Gen. xv. 16, of natural, individual procreation. But, in fact, the word very early stood for a much larger period of time, in the sense of a *race* of people, or a protracted *age* of time. Gesenius[1] (who is indebted to Simonis) explains the word more fully than other lexicographers. And it is strange that Dr. Colenso, who sometimes refers to Gesenius (p. 88, above), did not consult him on this important subject; and note the following remark, in relation to our present question :—" But the Hebrews, like our-
" selves, seem to have counted the life of man commonly thirty or
" forty years (see Job xlii. 16), but at the time of the long-lived
" patriarchs, a hundred (Gen. xv. 16; comp. Comm. 14, and Exod.
" xii. 40); and, similarly, among the Romans, the word *seculum*
" anciently signified the life of man; afterward, Censorinus teaches
" us (*De Die Natali*, cap. 17), it came to mean a space of 100 years."
Here was a guiding line for Dr. Colenso. Two meanings of the word, "generation," are mentioned; one, between thirty and forty years, viz., for people generally; another, of 100 years, with especial reference to the patriarchs, and to Gen. xv. 16, the passage in question; but neither of them anything like Dr. Colenso's fifty-three years and three-fourths, or four arbitrary divisions of 215 years. Of the very early use of the word דור, in the sense of *race* and *an age*, examples may be found, at the places mentioned below.[2] Thus, " Inquire, I pray thee, of the former age; " " the generation to come of your children, that shall rise up after you; " " a very froward generation, children in whom is no faith." It is certain, then, that דור, even in its earliest uses, always means an undefined and varying cycle of time; and sometimes the period of a whole *race* of people, or determination of an *age*.

Here I shall call attention to a curious fact, not as an argument, but as a hint, to men with Scriptural instinct, men who feel (by God's grace) implicit confidence in the Holy Bible. One of the

[1] Gesenius' Thesaur., p. 330; Simonis' Lex., p. 383; Fürst's Concord., pp. 275, 276.
[2] Job viii. 8; Exod. i. 6; Num. xxxii. 13; Deut. ii. 14; xxix. 22; xxxii. 5, 24.

passages referred to above (Exod. i. 6), is as follows, "And Joseph died, and all his brethren, and all that generation." Supposing we took this as an inspired intimation how to determine "the fourth generation" of Gen. xv. 16. Joseph died seventy-one years after Jacob and his other sons went down to Egypt, in the second year of the famine (Gen. xlvi. 1); let us amuse ourselves, therefore, by taking seventy-one years as the limit of the first generation of the captivity, then three such generations would be 213 years of the 215; and it would be true, in this sense, that Israel left Egypt, in the "fourth generation" of the captivity. This takes the word *generation*, in the first sense, viz., *limit of life;* and not in the second, viz., *power of begetment*.

However, to proceed, דור stands for any undeterminate cycle of time. Yet, to test the fulfilment of a particular promise, depending upon its meaning, it must be referred to some selected standard, for measurement. Now, the promise to Abraham was (Gen. xv. 16), " in the fourth generation, they" (viz., thy seed) "shall come hither again." And the selected standard, by which to prove the fulfilment of this prophecy, or promise, was, *the Patriarchate;* the headship of the whole family; the generations of the whole family being thus parcelled into fours, by the Patriarchate. "In the fourth generation of the Patriarchate, after going down, they shall come up again." In other words, the head of the whole house, filling the place of Abraham, was to be, at the time of the Exodus, in the "fourth generation," from Jacob, under whose Patriarchate they went down there. And this without limitation of the natural procreations of other branches of the family. The promise, thus made to Abraham, would be literally fulfilled if Israel were brought out of Egypt, during the fourth generation of the patriarchal family, reckoning from Jacob. And to prove such fulfilment we have the genealogy of Moses and Aaron given us at Exod. vi. 16—27. To that genealogy Dr. Colenso refers; but seems not to understand its use.

Moses and Aaron were fourth in descent from Jacob, through Levi:—Jacob, Levi, Kohath, Amram, and Aaron-with-Moses. And we know, as matter of fact, that, so it pleased God, the Patriarchate, or headship, over all Israel was, by special appointment, vested in Moses and Aaron. Moreover, we may trace (in Exod. vi.) certain providential circumstances which all tended to the same end of giving the tribe of Levi this Patriarchate. The Jews say, and

Exod. vi. 16, seems to justify the idea, that Levi outlived all the other Patriarchs. Clearly he outlived Joseph; and all the others seem to have been dead when Joseph died. (Exod. i. 6.) Of Levi and his sons alone, patriarchal ages are there recorded. Levi, 137 years; Kohath, 133 years; Amram, 137 years (Exod. vi. 16, 18, 20); and Aaron dying in the fortieth year of the Exodus, lived about 122 years. Further, Levi was Jacob's third son; and if anything had happened to displace Reuben and Simeon, his two elder brothers, the Patriarchate devolved on him by right. Now Reuben had been formally forbidden the Patriarchate by Jacob, for his crime mentioned at Gen. xlix. 4, "Unstable as water, thou shalt not excel," *i.e.*, "ungovernable in thy passions, as seething water, thou shalt not have rule over thy brethren." Simeon and Levi were both to be divided in Jacob, and scattered in Israel. (Gen. xlix. 5—7.) But, whatever prevented Simeon's obtaining the Patriarchate, whether early death or any other cause, is of little moment to the subject, seeing that we know, as matter of fact, it was given by the Almighty to the family of Kohath, the son of Levi. The genealogist carefully mentions the children of Reuben and Simeon, and then proceeds to trace the patriarchate of Levi, in the sons of Kohath; no doubt, that it may be distinctly observed he does so in the consciousness, except for intervening circumstances, of the naturally prior claims of Reuben and of Simeon. What those circumstances were, in the case of Simeon, we are not informed; neither are we informed why Kohath, Levi's second son, was preferred to Gershon, the eldest. Neither are we instructed why Moses, Amram's second son, was chosen as leader and lawgiver to Israel; while Aaron, the eldest, in a subordinate position himself, received, in his sons, the high-priesthood, as a Patriarchate, through many successive generations. In the genealogy of Exod. vi. 16—27, as in other genealogies, which Dr. Colenso so little understands, the annalist has a particular business before him, viz., to detail the Patriarchate of Levi, and his sons to the third generation; and he does so, not concerning himself with collateral matter.

Yet, it is curious to observe that, as to Levi's having acquired the Patriarchate, there are additional considerations glanced at in the narrative. The Israelitish blood of Levi seems to have been kept pure (Exod. vi. 20); and, besides the long lives, already referred to, of Levi's sons, Gershon and Amram, the fact of the adoption of

Moses, by a person so great and influential as Pharaoh's daughter, suggests reasons why the Patriarchate which had devolved upon Levi, the last survivor of Jacob's sons, was continued to his posterity.

Should it be observed that the royalties of the firstborn, the kingship, had been given to Judah (Gen. xlix. 10), it may be justly answered, they had been given predictively, but Israel would know, and Judah's sons also, that it was no part of their duty to anticipate the providential fulfilment of that prediction. The headship of the house was ostensibly Levi's, as Judah's elder (and, probably, surviving) brother; and circumstances, at the time, pointed to the perpetuation of that headship in his family. Yet, in connection with this part of the inquiry, we may note that Aaron married the sister of Naashon, the head of the house of Judah, (Exod. vi. 23); so that, already, the house of Judah had some personal interest in supporting the claims of Aaron. The sacerdotal, and royal, tribes were at the moment united. Nor is it unreasonable to infer, considering that the family of Levi was eventually destined for the service of the tabernacle, and that of Aaron for the government in the high-priesthood, that it had pleased the Almighty to impart to Israel some traditional influences tending in that direction.

I conclude, then—

1. That, critically, Dr. Colenso has no manner of right to limit the word "generation," in Gen. xv. 16, to the meaning of natural, individual, begetment.

2. That common sense says 215 years must count for more than four natural generations, as begetments; and that it is absurd to give fifty-three years and three-fourths, to one such.

3. That the case of Ephraim's children (Gen. l. 23), is itself a sufficient refutation of the idea.

4. That "the fourth generation" intended, in Gen. xv. 16, is the "fourth generation" of the Patriarchate; reckoning from Jacob, in whose Patriarchate the descent into Egypt took place; and that the four steps were these—Levi, Kohath, Amram, and Moses-with-Aaron.

§ XX. THE NUMBER OF ISRAELITES AT THE EXODUS.

This important conclusion breaks up all that Dr. Colenso has said about the numbers of Israel, and their several tribes, at the Exodus;

the chapters concerning which form, perhaps, the most serious part of his book; or, at least, the part most likely to mislead the general reader. Besides, it should be observed, that the Bishop has made a serious mistake in venturing to base any part of his calculations as to the number of the people upon the pedigrees given in Holy Scripture. They contain no sufficient *data* for such a purpose. Nor, having regard to the object of revelation, was it likely that they would. They are given for specific purposes, sufficiently exhibited. But, to meet the Bishop's ideas, we should have needed a minute record of births, deaths, and marriages. Now, Moses does not profess to be a registrar-general. We are not acquainted with the principle upon which tribes were divided into families; nor whether they were so, upon any fixed principle whatever. That unrecorded circumstances affected this matter, we are sure, from Num. xxvi. 19, 38, where the full five families are given to Judah, for his five sons, by including Hezron and Hamul; and only seven families given to Benjamin, for his ten sons; and that by the inclusion of two grandsons, the sons of Bela; so that three whole families were reckoned to Bela, one of Benjamin's sons, and four of his other sons were entirely excluded. We are not informed as to the principle upon which families were selected to be heads of tribes; nor from how many, or what, causes the first-born (like Reuben) might be set aside for the elevation of a younger. We are not told how this other was determined on; nor, generally, what extraneous influences might have affected, or even have suspended, the laws of descent. In Jewish pedigrees, it was customary not to include the women; and yet, it is manifest, the deaths, and births, and ages, and numbers, and degrees of relationship, of the women must have had the greatest influence upon the pedigree. To proceed, however, to the *numbers*, the Bishop observes:—

"In the first place, it must be observed, as already noted, that we nowhere read of any *very large families* among the children of Jacob, or their descendants, to the time of the Exodus. We may suppose, in order that we may have the population as large as possible, that very few died prematurely, and that those, who were born, almost all lived and multiplied. But we have no reason whatever, from the data furnished by the Sacred Books themselves, to assume that they had families materially larger than those of the present day. Thus we are told in Gen. xlvi. that Reuben had 4 sons, Simeon 6, Levi 3, Judah 5, Issachar 4, Zebulun 3, Gad 7, Asher 4, Joseph 2, Benjamin 10, Dan 1, Naphtali 4. It is certainly strange that, among all the 69 children and grandchildren and great-grandchildren of Jacob, who went down with him into Egypt, there should be only *one* daughter mentioned, and *one* granddaughter. The very numbering of these two among the 'seventy souls' shows that the females 'out of the loins of Jacob' were not omitted *intentionally*.

"117. Some, indeed, have suggested that these two only were inserted, because they were either notorious already, as Dinah, or may have become notorious in after days, as may possibly have been the case with Asher's daughter, Serah, ver. 17, though the Bible says nothing about it. But it is plain that this is only perverting the obvious meaning of the Scripture in Gen. xlvi. It is certain that the writer intends it to be understood that these seventy were the *only* persons, and these two the *only* females, who had at that time been born in the family of Jacob. And, though the fact itself, of this wonderful preponderance of males, may seem very strange, and would be so indeed in actual history, it is only another indication of the unhistorical character of the whole account. For the present, however, we may admit it as *possible* in the nature of things, that there should have been, at first at all events, such a preponderance of males, and even *probable*, if the house of Israel was to increase with extraordinary rapidity.

"118. The twelve sons of Jacob, then, as appears from the above, had between them 53 sons, that is, on the average 4½ each. Let us suppose that they increased in this way from generation to generation. Then in the *first* generation, that of *Kohath*, there would be 54 males (according to the story, 53, or rather only 51, since Er and Onan died in the land of Canaan, ver. 12, without issue)—in the *second*, that of *Amram*, 243,—in the *third*, that of *Moses* and *Aaron*, 1,094,— and in the *fourth*, that of *Joshua* and *Eleazar*, 4,923; that is to say, instead of 600,000 warriors in the prime of life, there could not have been 5,000.

"Further, if the numbers of *all* the males in the four generations be added together (which supposes that they were all living at the time of the Exodus), they would only amount to 6,311. If we even add to these the number of the *fifth* generation, 22,154, who would be mostly children, the sum-total of males of all generations could not, according to these data, have exceeded 28,465, instead of being 1,000,000."

All of which becomes valueless when we remember that Dr. Colenso is wrong in the application he makes of the expression "fourth generation"; and that instead of four natural generations in 215 years, there ought to be reckoned seven at the fewest. Indeed, Gen. l. 23, as written of Ephraim's children, gives us some right to reckon one generation, or begetment, to every twenty-five or twenty-six years. There might have been, therefore (as reason suggests there were), eight, or at least seven, generations, in 215 years. Let us take thirty years as a generation, in the sense of a sum of *natural begetments*.

1. The Bishop observes that "we have no reason whatever, from "the data furnished by the Sacred Books themselves, to assume that "they (the children of Jacob) had families materially larger than "those of the present day. Thus we are told, in Gen. xlvi., that "Reuben had 4 sons, Simeon 6, Levi 3, Judah 5, Issachar 4, "Zebulun 3, Gad 7, Asher 4, Joseph 2, Benjamin 10, Dan 1, "Napthali 4." But this takes no account of two elements of calculation most important on this part of the subject, viz., 1. The comparative youth of the Patriarchs when Jacob removed into Egypt; 2. That their social status was entirely changed by their going there. We shall presently see that the average age of Jacob's twelve sons, at the descent into Egypt, was not forty years; while, as the Bishop admits, Benjamin was a lad twenty-two years old. Are we to suppose that these twelve men had no more children after they settled in Goshen? Dr. Colenso boldly replies, p. 23, "Certainly, if "the plain meaning of the text of Scripture will not allow us to "suppose the contrary." The text of Scripture will allow us to suppose the contrary; requiring us only to understand that the seventy persons, who went down into Egypt, were those from whom the multitude, that came out, was descended. The conclusion that they had no more children born in Egypt would be unreasonable, and contrary to all human probability. Let us remember the recorded dispositions of these sons of Jacob, as indicated by Reuben's conduct (Gen. xxxv. 22), by Judah's (Gen. xxxviii. 15), and by the fact that the possession of concubines is recorded in the case of two of them, Simeon (Gen. xlvi. 10) and Benjamin, who having ten sons when he was but twenty-two years of age, must have had them by more than one woman; or, as Dr. Colenso says, p. 24, "possibly by more than one wife." With such facts as these before him, and with the example of Jacob, who had two wives and two concubines, it is strange to find the Bishop asserting, pp. 117, 120, that "there is no indication that polygamy *did* prevail among the "Hebrews of those days;" stranger still, when we remember that polygamy and concubinage were expressly provided for by the Levitical law at the time of the Exodus. (Exod. xxi. 7—11; Deut. xxi. 15—17.) Which provision distinctly implies both that polygamy and concubinage did then exist, and also were likely to be continued. And we know that they were continued. Surely, if Scripture is to guide us, there can be no doubt that polygamy and

concubinage were general among the Hebrews, from the time of their descent into Egypt to the time of their coming out. We cannot rationally suppose that these twelve patriarchs had no more wives, concubines, nor children, after they became settled, as brethren of the Prime Minister, in a country where Potiphar's wife, and Mr. Lane's recent researches,[1] may vouch for the normal character of the ladies. Probably Joseph's conduct (Gen. xxxix. 8) is thrown into bold contrast with his brethren's, in order to impress all readers with a deep sense of his eminent piety towards God. Let us remember, also, the laws of descent which obtained similarly among Hebrews and Egyptians, viz., that the children of concubines inherited upon equal terms with those of lawful wives. And though polygamy seems to have been rare among the Egyptians,[2] it was permitted, as was also concubinage; and divorce, to any extent. The children of concubines and slaves, were treated as if the children of wives. This is proved in Jacob's case, in Simeon's, Judah's, and Benjamin's. And that such wives or concubines, with their children, would be reckoned as Israelites, is clear from these cases; and the children of Egyptian women also as such, from Joseph's, as well as from the direct testimony of Holy Scripture. In regard to the question whether the patriarchs had, individually, more children born after their descent into Egypt, it is curious to notice that the Septuagint gives Joseph nine children, viz., two already born when Jacob arrived in Egypt, and seven more some time afterwards. (See Sept., Gen. xlii. 27; Exod. i. 5.)

The average number of children in each family of Jacob's sons, born before the residence in Egypt, is no fair test of the probable size of the Hebrew families subsequently born in that country. Their social existence was entirely changed when they resided in Egypt. In Canaan they had little inducement to extend their alliance with the natives; in Egypt they had the greatest. They knew that the Canaanites were doomed to be thrust out, to make room for them. (Gen. xv. 16—21.) Canaan was at that time comparatively but thinly peopled; Egypt was already populous. In Canaan, they were known, though respected, merely as most prosperous shepherds; in Egypt, they were known as the same, and also as brethren of the monarch's chief favourite.

[1] Lane's Mod. Egypt, vol. i., p. 219, &c.
[2] Wilkinson's Anc. Egypt., vol. ii., pp. 62—64.

Temptation to sexual indulgence was, in Canaan, not unusually great; in Egypt it became peculiarly so. Every probable consideration suggests that the families of Hebrews would be in Egypt much larger than they were before; and Scripture asserts that they were so to an extraordinary degree. (Exod. i. 7.)

Nor does Scripture furnish us with any numeration of the children in Hebrew-Egyptian families such as to enable us to draw general conclusions on the subject. Dr. Colenso has endeavoured, p. 105, to establish the inference that the families in Egypt were even smaller, on the average, than they were in Canaan. He does so, without success, by appealing to Exod. vi., which records some particulars concerning the families of Levi, Reuben, and Judah; but none which will justify any conclusion as to the size, generally, of Hebrew-Egyptian families. Is it safe to draw a general inference, respecting a whole nation, from certain peculiarities affecting one, or two, or three, families?

2. The Bishop says (p. 104), that, as the object of the Egyptian " King was to keep down their numbers, it is not to be supposed " that he would allow them to take wives freely from among his own " people, or that the women of Egypt (at least those of the genera-" tions of Amram, which gave birth to Moses, and after it,) would be " willing, generally, to associate their lot with a people so abject and " oppressed as the Hebrews. Besides, we are told expressly that, in " childbirth, ' the *Hebrew* women were not as the Egyptian women ' " (Exod. i. 19), by which it is plainly implied that the wives of the " Hebrews were also Hebrews." Which remark is erroneous in three particulars. Doubtless, it was the object of Thotmes III., who lived when Moses was born, to destroy the *male* children (Exod. i. 16); but only the males. The girls were to be spared, and might become the wives of other Hebrews; or even of Egyptians, who, casting in their lot with Israel, would be esteemed as Hebrews; as, doubtless, the husbands of Dinah and Zerah were; and as, indeed, Scripture gives us express reason to believe: Exod. xii. 48; Num. ix. 14; Deut. xxiii. 8; 1 Chron. ii. 34, 35. Besides, there is no evidence that the peculiar persecution, adopted against the male children, was continued long, or very successful while continued. The answer of the midwives shows that they concerted an evasion of the order they had received; and should be regarded as a reply, framed for the express purpose of deceiving Pharaoh. It also proves, in direct

opposition to Dr. Colenso, that certain Egyptians were, at that very time, favourable to the Hebrews, and probably by no means so averse to alliance with them, as the Bishop supposes. But, if they were, the Israelites had, at this time, flourished exceedingly for about 135 years; had, during all that time, intermarried, and cohabited with, Egyptians; had formed extensive connections among them; and marriages with pure Egyptians would be no longer necessary; though it is likely the persecution by Pharaoh would not have prevented them, if they were. The supposed contrast, which Dr. Colenso draws, between Hebrew women and Egyptian, as to their parturition, is easily explained away, either by the fact that the midwives meant simply to deceive Pharaoh; or by the fact, that Hebrew wives descended from Egyptian marriages, were esteemed Hebrews, and spoken of accordingly.

3. Dr. Colenso stubbornly refuses to believe in the singular fruitfulness of the Hebrews, when in Egypt. He says (p. 106):—
" The Scripture implies no such fecundity among the Hebrews,
" either in Gen. xlvi., or in Exod. vi., or in Exod. i. 19, where
" the midwives say, of the Hebrew women, 'They are delivered
" 'ere the midwives come in unto them,' which could hardly have
" been said, if three or four children were often born at a time."
I do not know that; for when Hebrew parents knew that their boy-babies were likely to be murdered, they might not have been over-hasty to send for a nurse, who was supposed to act in obedience to the Egyptian King. Besides which, as just now explained, the answer of the midwives was framed expressly to deceive; and, even when not friendly, if they failed to be in time, they would, naturally, seek to screen themselves from suspected complicity. It is not usual for unbelievers to contradict the testimony of heathen, in matters affecting the Christian religion. Why does Dr. Colenso refuse the testimony of Aristotle (*Hist. Anam.*, vii. 4), and of Pliny (*Nat. Hist.*, vii. 3), who (Kalisch, and others, have noted) expressly say, that women, in Egypt, bore three, four, or even five, children at a time? And, (Dr. Colenso's attempted contrast, notwithstanding,) Hebrew wives, after 135 years' residence of the people of Israel, in Egypt, were, to all intents and purposes, Egyptian women. But Scripture does speak specifically of the extraordinary fecundity of the Hebrews in Egypt. (Exod. i. 7.) And, as to the Bishop's references above, Gen. xlvi. is of the people in Canaan, and has

nothing to do with the question; and Exod. vi. is, more particularly, of the family of Amram; and will be considered in its proper place. Meanwhile, it is enough to say, that Bishop Colenso is mistaken in his reading of that genealogy; and that, if he were not, he cannot safely venture to reason as to the condition of a whole people, from that of two, or three, particular families. There is good reason to believe that the family of Levi avoided, to a great extent, the blandishments of the Egyptian women round them. And we may close this part of the subject by observing, that Dr. Colenso's reference to the small family of Zelophehad, p. 105 (Num. xxvii. 1), is as little to the purpose, as that to Gen. xlvi.; for it has regard to a date nearly forty years after they had left Egypt.

On the whole, there is the express testimony of Holy Scripture; there is the testimony of heathen writers; and there is every natural probability; to lead us to conclude that the Hebrews had much larger families, in Egypt, than before.

4. Dr. Colenso, in reckoning the progenitors of Israelites in Egypt, has excluded all the twelve Patriarchs, who, when they went down thither, were in the prime of life. This is a serious mistake. It appears that all Jacob's sons, except Benjamin, were born within seven years of each other; taking Reuben as the eldest, and Joseph and Zebulun as the youngest two. For Jacob, after seven years' service with Laban, obtained his two wives, Leah and Rachel (Gen. xxix. 21—30); and, as soon as Joseph had been born, viz., at the end of seven years' service for Rachel (Gen. xxx. 22—26, and xxxi. 41), and before his six years' service for cattle, he desired to return home. All, therefore, but Benjamin, were born within seven years of each other. Now, Joseph was thirty-nine years old, when Jacob and his other sons went into Egypt (Gen. xli. 46), for Jacob went down in the second year of famine; and Joseph was already thirty years old, "when he stood before Pharaoh." (Gen. xli. 46.) And Judah was three years older than Joseph, or forty-two years old, at the descent into Egypt. Judah was Jacob's fourth son; so that Reuben appears to have been, at that time, about forty-five years old. (Gen. xxxix. 31—35.) We cannot be quite certain of the relative ages of all the other sons; but it appears, that Jacob was, during these seven years, cohabiting with his two wives, and their two handmaids; and that the ages of the several sons will be nearly as follows:—Reuben,

forty-five years; Simeon, forty-four; Levi, forty-three; Judah, forty-two; Dan, forty-one; Gad, forty-one; Naphtali, forty; Asher, forty; Issachar, forty; Zebulun, thirty-nine; Joseph, thirty-nine; Benjamin, twenty-two; at the going down into Egypt. So that the average ages of the eldest eleven sons was about thirty-eight years; and the youngest was only twenty-two. Surely it is a sad mistake of Dr. Colenso to have assumed that these men had no more children born in Egypt.

Further, at the time of going into Egypt, these men had, among them all, about twelve marriageable sons, one marriageable sister, and one marriageable daughter. I say, twelve marriageable sons, because I reckon three each to Reuben, Simeon, and Levi; and one each to Judah, Dan, and Gad. Judah's two elder sons had died in Canaan. There were, altogether, then, twenty-six persons, at the descent into Egypt, from whom the multiplication of children might have commenced, at the very beginning of the 215 years.

I have already explained how unreasonable is Dr. Colenso's first assumption, that the families of Israelites in Egypt averaged only four and a-half. He seems to have felt so himself; for afterwards, he does not object to take them at six,—viz., three sons and three daughters. For he observes (p. 105):—

> "If we take all the families given in Exod. vi. 14—25, together with the two sons of Moses, we shall find that there are thirteen persons who have born them thirty-nine sons, which gives an average of three sons each. This average is a fairer one to take, for our purpose, than the former; because these persons lived at all different times in the interval, between the migration into Egypt, and the Exodus. We may suppose, then, that the average of *children* is still as large as before, or even larger; so that each man may have had, on the average, six children, viz., three sons and three daughters."

Such is Dr. Colenso's allowance, not admitting the existence of polygamy, nor even of concubinage. That they did exist among the Hebrews in Egypt, and out of it, from their descent into Egypt, and at the Exodus, and long after, is a fact which Scripture attests, and which cannot be rationally denied.

Even in this nipping climate of the North, the possession of two wives would not be very injurious to the physical constitution of a man; and it might, in many cases, tend to the health and increased fruitfulness, of both the women. Surely, in the sun of Egypt, the supposition that each Hebrew may have had, on the average, the society of two women, is not unreasonable; nor that, of these two women, ten children, on the average, or five each, may have been born. For the Hebrew men married at about twenty years, and Egyptian girls usually at sixteen: they were marriageable before.[1] I shall, therefore, take a lower average than Dr. Colenso's highest, and assume that every married woman, and every concubine, among the Hebrews, had, on the average, five children, viz., one-half more than Dr. Colenso's lowest, and unfair, average, four and one-half. Here, I would beg to inform my lay brethren that the cost of keeping a family in Egypt, was extremely small;[2] being about thirteen English shillings a-year, for each child. Even in the cold and dreary towns of England, ten children in one family, of one wife, are by no means rare. The case would, doubtless, be much oftener so, were we not crowded into unhealthy towns, in a bleak climate, and under social conditions which render early marriages inadvisable, and super-induce vices, which secure physical degeneration. I shall reckon, therefore, ten children, on an average, to each man, by two women, viz., five sons and five daughters.

Dr. Colenso has attacked the Pentateuch upon some *hypotheses:* we may well be permitted to defend it upon others, of a far different character.

My object will be to put before the reader, one, only one, clear and reasonable hypothesis, by which it may be seen that the Israelites may, possibly, have increased naturally to the extent asserted in the Pentateuch, but denied by Dr. Colenso. I have already shown that, at the very day of the descent into Egypt, there were at least twenty-six able-bodied adults, from whom the increase of the people might have instantly proceeded; but that Dr. Colenso studiously and unfairly leaves out the twelve patriarchs; starting with fifty-four males, in the first generation, Kohath's. (See p. 102, above.) For the sake of the argument, I shall do, in effect, the same; and also, for the sake of the argument, I shall come very closely to Dr. Colenso's lowest, and unfair, average of four and a-half children to each man. I shall take five.

---

[1] See Lane's Mod. Egypt., vol. i., p. 194. Whoever will compare Wilkinson's Anc. Egypt., with Lane, may see how singularly they agree in their accounts of the people. [2] See Wilkinson's Anc. Egypt., vol. ii., p. 53.

We have 215 years to lay out in rearing families. And, since the whole number of *males*, reckoned to Jacob at the going down to Egypt, was 65, including Joseph and his two sons, but excluding Hezron and Hamul, I shall take the stock, for procreation, at the low number of 50. I shall throw off the first 15 years of the 215, to allow the lads to become men of 20 years old; and shall assume that not one of them was so bad as his Uncle Benjamin, who had 10 children when he was only 22 years of age. Should it be objected that some of the lads would scarcely be men by that time, I shall hope that this possibility is allowed for, and fairly met, by leaving out the 12 patriarchs, and *any additional children they and their adult sons may have had born in Egypt during those* 15 *years.* We have now 200 years left. I shall throw off 20 years more, at the end of the 200, in order that every male, to be reckoned at the Exodus, may be quite 20 years old. Lastly, instead of 53 descendants of Jacob, being the whole number 65 without the 12 Patriarchs, I shall take 50; thus leaving out Gershon, Kohath, and Merari, fathers of the Levites. These 50 descendants, at 5 sons each, for 6 generations, of 30 years each, are exactly equal to 781,250 men, above twenty years old, or 177,700 more than the fighting men given us at Num. ii. 32. Now, if the reader will refer to p. 46, above, he will see that the 603,550 men mentioned, for all the twelve tribes, at Num. ii. 32, are only the *fighting* men; men, that is, habitually fit for war. So that my calculation, allowing 5 sons, on the average, to each man, for 6 generations of 30 years, produces the number of fighting men required; and allows 20 years' produce for boys and girls under that age; also allows 177,700 men, not fit for fighting; and, lastly, reckons the whole number of women as equal to the whole number of men. In fact, it reckons all the people to have amounted to, at least, 1,562,500 adults, above 20 years of age.

Nor have I yet stated the case fully. Dr. Colenso will not admit that the sons of Israel took any servants with them into Egypt. He dares to affirm, p. 114,—

"(i.) There is no word or indication of any such *cortège* having accompanied Jacob into Egypt.

"(ii.) There is no sign even in Gen. xxxii., xxxiii., to which KURTZ refers, where Jacob meets with his brother Esau, of his having any such a body of servants.

"(iii.) If he had had so many at his command, it is hardly likely that he would have sent his darling Joseph, at seventeen years of age, to go, all alone and unattended, wandering about upon the veldt in search of his brethren.

"(iv.) These also are spoken of as 'feeding their flocks,' and seem to have had none of these 'thousands' with them, to witness their ill-treatment of their brother and report it to their father.

"(v.) Nothing is said about any of these servants coming down with the sons of Jacob to buy corn in Egypt, on either of their expeditions.

"(vi.) Rather, the whole story implies the contrary,—' they speedily took down every man his sack to the ground, and opened every man his sack,'— 'then they rent their clothes, and laded every man his ass, and returned to the city,'—' we are brought in, that he may seek occasion against us, and take us for bondmen, and our *asses*,' not a word being said about *servants*.

"(vii.) In fact, *their eleven sacks would have held but a very scanty supply of food for one year's consumption of so many starving 'thousands.'*

"(viii.) The flocks and herds did not absolutely require any ' servants' to tend them, in the absence of Jacob's sons, since there remained at home, with the patriarch himself, his thirty-nine children and grandchildren, as well as his sons' wives."

All of which, if worth anything, might go to prove that Jacob *never* had any great number of servants or retainers. How, then, did he take from the Amorite, with his sword and his bow, that extra portion which he gave to Joseph? (Gen. xlviii. 22.) How, then, did Simeon and Levi take each man his sword, and smite the whole people of Shechem to a man? (Gen. xxxiv. 26.) Dr. Colenso! it is clear, from Holy Scripture, that Jacob and his sons must have had a very large body of retainers. But let us agree, that like ungrateful hinds, they deserted their masters in the famine; or else, that Jacob, unable to maintain them, gave them leave to go. Is it too much to suppose that twenty-five, only twenty-five, cast in their lots with them, and went down to Egypt? Only twenty-five faithful retainers out of so large a body! Jacob and his sons took with them into Egypt their cattle and their goods (Gen. xlvi. 6); and would, doubtless, keep in view the business of breeding. But, Buffon informs us that, under such conditions, not more than 100 sheep, nor more than 50 goats, should be given to the charge of one man.[1] Supposing that, to the eleven able-bodied patriarchs, we add fourteen sons old enough to be trusted with sheep for such a purpose, and twenty-five adult men-servants, similarly, with the goats; then the breeding flock of Jacob may be taken at 2,500 sheep, and 1,250

[1] Buffon's Nat. Hist., vol. v., pp. 254, 274.

goats; or 3,750 altogether. A very small number to allow under the circumstances. But some one will say, they had cattle, and probably camels and asses. Aye! to be sure; and the greater the probability, therefore, that they had servants, and more servants than twenty-five. But let us be generous to Dr. Colenso, and take only twenty-five.

Then, at the same rate of increase, those twenty-five servants will make the whole number of people half as many again. In other words, we can afford to give up *one-third* of all the people on the scores of early death, comparative barrenness, wear and tear of work at the brick-making, and Pharaoh's slaughter. Or, again, in other words, we can afford to take an average family, by two women, at one-third of ten fewer, or six children and two-thirds in a family. So that, Dr. Colenso being willing to allow six to a family, without polygamy or concu-binage, we can afford to come to his own terms, two-thirds of a birth in each family only excepted, and still have men enough and to spare. Oh, Dr. Colenso! Dr. Colenso! no one blames you for not knowing Hebrew; but you ought to have been fairer at averages!

Some of my believing brethren may say, ' If all be so natural, wherein lies the miraculous nature of the people's increase, as plainly stated in Holy Scripture?' (Gen. xlvi. 3, and Exod. i. 20.) It lies in the fact, not that they *could* so increase, but that they *did* so increase; that, by especial protection of Providence, they were guarded, for so long a time, against the ravages of envy and hatred, on the part of strange people; that they were born so habitually in full vigour, and grew to full maturity; that they were preserved so generally from the diseases of the climate; that the more the iron heel of oppression stamped them down, the fresher, and stronger, and thicker they sprung up again; that their appointed murderers proved their friends; that they grew in the hearts of the Egyptian common people, notwithstanding they absorbed a great portion of wealth; and that, in the end, they came out with a strong hand, their proudest lords entreating them to go, and gladly yielding up their choicest treasures, in hopes of gaining, by that sacrifice, the favour of these serfs, once so despised. The losses of Israel, in Egypt, may have been great and natural; the wonder is they were not greater, since causes existed to make them *supernatural.*

For, I entreat Bishop Colenso to understand that, with all my soul, I believe in, and thank God for, the wonders of the Pentateuch.

§ XXI. THE NUMBER OF THE DANITES.

A very similar argument destroys all that Dr. Colenso has said about the Danites at the time of the Exodus. But their case has certain peculiar features, which will interest us.

> "When, however, we go on further to examine into the details of this large number of male adults, the results will be found yet more extravagant. Thus Dan, in the first generation, has *one* son (Gen. xlvi. 23); and that he had no more born to him in the land of Egypt, and therefore had *only* one son, appears from Num. xxvi. 42, where the sons of Dan consist of only one family. Hence we may reckon that in the fourth generation he would have had twenty-seven warriors descended from him, instead of 62,700, as they are numbered in Num. ii. 26, increased to 64,400 in Num. xxvi. 43.
>
> "In order to have had this number born to him, we must suppose that Dan's one son, and each of his sons and grandsons, must have had about eighty children of both sexes. We may observe, also, that the offspring of the *one* son of Dan, 62,700, is represented as nearly double that of the *ten* sons of Benjamin, 35,400. (Num. ii. 23.)"

The Bishop's first mistake is in saying that it is certain Dan had no sons born in Egypt, because at Num. xxvi. 42, there is only one family reckoned to him. The Jews say that Joseph had nine children, but only two heads of tribes were reckoned to him. Benjamin had ten children, but only seven families are reckoned to him. We are not acquainted with the principle which guided the Israelites in numbering their families under heads. No doubt there were various intervening, and contracting, causes; as we are sure (from the case of Pharez), that there were some extending causes. Sometimes a tribe would gain an additional family and its head; sometimes lose one. Nothing is more probable than that Dan's sons, by Egyptian women, should be counted under the head of Hushim. Be that as it may, we may venture to conclude, according to natural probability, that Dan, who was only forty-one years old when he went into Egypt, was not insensible to the attractions of its society; and had consequently sons born there. As, no doubt, the other patriarchs had; though no families are reckoned except in reference to Jacob's sons born in Canaan, as, *e.g.*, Hezron and Hamul were to Pharez (Num. xxvi. 1—51); and Ephraim and Manasseh, to Joseph.

Supposing, then, that Dan and Hushim were the only Danites who came from Canaan into Egypt, then, at the same rate of calculation as before, Dan being forty-one years old, and Hushim twenty, they are worth 31,250 fighting men at the time of the Exodus. This is in six generations of thirty years each at five sons a man, throwing off fifteen years at the commencement, and twenty years at the end, of the 215 years of captivity. But, it is manifest, there is no occasion for our throwing off these fifteen years, in the present case. We may fairly reckon the Danites at six generations and a-half, still giving up twenty years at the end. This half of a generation, being the last fifteen years of the 195 immediately preceding the twenty years given up, would make the whole number of fighting Danites, at the time of the Exodus, 78,125; somewhat in excess of the number 62,700, given in Holy Scripture. (Num. iii. 26.)

The above is without servants; whereas if we allow Dan and Hushim each a servant, the number becomes 156,250; and, as in other cases, we can afford to allow for casualties.

But there is a curious consideration connected with the Danites. All, who are acquainted with Holy Scripture, know that Dan's was peculiarly the *idolatrous* tribe. (Judg. xviii. 14.) Is it possible that Dan and Hushim consorted, from the first, with the Egyptians, even more thoroughly than their brethren? Had they more Egyptian consorts? Or were they so easy and social, finding little obstacle in religion, that Egyptian proselytes (who would be reckoned to the tribe) joined them in more than ordinary numbers? Such considerations may account for the fact that Dan's was the largest tribe (Num. i. 39). For Dan's was the largest, 62,700; and Manasseh's was the smallest, 32,200 (Num. i. 35); excepting Levi's, 22,000 (Num. iii. 39), to be presently referred to.

The Bishop contrasts, with great effect, the number 62,700 of Dan, who had one child, with the number, 35,400, of Benjamin, who had ten. It is a remarkable fact. Do we see here the effect of Joseph's piety? Remember how young was Benjamin; remember he was Joseph's own and beloved brother; remember that, of all Jacob's children, Joseph was distinguished for continence—is it unreasonable to think that Joseph's advice, and example, may have reformed his brother? How ashamed, and disgusted, that good man must have been, when he found that Benjamin has ten sons, when only twenty-two years old! May it not have been, of all, Joseph's deepest cause of regret, when he remembered his mother's early death, and his own cruel separation from the little brother, the נער of the family? Is it not likely that Joseph kept him near his own person, and so powerfully influenced his future principles, and the conduct of his descendants, that they, courting Joseph's patronage (who lived more than two generations after the arrival of Benjamin), may have specially avoided those snares, which tended so extremely to multiply the sons of Dan? Is it unreasonable to think that this early bias in Egypt may have generally influenced Benjamin's posterity all through the 215 years of captivity?

Excepting Levi's, the smallest tribe was Manasseh's, Joseph's eldest son; the next smallest was Ephraim's, Joseph's second son, to whom, however, peculiar fruitfulness had been promised (Gen. xlviii. 19); and the next smallest was Benjamin's, Joseph's beloved brother. Was the same influence at work in each case? And the smallness of the tribes of Joseph's sons is the more extraordinary if (as the Jews say) Joseph had seven sons born after Jacob's blessing.

§ XXII. THE NUMBER OF LEVITES AT THE EXODUS.

It will, probably, occur to the reader at once that if Dr. Colenso has been so singularly mistaken as to the meaning of the term "fourth generation," and so incorrect in his assumed averages for the size of Hebrew families in Egypt, it follows, as matter of course, that he is as much in error regarding the number of the Levites.

There is, however, one consideration which makes their case peculiar, and which we ought carefully to bear in mind. I have explained at p. 98, above, that the prophecy, or promise, of deliverance from Egypt, in the "fourth generation," had reference to Abraham's descendants only in the patriarchal family. That family, whichever it might be, whose head should occupy the place of Abraham in the patriarchate of all Israel at the time of the Exodus, and in the "fourth generation" from the patriarch Jacob, was to be the test of the fulfilment of the prophecy, and the standard representative, as chief, of the family of the whole house. That patriarchal family was Levi's; and among Levi's children, Kohath's; and among Kohath's children, Amram's; and the promise, or prophecy, was literally fulfilled in Moses and Aaron, who were the heads of the whole house, and in the "fourth generation" from Jacob.

The question arises, Since Amram's family was in the "fourth generation" from Jacob, ought we to conclude that all other Levites were? In other words, Ought we to conclude that, as of the patriarchal family so of all Levitical families, there were but four generations in 215 years?

This is the assumption which Dr. Colenso has made for all the children of Israel, but without reason. And this is the assumption which he has made for the sons of Levi, with as little.

The case of the patriarchal family Kohath's, as a son of Levi, is evidently treated as peculiar. And Dr. Colenso, when hunting up pedigrees to establish, from the Holy Bible, his theory of the " fourth generation," could only find (as we observed at p. 92 above) eleven cases, although he called to his assistance the books of Joshua, Ruth, and even Chronicles, besides the Pentateuch. These eleven cases reduce themselves to two; for five of the eleven concern the tribe of Levi, in the single family of Kohath; two more are of Reuben, through Pallu; and of the others, not one is strictly to the purpose. And, certainly, not at all to Dr. Colenso's purpose. Besides which, three of the remaining four are of Pharez, whom he incorrectly asserts to have been an 'adult grandson' of Jacob, when he went down into Egypt.

Dr. Colenso appears, in a manner perfectly astounding, not to understand the Levitical genealogy recorded in the sixth of Exodus. I have read what he says again and again, and have put down the book amazed that any clergyman could have written such stuff; and more amazed still that one who could do so should have found his way to the number of the Bishops. But let the objection he makes be stated in his own words:—

> "Again we have in Exod. vi. the genealogy, before quoted, of the three sons of Levi, who came with Jacob into Egypt,—Gershon, Kohath, Merari.
>
> "(i.) These three increased in the *second* (Amram's) generation to 8 (not to 9, as it would have been if they had had each three sons on the average), viz., the sons of Kohath 4, of Gershon 2, of Merari 2. (Exod. vi. 17—19.)
>
> "(ii.) The 4 sons of *Kohath* increased in the *third* (Aaron's) generation to 8 (not to 12), viz., the sons of Amram (Moses and Aaron) 2, of Izhar 3, of Uzziel 3. (Exod. vi. 20—22.) If we now assume that the 2 sons of *Gershon* and the 2 sons of *Merari* increased in the same proportion, that is, to 4 and 4 respectively, then all the male Levites of the *third* generation would have been 16.
>
> "(iii.) The two sons of Amram increased in the *fourth* (Eleazar's) generation to 6, viz., the sons of Aaron 4 (of whom, however, 2 died, Num iii. 2, 4), and of Moses 2. Assuming that all the 16 of the third generation increased in the same proportion, then all the male Levites of the generation

of Eleazar would have been 48, or rather 44, if we omit the 4 sons of Aaron who were reckoned as priests. Thus the whole number of Levites who would be numbered at the first census would be only 44, viz., 20 *Kohathites*, 12 *Gershonites*, 12 *Merarites*, instead of 8,580, as they are numbered in Num. iv. 48, viz., 2,750 *Kohathites*, 2,630 *Gershonites*, and 3,200 *Merarites*, vers. 36, 40, 44.

"127. Or we may put the matter in another, and a yet stronger, light, *using only the express data of Scripture*, and omitting all reference to the 215 years' sojourn in Egypt and to the four generations,—in fact, *making no assumptions of our own whatever.*

"The Amramites, numbered as Levites in the fourth (Eleazar's) generation, were, as above, only two, viz., the two sons of Moses, the sons of Aaron being reckoned as priests. Hence the rest of the Kohathites of this generation must have been made up of the descendants of Izhar and Uzziel, each of whom had *three* sons. (Exod. vi. 21, 22.) Consequently, since *all* the Kohathites of Eleazar's generation were numbered at 2,750 (Num. iv. 36), it follows that these *six* men must have had between them, according to the Scripture story, 2,748 sons, and we must suppose about the same number of daughters.

"128. There are some variations in the account given of the Levite families in the book of Chronicles from that which we find in Exod. vi. We have already had reason to see (113) that the statements of the Chronicler are not always trustworthy. But it may be well to consider how far they would oblige us to modify the results we have just arrived at.

"Thus, in Exod. vi., the sons of Libni and Shimi, ver. 17, are not mentioned. But in 1 Chron. xxiii. we are told that the sons of Laadan (Libni) were three, ver. 8, and the sons of Shimei (Shimi) three, ver. 9, whose names are given as 'Shelomith, Haziel, and Haran, three.' In the very next verse, however, we read 'the sons of Shimei were Jahath, Zina (or rather Zizah, ver. 11), Jeush, and Beriah; these *four* were the sons of Shimei'; and it is obvious that their names are totally different from the three former names. It is added, ver. 11, 'And Jahath was the chief, and Zizah the second: but Jeush and Beriah had not many sons; therefore they were in one reckoning, according to their father's house.'

"Again, in Exod. vi., while the sons of Amram, Izhar, and Uzziel are mentioned, no sons are assigned to their brother Hebron. In Num. iii. 27, however, we read of 'the family of the Hebronites'; and in 1 Chron. xxiii. 19, *four* sons of Hebron are mentioned.

"So in Exod. vi. 21, 22, the sons of Izhar are *three*, and the sons of Uzziel *three:* but in 1 Chron. xxiii. 18, 20, Izhar has only *one* son, and Uzziel *two*.

"Collecting, however, the Chronicler's statements, we find that, in the *third* generation, the Gershonites were 7, viz., the sons of Laadan 3, of Shimei 4,—the Kohathites 9, viz., the sons of Amram 2, of Izhar 1, of Hebron 4, of Uzziel 2,—the Merarites 5, viz., the sons of Mahli 2, ver. 21 (but one of these had no sons, ver. 22), of Mushi 3, ver. 23.

"Thus, according to the Chronicler, all the male Levites in the *third* generation were 21, of whom one had no sons; whereas in (126) we have reckoned them as 16. It is plain, then, that the results of the *fourth* generation will not be materially different, if we take his data, from those which we have already arrived at."

The errors of the above statement are so palpable, that I cannot believe the reader has not already noticed them. Dr. Colenso states that Gershon, Kohath, and Merari had increased to eight people in Amram's generation. And the eight persons are these— Libni, Shimi, Amram, Izhar, Hebron, Uzziel, Mahali, and Mushi. But they are mentioned as heads of *whole families*, without the slightest indication that they were all the Levites to be reckoned to that generation; and with as little respecting the number of people to be counted under each. We have no right to assume, in Hebrew genealogies, that all the souls proceeding from the stock being traced, in other words, the *begetments*, of the man referred to, are included. For the reader should be apprized, that in Exod. vi. 16, 19, the sacred writer uses for the word "generation," not דור, but הולדה, quite a different word, and having especial reference to actual *generation*, or begetment, and not to any cycle of time expressive of a race or generation, as a succession of men taken within certain limits. When Libni and Shimei are mentioned as sons of Gershon, or Mahali and Mushi, as sons of Merari, "according to their families," we have no right to assume that they were Gershon's, and Merari's, only children, or only sons; they are mentioned as the heads of their brethren, born by whomsoever, or whensoever, of Gershon, and of Merari, as to whose number we have no information. I have previously observed, at p. 113, that we are not acquainted with the principles upon which the Hebrew tribes were divided into families. Nor do we know certainly what sons, or how many in each case, were taken as heads of their brethren. Here and there Scripture gives us a hint, but not sufficient for a sure determination of the inquiry. Of this, however, we may be convinced, viz., that all were not included; as, *e.g.*, the wives and daughters were habitually omitted; and sometimes some of the sons. The absence of *names* is no proof of the non-existence of families. The line was traced through certain persons for some definite purpose, as, for instance, to mark the headship of families; or, as in the case of Amram's family, to point clearly along the line of the high priesthood.

Now, whoever will carefully examine Exod. vi. 14—27 (the Scripture in question), will be able to observe instantly that the limited genealogy contained in it answers two purposes :—1. It gives the *heads* of the different families of the first three tribes, Reuben, Simeon, and Levi; and, 2. It gives the pedigree of the high priest, down to Phinehas, who was the high priest presumptive, when the people entered into Canaan. The historian commences thus (ver. 14)—" These be the heads of their fathers' houses." How many each house contained is another matter. He then mentions four sons of Reuben, as heads of all the families of Reuben, but without prejudice to the question whether Reuben had more sons born in Egypt; as, doubtless, he had. He then names, similarly, six sons of Simeon, as those sons which were heads of all the families of Simeon. He then proceeds more minutely to the Levites; telling us (ver. 17) that all the sons of Gershon, no matter how many there were, were reckoned under two heads, viz., Libni and Shimei, and the sons of Merari (ver. 19), under two heads, Mahali and Mushi. That is, the Gershonites and the Merarites were each divided into two families, or clans, at the time of the Exodus. He also enumerates the privileged family (Kohath's) under four heads—Amram, and Izhar, and Hebron, and Uzziel. Not that he means to say these were all the children, or even all the sons, of Kohath, born to him in about 110 years (for he lived to be 133 years old), but that these were those sons of his under whom all their brethren, and their sisters, and their children, were to be reckoned, as the heads of the families of Kohath. Having done this, he winds up that part of the subject with the observation, "These are the families of Levi, according to their generations" (ver. 19); *i.e.*, 'inclusive of all the children begotten,' no matter how many there were, or in what space of time begotten. Next, he proceeds (Exod. vi. 20) more minutely with Amram's family; his first object being, apparently, to trace the patriarchate by age—for of Levi, Kohath, and Amram, alone, are patriarchal ages there affirmed. Levi lived 137 years (ver. 16); Kohath lived 133 years (ver. 18); Amram lived 137 years (ver. 20); and, since Aaron was eighty-three, and Moses eighty years old at the Exodus, each of them must have been about 120 years old when they died just before the entrance into Canaan. Here you have carefully put on record "the fourth generation," דור רביעי, *patriarchal.* Four patriarchal cycles of time, without reference to individual תולדות *begetments*, or procreations. Having mentioned so carefully the sons of Amram, and having specified also those of Korah, the leader in the rebellion, mentioned at Num. xvi. 1 (which I believe to have taken place before the book of Exodus was written), he leaves us no room for misapprehension, by adding at ver. 25, "These are the heads of the fathers of the Levites, according to their families." As though he would say, 'Do not suppose I have mentioned all the sons of Kohath, Gershon, and Merari; nor even all the fathers of divisional families; for I have mentioned only the heads, or chiefs, of the fathers,' אלה ראשי אבות. In short, we cannot, for a moment, venture to draw a certain inference as to the whole number of Kohathites in (what Dr. Colenso calls) the *second* generation, viz., Amram's, from the partial genealogy given us in Exod. vi. 16—25. And it is great error in the Bishop to have done so.

It is worthy of notice (see above, p. 92), that the only two pedigrees, out of Levi's family, found in the Pentateuch by Dr. Colenso, are those of Dathan and Abiram; two brothers, sons of Reuben, through Pallu; and in the fourth generation. Their pedigree is, in effect, but *one;* and is given, probably, because, being such sons of the *firstborn* Reuben, and in the fourth generation, they considered they had a legal right to the government: hence their revolt, as recorded at Num. xvi. 1; Korah joining with them, with a view to the High-priesthood.

One often notices that objectors to Holy Writ continually touch upon Scriptures which refute their objections, without themselves being aware of it. Every now and then Dr. Colenso runs away from his subject, and dives into Chronicles—I regret to say with no good feeling or intention. With what singular darkness, or unfairness, he has done so in regard to the sons of Levi we cannot fail to perceive, when we remark that the extract above given, which contains his allusion to Chronicles, respecting sons of Levi, furnishes us with two most important particulars concerning the divisions of Hebrew tribes into families, and concerning the sons of Levi in particular.

For, 1. We see that, sometimes, the sons of the same man, as, *e.g.*, Gershon or Merari, were shut up (so to speak)—telescopically included—under their brethren as "heads of families." Thus, "the sons of Shimei were Jahath, Zina, Jeush, and Beriah: these four were the sons of Shimei. And Jahath was the chief, and Zizah the second. But Jeush and Beriah had not many sons; therefore they were in one reckoning according to their father's house." They had sons, but we know not the number; they may have had very many daughters—but inasmuch as neither of them had many sons, both were included, with all their sons and all their daughters, under one head. This, probably, is the reason that Benjamin's ten sons are counted under only six heads at Num. xxvi. 38, and then one of these six divided into two. Families seem to have been allotted according to the number of *sons*, and, accordingly, sometimes they were extended, sometimes contracted, in number.

2. It may be seen, from this reference to Chronicles, that we are quite right in concluding that the sacred writer did not intend to mention all the families of the Levites in Exod. vi. 16—25. For all the Hebronites, sons of Amram, are omitted in Exod. vi., but are carefully mentioned both at Num. iii. 27, and at 1 Chron. xxiii. 19. Also we notice, from 1 Chron. xxiii. 14—17, that the sons of Moses were reckoned to the tribe of Levi; and yet Moses says not a word about them in Exod. vi. One reason of his silence was, doubtless, that Gershom and Eliezer were comparatively young, had not at that time children to form a house, and, therefore, were reckoned under one of Amram's sons. Afterwards the Chronicler tells us that Gershom had several sons, but they were all reckoned under one chief, Shebuel; and that Eliezer had very many grandsons, but all reckoned under Rehabiäh as one chief. In short, we cannot venture to reckon, from the names, or number, of the chiefs, how many families, or sons, there were. Exod. vi. 16—25 gives no certain *data* from which to justify Bishop Colenso's reasoning. The *heads* of families of Kohath's generation were eight; but how many living souls there were, of the same, is a question which we cannot answer.

Dr. Colenso's appeal to Chronicles, respecting the number of Levites at the Exodus, was singularly perilous, and one is surprised that it did not, at least in some degree, set him right in his interpretation of Exod. vi. 16—25. Let us briefly compare the Levitical pedigrees given in 1 Chron. xxiii. 6—23, with those to be found at Exod. vi. 16—25, and Num. xxvi. 57—62.

At Exod. vi. 18, Hebron, the son of Kohath, is mentioned, but no children are assigned to him, though the names of children of his three brothers, Amram, and Izhar, and Uzziel, are carefully recorded. Are we to assume, as Dr. Colenso to be consistent ought to have done, that Hebron had no children? Were we to do so, we should be very wrong, for at Num. xxvi. 58 we find carefully given " the family of the Hebronites;" the explanation being, probably, this, that at the time of the Exodus the children of Hebron, male and female, were reckoned under one of his brethren, and not as a separate house; but, at some time during the sojourning in the wilderness, they were separated as a family by themselves, and recorded as such, just before the entrance into Canaan. The absence of their *names* from Exod. vi. 16—25 does not imply non-existence.

In Exod. vi. 17 the families of Gershon are carefully given as two, under Libni and Shimi. In Num. xxvi. 58 the Gershonites are given as only one family, " the family of the Libnites." Where are the Shimites gone? Are they all dead, because not mentioned? No; for at 1 Chron. xxiii. 7 they are most carefully mentioned, and, as it would appear, formed the grandest division of the Gershonites. It would seem that while only three sons are reckoned to Laadan, *i.e.*, Libni, seven sons are reckoned to Shimei, *i.e.*, Shimi; and that of these seven sons, three were passed over to the chieftainship of Libni, the elder brother; while the other four were counted under Shimi, their progenitor. Perhaps, at Num. xxvi. 58, we may venture to conclude that the absence of Shimi's *name* does not warrant us in inferring, as Dr. Colenso would, the non-existence of children; perhaps, too, we may conclude that, while at Num. xxvi. 58 they were, for some unexplained reason, all included under the name of Libni, they were afterwards opened out by the selection of four sons to make a separate house, with regard to which it is also distinctly added (1 Chron. xxiii. 11) that the children of the four sons were reckoned under only two heads of houses.

Now Dr. Colenso (see above, p. 117) takes the seven sons of Shimei to be but three, or four, although he oddly refers to the difference of their names. If he had translated, " these four were sons (not *the* sons) of Shimei," he would have seen the meaning more clearly.

Again, in Exod. vi. 18—24, children of Kohath are carefully given, as Amram, Izhar, Hebron, and Uzziel; and children, with equal care, of Amram, Izhar, and Uzziel. Also, for a reason already referred to, heads of the families of Korah, the grandson of Kohath. But, at Num. xxvi. 57, 58, where are all the Kohathites? They are mentioned, generally, as " the family of the Kohathites," but when we seek for their divisions, under heads (of which no fewer than eight are mentioned at Exod. vi. 21—24, besides the family of Amram), we find them all classed under "Hebronites" and "Korahites;" Korah being only a grandson of Kohath, and Hebron having had no children assigned him before. Where are the children of Izhar,—where are those of Uzziel? Does the absence of their *names* imply non-existence, as Dr. Colenso would suppose? And, if so, what has become of the Kohathites as a grand division of the tribe of Levi? Turn to 1 Chron. xxiii. 20, and you will find that no such inference would be just. The four sons of Kohath are still to be counted, with additional particulars,—viz., 1. That the Amramites were much increased by the descendants of Moses (ver. 15—17.) 2. That the sons of Izhar were reckoned under one chief, Shelomith. 3. That the sons of Hebron were counted under four heads. And 4. That the sons of Uzziel were counted under two,—the heads being given here, also, without special mention of the number of living souls under each.

Observe, again, that the Chronicler intends to enumerate the heads of the families of Levi, as they were numbered, for the service of the tabernacle, two years after the Exodus (1 Chron. xxiii. 7—23); where he says distinctly only "the chief of the fathers" were counted. And, however it may suit Bishop Colenso to call in question the veracity of the Chronicler, we may at least take him to have been a Jew competent to express a Jew's idea of certain conventional arrangements, made regarding the numbers of a section of his people. Dr. Colenso would like us to believe, at p. 108, that the whole number of Levites at the first numbering was 44 instead of 8,580. But the Jewish Chronicler says that the number of chief-heads, not of heads of families only, but of chief-heads of families, was at the time of that numbering 21; so that, putting the Jew Chronicler in opposition to the Gentile Bishop, there would be just a little more than two living souls to reckon under each chief-head. I think we need not hesitate which explanation of Exod. vi. 16—25, and Num. xxvi. 57—62, to take as the more reasonable: Dr. Colenso's, or the Chronicler's. And Dr. Colenso has drawn his absurd conclusion, in the face of the Chronicler, notwithstanding he uses such expressions as "the chief of the fathers," "the sons of Rehabiah were very many," and others which tend to indicate the numerous persons composing the tribe of Levi at the numbering in the wilderness. I do not think the Bishop gained much advantage by his reference to Chronicles, and hope that we have sufficiently proved—

1. That, in treating of Exod. vi. 16—23, Bishop Colenso has erred in taking the number of *fathers*, as the exact number of living souls.

2. That the absence of certain names, in such a pedigree, does not imply the non-existence of other living descendants.

3. That the enumeration of persons, and even of whole families of persons, varied in such pedigrees, according to the circumstances of the time.

4. That such pedigrees afford us no *data* from which to reckon the exact number of souls comprised in them. Dr. Colenso commits the fatal error of assuming that they do.

Surely, it cannot be necessary to say more in exposure of the Bishop's wonderful conclusion, that, in 215 years of Egyptian lifetime, Levi's three sons, Gershon, Kohath, and Merari, had increased to only sixteen souls! The assertion is itself an exposure of its absurdity; and affords one of the best proofs we could have that, all through his argument, the Bishop misapprehends the meaning of the expression, "fourth generation." There is no reason for doubting that the sons of Levi increased in Egypt, as any other man's children would. Nor, for thinking, that thirty years is too short a time to reckon as one natural generation; having regard to individual begetments. Probably, it is too long, by nearly ten years.

Now, I entirely demur to the Bishop's third assumption, at p. 108, that the sons of Amram, in the times of Moses and Aaron, give a fair average of increase for all the Levites. It is manifestly unfair. For, not to reason on any special intervention of the Almighty, which may be considered as probable, in the case of two men destined for offices so high as theirs, we are sure that Moses and Aaron abstained from polygamy and concubinage. And, perhaps, the idea may not be unreasonable that, so soon as the Patriarchate was known to be fixed on the family of Kohath, and in the person of Amram, purity of race was studiously sought after in that family. We are told, by the Jews, that one reason why so little is said by Moses of his own sons, is, that they were born of an Ethiopian woman. A dishonour with which his sister Miriam reproached him. (Num. xii. 1.) For this purpose of purity of race, it may be that

Amram married a Jewess, a daughter of Levi, who must, nevertheless, have been so many years his elder. And, if so, the patriarchal family, Amram's, can afford us no average from which to reason fairly as to the generation, *i.e.*, begetments, of Levi's other sons; and, particularly, not upon which to reckon the increase of the children of Gershon and Merari, whose connection with the Patriarchate was so remote.

But, supposing we were to assume that the sons of Levi multiplied exactly at the same rate, as we believe may fairly be understood for all Jacob's other sons, then the number of male Levites, at the Exodus, might have been considerably more than as stated. For all other descendants we reckon only six generations in 215 years; one reason for our doing so being that all the men of other tribes were to be taken as at twenty years old, at the Exodus. But the Levites were to be numbered from only *one month* old and upwards; so that we may count seven generations of thirty years each to the sons of Levi, Kohath, Gershon, and Merari, who were of about marriageable age when they went down to Egypt.

Supposing, then, that we left out Levi, and commenced the stock with Gershon, Kohath, and Merari; reckoning thirty years to one generation; and allowing, on the average, five sons to each man, the male Levites above five years old, at the Exodus, would be in seven generations 234,375. This is without reckoning any increase from supposed servants, or additional sons of Levi, but confining the tribe of Levi strictly to sons of Gershon, Kohath, and Merari.

But at Num. iii. 39 the whole number of Levites given, from one month old and upwards, is only 22,000; which, when compared with other tribes, even with Manasseh's, indicates singular continency on their parts; and, probably, corresponding purity of race. What influence was exerted, or when, so to influence the Levites, we are not informed. But Amram lived to be 133 years old; and if we suppose that, during the last three natural generations, and when the Patriarchate was known to be fixed in Kohath's family, this influence to continency and purity of race was exercised among the Levites; then, taking them for the last three generations of the seven, at an average of five children in a family, or only two and a-half sons, the number of Levites above five years old at the Exodus would be seven-eighths above 29,296. In fact, very great continency is indicated in the tribe of Levi; though it is impossible to say at what period of the captivity it began to affect the numbers of their tribe.

That the Levites *might* have increased to many, very many, more than 22,000 sons, above one month old, at the numbering in Sinai, *i.e.*, in more than seven generations of thirty years, reckoning the stock from only three fathers, viz., Gershon, Kohath, and Merari, we are sure.

But really Dr. Colenso is hard to please. One tribe of Israel increases too much, another too little; and the same tribe, at different times, is found offending against the Bishop's notions of propriety in very opposite ways.

Now here is the tribe of Levi. We have just seen how creditable it is to it, that it numbered only 22,000, by its males of a month old, at the numbering at Sinai. Dr. Colenso is quite out of patience with these poor fellows that they only increased by 1,000 in about thirty-eight years after. Surely it was no fault of theirs.

> "The number of the Levites at the second census when compared with that of the first, involves also a great inconsistency. We are told, (Num. xxvi. 62), that, at the *second* census, 'those that were numbered of them were 23,000 all males from a month old and upward.' And, at the *first* census, (Num. iii. 39), 'All that were numbered of the Levites, all the males from a month old and upward, were 22,000. Hence during the thirty-eight years in the wilderness, they had only increased in number 1,000 upon 22,000.
>
> "Now either the Levites were included in the sentence passed upon the congregation generally that they should die in the wilderness, or they were not. The former supposition seems to be precluded by the fact that Eleazar, the son of Aaron, at all events, was alive, according to the story, even after the death of Joshua. (Josh. xxiv. 33.) And Eleazar was a full-grown priest at Sinai (Exod. xxxviii. 1), and was therefore, we must suppose, above the age of twenty, or even that of thirty, at which the Levites were first allowed to do service in the Sanctuary. (Num. iv. 47.) We must conclude, then, that the Levites were not involved in the general doom; and, in fact, it is repeatedly said (Num. ii. 33, and xxvi. 62), that they were not numbered among the children of Israel, and the doom in question is evidently confined to 'the children of Israel,' except Joshua and Caleb. (Num. xiv. 2, 10; xxvi. 62—65.)
>
> "130. Now the population of England increases at the rate of about 23 per cent. in ten years. Upon the same scale, then,—that is to say, at no greater rate of increase than this,—the 22,000 Levites (since these were *all* the males of all ages, 'from a month old and upward,' and therefore may be reckoned as about half the whole mixed population of Levites, male

and female) should have increased in ten years to 27,060, in the next ten years to 33,284, in the next ten to 40,939, and in the last eight to 48,471— instead of which the number of this favoured tribe is given only as 23,000. In other words, they *should* have increased by more than 26,000; but they are represented as increased by only 1,000.

" On the other hand the tribe of Manasseh increased in the thirty-eight years from 32,200 (Num. i. 35), to 52,700 (Num. xxvi. 34), and all these were men in the prime of life, and not one of the 32,200 was numbered among the 52,700. Whereas the 22,000 were males of all ages, 'from a month old and upward,' and a large proportion of these, we may suppose, survived the thirty-eight years; and yet these, with their children, were only increased by 1,000 in the same interval."

" This favoured tribe!" Is it a sneer? Yes, they were a favoured tribe; favoured by the very virtues which kept back their population. I have already pointed out that great continency is intimated on the part of the tribe of Levi; suggested, probably, by the fact that they knew, towards the end of the captivity in Egypt, that they were selected as the patriarchal tribe; suggested, therefore, by the desire of keeping their Israelitish blood as pure as they could. This, probably, had checked their increase for several generations.

Moreover, there are certain causes hinted at, which would check their increase in the desert. Priestly tribes are seldom popular; though they may be powerful. My lay brethren will-pardon me; but, if the truth be told, they none of them like *parsons*. Now, there can be little doubt, but that a similar prejudice extended to all the tribe of Levi; of which, some were ruling priests; all were devoted to the service of the Tabernacle, and pledged to support the priesthood; and all of them kept (some would say, like lazy fellows —consumers, not producers,) at the public expense. What smart man of business, or clever, professional gentleman, ever liked tithes, or firstfruits, or Easter-offerings; unless, indeed, he had to take them; or had got them into his family by *mis*-appropriation? We may rely upon it, that the sons of Levi had to pay the penalty, levied, by all mixed societies, against the privileged caste!

Besides which, the Levites were the public avengers of morality and religion; and at times exhibited a muscular piety, of which certain Christian philosophers of the present day would scarcely approve, notwithstanding all their boasted practical energy and vigour. An event had occurred, at the very commencement of Israel's residence in the desert, for which the Levites could never expect to be forgiven. When all Israel apostatized at Horeb, the patriarchal tribe alone remained faithful. No doubt their brethren accused them of doing so from interested motives; still, they did remain faithful. "Then Moses stood in the gate of the camp, and said, Who is on the Lord's side? let him come unto me. And all the sons of Levi gathered themselves together unto him;" and then slew "about three thousand men." (Exod. xxxii. 25—29.) "Put ye on every man his sword by his side," was a command which must have sounded terribly in the ears of Israel, when addressed to the sons of Levi. In after-days, Phinehas, the son of Eleazar, the son of Aaron, the High Priest, kept up the tradition of his tribe. (Num. xxv. 7.) On such occasions, we can easily imagine, a little personal severity for slights, real or imagined, may have mingled itself with Levi's religious zeal; but, at any rate, the tribe was open to the suspicion; and, we may fairly conclude, suffered from having evil motives attributed to them; as well as from the fact that they so actively, and unflinchingly, avenged the law.

The natural effect of such circumstances would be, to isolate the tribe of Levi; and the consequence of such isolation would be, that they would intermarry much among themselves. Which habit would, probably, be confirmed, by a desire, on their parts, to insure the tenure of their exclusive privileges, by seclusive alliances. And the natural tendency of this marrying in and in, among themselves, would be, to retard their marriages, and to diminish their rate of increase.

Now, as regards the perishing in the wilderness of all the men, above twenty years of age, that came out of Egypt, Dr. Colenso has thought proper to say:—" Either the Levites were included in the " sentence passed upon the congregation generally, that they should " die in the wilderness, or they were not."

But, suppose we state the proposition for him thus:—" Either " the Levites were *entirely* included in the sentence passed, or " *not at all*." Does he not see the fallacy? At any rate, we do.

The Levites, as a tribe, were not included in the sentence passed upon the whole of the congregation. They were, upon the whole, a faithful tribe throughout. But this admission will not negative the probability that many of them may have sympathized with the rest of Israel, and have paid the penalty accordingly.

Yet, after all, what was this penalty? Merely this, that one whole generation died off in about forty years; when, we may add, with reverence, it was time for them to die. The youngest of these, who so died, would be about sixty years old: the majority of them, very much older. Dr. Colenso alludes to the " doom," as he calls it, as if it were something awful, and extraordinary, and must have had some serious effect upon the procreating power of the tribes. He misapprehends the case. The time of these men, for purposes of multiplication, we believe to have been passed. What children they were to have, they had had; and left behind them. Their " general " doom" did not otherwise affect the numbers of Israel, than by the withdrawal of themselves. And, when Dr. Colenso asks, with affronting incredulity, at p. 111,—What are we to say " of the " whole body of 600,000 fighting men being swept away, during " the forty years' sojourning in the wilderness?" he forgets, what an arithmetician ought to have remembered, that it was in the natural course of things that they should die so. That forty years of travelling and hardship in the wilderness, would wear down almost any man, who started, at twenty years of age, from the cucumbers and onions of Egypt. If it be asked,—In what, then, consisted their punishment? the answer is plain. Dr. Colenso misapprehends the Scripture. Their punishment lay in the fact that they were not permitted to enter Canaan on their first arrival at its borders (Num. xiv. 23); and also bore a close parallel to that of Moses. (Num. xxvii. 12—14.) God's peculiar blessing was withdrawn from them. He would not protract the life of any one of them, save Caleb and Joshua, to see "that good land;" but interfered that all should perish in the desert. It was no marvel that the majority of them died in the wilderness; but it was a marvel that not *one* of them survived to enter into Canaan.

Dr. Colenso thinks it an objection that the sons of Levi had increased by only one thousand in thirty-eight years. Might not physical causes so operate in the wilderness, as to diminish procreation? Might not the withdrawal of Egyptian women have tended to the chastity of the young men in all the tribes of Israel? Might not constant harassing and danger, alarm and hardship, with famine or

K

drought threatened every now and then, have checked the amorous propensities of the warmest? Might not the adhesion of some of the "mixed multitude," who went up with them out of Egypt (Exod. xii. 38), have increased some tribes; and the avoidance of this very adhesion, have kept others nearly stationary? It is plain, a hundred questions may be raised, affecting the generation of people in the desert, which Dr. Colenso would not be able to answer. In other words, there is necessarily an absence of *data* upon this subject, more than enough to prevent the Doctor from attacking the Pentateuch, in respect to it, at least with any show of reason.

But why has he not compared the numbers of all the tribes, at the time they left Egypt, and at the time when they entered Canaan? He is so fond of averages! Now some very useful hints may be gathered by our doing so.

When Israel left Egypt, the fighting men numbered, of

Reuben	46,500	Simeon	59,300	Gad	45,650
Judah	74,600	Issachar	54,400	Zebulun	57,400
Ephraim	40,500	Manasseh	32,200	Benjamin	35,400
Dan	62,700	Asher	41,500	Naphtali	53,400

Total . . . 603,550. (Num. i. 1—46.)

And when Israel entered into Canaan, the fighting men numbered, of

Reuben	43,730	Simeon	22,200	Gad	40,500
Judah	76,500	Issachar	64,300	Zebulun	60,500
Ephraim	32,500	Manasseh	52,700	Benjamin	45,600
Dan	64,400	Asher	53,400	Naphtali	45,400

Total . . . 601,730. (Num. xxvi. 1—51.)

Being, in the following tribes, increase for,

				Issachar	9,900
Judah	1,900	Zebulun	3,100	Manasseh	20,500
Benjamin	10,200	Dan	1,700	Asher	11,900

Total Increase . . . 59,200.

But, in the following tribes, decrease for

Reuben	2,770	Simeon	37,100	Gad	5,150
		Ephraim	8,000	Naphtali	8,000

Total Decrease . . . 61,020.

What does Dr. Colenso mean? Is he prepared to quarrel with the historian because he asserts that some tribes varied but little in the number of their fighting men, some tribes increased much, and some decreased more? Would it be reasonable to make each fact a cause of difference with the historian? If not, on which is Dr. Colenso prepared to take his stand? Would it not be more reasonable to conclude that the numbers, in twelve tribes, thus arbitrarily intervaried, are stated truly; and were severally determined by various causes, differently affecting the several tribes, which the historian did not feel it needful, or had not the means sufficiently, to explain? For instance, in the case of Simeon, so wonderfully reduced, might not Providence have been overruling circumstances so as to fulfil his predicted punishment, " I will divide them in Jacob, and scatter them in Israel."? (Gen. xlix. 5—7.) Might not the diminution of the tribe have been preparatory to this? And, similarly, as to Levi's very small increase; for he had to share this punishment with Simeon. God's "favoured tribe" was never exempt from chastisement. Or, again, as regards the great decrease of Ephraim and Naphtali, is it quite inconceivable that they might have been among the most unruly tribes; and have met, in the various plagues of the desert, chastisement in proportion? Or, again, as regards the great increase of Manasseh, Benjamin, and Asher, is it too much to remember that Joseph's and Benjamin's were favoured tribes, and that the increase which was perilled, through the faults of Ephraim, may have been abundantly made up to the fidelity of Manasseh? Or, again, as regards Manasseh, Benjamin, and Asher, is it absolutely foolish to imagine that some of the " mixed people "' may have longed for the privileges of Israel, and particularly in conjunction with a tribe upon whom were to fall the blessings of Joseph? (Gen. xlix. 22—26.)

In short, there are so many ways of rationally conceiving why the tribes of Israel should have varied in the desert, by increase or decrease among themselves, that I venture to say it is hopeless in Dr. Colenso to expect to attack the Pentateuch, successfully, on any such account. On the other hand, it must be admitted that the statement of a gross total decrease on the number of fighting men of only 1,820, is reasonable in itself, considering all the circumstances of the people in the desert. Taking these fighting men as *indices* to the numbers of the several tribes, it is manifest that the rate of increase of all the people had been considerably diminished from what it was in Egypt. The peculiar blessing of God upon them, to that end, had now been withdrawn, because no longer needed; the natural means, furnished in Egypt, had been removed; and the people now were generated only at a rate which indicated sufficiently the hardships of the desert. Lastly, it should be remembered that the numbers given are only of the men fit for habitual war (Num. xxvi. 2; and see pp. 44—46, above); and may be, therefore, but very imperfect indices, after all, to the relative sizes of the tribes.

For all which reasons I conclude—

1. That the historian gives Dr. Colenso no sufficient *data* by which to enable him, rationally, to assail the Pentateuch on the score of the numbers at the second numbering. (Num. xxvi. 1.)

2. That we can easily conceive causes for the very limited number of the Levitical tribe at the Exodus, and for their very limited increase in the desert.

§ XXIII. THE NUMBER OF THE FIRSTBORN.

In no part of Dr. Colenso's work does his one-sidedness in argument, or the prejudiced and morbid state of his mind, appear in a more lamentable degree than in that concerning "the number of the firstborns compared with the number of male adults." Having resolved to impugn the accuracy and veracity of the Pentateuch, there is apparent, all through his book, a determination to magnify its difficulties, and to see clearly nothing which deserves consideration on the other side.

Let me select from this, his fourteenth chapter, a few illustrations of such dangerous partiality.

1. Kurtz (in making a very unconvincing attempt to explain the difficulty connected with the firstborn) suggests that "polygamy was rare" among the Hebrews; on this Dr. Colenso observes, " which, indeed, " Kurtz assumes without proof." Yet in another part of his book he will not, for one moment, allow that polygamy did prevail among the Hebrews. He not only, at p. 117, confronts Kalisch (who acknowledges the polygamy) with Kurtz (who denies it), but adds, at p. 120, the determinate assertion of his own: " There is no " indication that polygamy did prevail among the Hebrews of those " days;" and that (as we saw at pp. 103, 104, above) in contradiction to the plain evidence of Scripture.

2. Kurtz ventures to suggest that the Israelitish mothers gave birth to an unusual number of children. "This, again," says the Bishop, at p. 85, " is assumed without proof, or, rather, directly in " the face of all the facts which are given us, by which to judge of " the size of Hebrew families." And, as evidence, he recurs to Jacob's families born in Canaan, before the time for fulfilling the promise of special increase in Egypt; and also to the family of Amram, which we have already spoken of as peculiar. The truth is, as explained at pp. 103—106, above, Holy Scripture gives us no *data* sufficient to enable us to estimate fairly the size of Hebrew-Egyptian families. But the Christian Bishop steadily refuses to remember, or to confess belief in, the miraculous increase which Holy Scripture distinctly promises to the Jews in Egypt in the very name of God, " I will make of thee there a great nation." (Gen. xlvi. 3; Exod. i. 7—12.) And he as steadily refuses to see, or to admit, the testimony of heathen to the mere historical, physical, fact that the native women of Egypt (and Hebrew mothers *there* were native women) habitually produced two, three, four, and sometimes five children at a birth. A fact for which Kalisch has properly quoted Aristotle, *Hist. Anam.*, vii. 4, and Pliny, *Nat. Hist.*, vii. 3, as witnesses.

3. Kurtz ventures to suggest that the firstborn child in a family is usually a girl. Dr. Colenso, without being able to deny this physical, statistical, fact, stubbornly refers to the peculiar cases of " the children of promise," through Abraham, Isaac, and Jacob. Forgetting, or refusing to remember, that the whole status and condition of the Patriarchal family, before they went into Egypt, was very different from what it afterwards became, and was intended by the Almighty to be so. Forgetting, also, or refusing to remember, that, in order to refute the argument of Kurtz, he ought to have shown, by tables of statistics, that it was unsound.

4. The Bishop's prejudice and partiality are so resolute as, on one occasion, to betray him into a remark literally absurd. Although we ought to notice, in justice to him, that, since his reply touches on a piece of Hebrew criticism, we have other means of accounting for its absurdity, besides those of prejudice and partiality. What they are, all his book has painfully displayed. Hävernick, following Michaelis, maintains that the word בכור *firstborn* had, among the Israelites, a very peculiar and limited meaning, which (if the fact be so) utterly destroys Bishop Colenso's objection to the paucity of

their number. And, in support, he refers to Gen. xlix. 3, and other passages. Exclaims Dr. Colenso, at p. 88, "What is the use of "quoting such passages as Gen. xlix. 3, 'Reuben, thou art my first-"born;' Num. i. 20, 'Reuben, Israel's eldest son;' Ps. cv. 36, 'He "smote all the firstborn in the land;' or Deut. xxi. 15—17, where "the *man's* firstborn is not to be disinherited upon private affection?" Why, every use, if only Hävernick's criticism be correct. And such a question (if really believed by Dr. Colenso to be sensible) only shows, like all his book, that he is utterly devoid of Hebraistic instinct; no feeling of sympathetic intelligence thrills through his arithmetical mind as he reads, or tries to read, that language; he is all made up of roots, and squares, and *logs*, and decimals, and powers to the nth; but he has not a fraction of that power, which we all need for reading the Hebrew Bible, viz., a natural capacity to bow down before the genius of that mighty and blessed language—the language of Eden and the language of heaven (Acts xxvi. 14); nor has he even that intimate acquaintance with the Hebrew Bible, the mere result of drudgery at reading, which can make him competent to judge of a construction, or intuitively to recognise a familiar idiom.

Yet, supposing it should be the case that בכור *firstborn* did mean among the Hebrews—*first*, the firstborn son both of the father and the mother, and not merely the firstborn on the mother's side; *second*, the firstborn son of a whole family by the first virgin-wife, no matter how many other wives, or concubines, the father had; *third*, that the word was used in a sense implying certain functional privileges, and limiting the number of *firstborn* accordingly—then the natural proportion between the firstborn and other male children, is instantly and extensively changed; and we see, at a glance, the folly of asking, "What is the use of quoting such passages as Gen. xlix. 3, 'Reuben, "thou art my firstborn,'" &c., &c.

The Bishop's objection is stated thus, at p. 84:—

"93. *All the firstborn males, from a month old and upwards, of those that were numbered, were twenty and two thousand two hundred and threescore and thirteen.* (Num. iii. 43.)

"Let us see what this statement implies, when treated as a simple matter of fact. For this purpose I quote the words of Kurtz, iii., p. 209:—

"'If there were 600,000 males of twenty years and upwards, the whole number of males may be reckoned at 900,000 [he elsewhere reckons 1,000,000], in which case there would be only *one* firstborn to *forty-two* [forty-four] males.

In other words, the number of boys in every family must have been on the average *forty-two*.'

"This will be seen at once if we consider that the rest of the 900,000 males were *not* firstborns, and, therefore, each of these must have had one or other of the 22,273 as the firstborn of his own family—except, of course, any cases where the firstborn of any family was a *daughter*, or was *dead*, of which we shall speak presently.

"And these were not the firstborn on the *father's* side, as Michaelis supposes, so that a man might have many wives and many children, but only one firstborn, as was the case with Jacob himself. They are expressly stated to have been the firstborn on the *mother's* side—' all the firstborn that openeth the matrix' (Num. iii. 12). So that, according to the story in the Pentateuch, *every mother of Israel must have had on the average forty-two sons!*"

I shall, first, reply to this difficulty, taken just as stated by Dr. Colenso. It amounts to a serious deficiency of firstborn sons, who are given only as one to forty-two, taking the males alone, or as one to eighty-four, taking the females also, and assuming the firstborn daughters to be, in number, only just the same as the firstborn sons. Or, in the Bishop's own words, "And 44,546 firstborn " children" (males or females) "among a population of 1,800,000 " souls, would imply that each mother had, on the average, " forty-two children as before, but twenty-one sons and twenty-one " daughters."

The real difficulty, therefore, lies in conceiving each family in Israel to have numbered forty-two children; taking their whole number even as low as 1,800,000. But is there real cause for forming such a conception. There is a great truth, admitted by Dr. Colenso (indeed, it cannot be denied), viz., that all cases must be allowed for, in which the firstborn was a girl, or was dead. Have we any means of discovering how often either of these cases may have occurred? None whatever; and, therefore, if we kick against the numbers given, we must do so like men suspended in the air.

Now, Dr. Colenso has said, at p. 88, in reply to a remark by Hävernick, "I am wholly at a loss to understand the meaning of the " above paragraph." And I ask the Bishop's permission to quote two remarks of his own, which seem to me deserving of similar distinction. He says, at p. 85, "And the result is, as before, that " there are reckoned only 22,273 firstborn sons of all the mothers of " Israel, after one or other of whom the other males must all be " ranged in their respective families (except, as before, cases where "the firstborn of a family was either a female or was dead), so that "each mother must have had, on the average, forty-two sons." Yes, no doubt, "except as before;" but then the exception admits of such extension as to neutralize the whole conclusion. Supposing, for example, we selected 6,000 English families, containing 60,000 souls, and from them all enrolled 18,000 militiamen, among whom we found 2,500 firstborn sons, where is the sense of saying that all the other 15,500 men must be ranged "after one or other" of these 2,500 "in their respective families"? Such a statement is ridiculous; and when every case in which the firstborn son had died, earlier or later, or had been stillborn, and the cases in which the firstborn child was a daughter, had been counted up, we should find the seeming deficiency of firstborn sons made up; and that only a part, and perhaps only a small part, of the 15,500 men, not firstborns, had to be reckoned "under one or other" of the 2,500 who were such; but all the others must be remitted to their several distinct families.

Again, Dr. Colenso says, at p. 85, "Besides which, the number of "*mothers* must have been the same as that of the firstborns, male and "female, including also any that had died. Hence there would have "been only 60,000. Hence there would have been only 60,000 child-"bearing women to 600,000 men, so that only about one man in ten "had a wife or children." Upon the Bishop's hypothesis, which, as we shall see, is very unfair. But, even then, how can the conclusion be sound? Because, at any given time, a population of 1,800,000, containing 600,000 fighting men, can reckon only 60,000 firstborns, living or dead, above one month old; therefore there are but 60,000 child-bearing women, and only one man in ten has a wife or children? Indeed! how about those few men whose wives were barren? How about those many more, whose wives had not yet borne, though married (it may be) a year or two; but who, in all probability, would bear? How about the young men whose wives had borne their first child, but not so long ago as thirty days? Now, has Dr. Colenso really forgotten what he told us so kindly, and accurately, at p. 62 of his remarkable "Chronicles," that the births in such a population would have been 264 a-day; so that there may have been, at the time the firstborn were numbered, 29 times 264, *i.e.*, 7,656, little children under one month old, of whom many would be, undoubtedly, firstborns? And, lastly, how about the young men who had been married, we must suppose, within the 9 months immediately preceding the numeration of the firstborn, and whose wives had not yet been confined, though that interesting event might hourly be expected? I wish the Bishop had given us the probable rate of marriages per day, " in a population like that of London " (p. 62); so that we might have multiplied them by about 8 months, or 240 days. He has not done so; but the marriages in London in the year 1861 were 26,918, or 73 a day, and a little more. Let us take for Israel the same rate, for 8 months of 30 days, or 240 days, and we are provided with just 17,520 young Jews, who have wives, but no children; though every prospect of being blessed with them. Surely, for once, Dr. Colenso is wrong in his calculation, when he says that 60,000 firstborns to 600,000 men implies only 60,000 child-bearing women; or that only 1 man in 10 had a wife, or children. But there he was wrong, too, when he calculated the families of goats and sheep : see p. 54, above.

And, besides, I have not alluded to those older men, who, though they had no wives, were *widowers;* and, probably, had learned to bear the loss with becoming resignation.

Again (just one little word more), Dr. Colenso says, at p. 87:— " Still we cannot suppose any unusual mortality of this kind," viz., of the firstborn, " without checking in the same degree the increase " of the people." The loss of every child checks, of course, in its degree, the increase of a people ; but not the loss of the firstborn in particular. We can conceive, in a multitude of cases, the death of the firstborn to have been followed by a very numerous progeny. Indeed, were statistical tables prepared to that end, how frequent, perhaps how general, would be the loss of the firstborn child, is a matter to be glanced at more distinctly a little further on.

I said, at p. 135, above, that the real difficulty about these firstborn, as stated by Dr. Colenso, lay in finding but 22,273 in an assumed population of 900,000 males, *i.e.,* 1 in 42. I believe the figures are not quite accurate. But, accepting them as thus given, suppose we admit, at once, that these 42 males, instead of being reckoned to 1 family, ought to be counted to 7. Then the firstborn sons are deficient in 6 families out of every 7. Or, state the case in another way,—A population of 1,870,932 souls, with only 22,273 firstborn sons, gives 1 firstborn son to each 84 souls. Then, dividing these 84 souls into 12 families of about 7 each, the proportion of firstborn sons is as 1 to 12 families. Now, Dr.Colenso is utterly unable to meet, or to refute, the statistical fact that the firstborn child is, usually, a girl; nor does he attempt to do so. Let us suppose that, out of the 12 families of 7 souls each, 8 of them, or two-thirds, have daughters firstborn. The proportion is not unreasonable. Then the deficiency of firstborn sons is 3 out of every 4.

It seems to me, I venture to repeat, that these two admissions, which cannot be refused us, viz., 1. That, usually, the firstborn is a girl; and 2. That the firstborn child often dies; dispose of all the difficulty, arising from an imagined deficiency of the firstborn sons among Israel. And for this simple reason, that we have no means of certainly determining to what extent each admitted reason for deduction will operate. If we allow, for instance, that 2 out of every 3 firstborns were girls, surely no very strong imagination is required for perceiving that in a population of 1,870,932 people, circumstanced like the Hebrews in Egypt, 3 out of every 4 firstborn sons were violently killed by Pharaoh, or had died naturally, or had perished in the birth.

For, as to this deficiency of firstborn sons, there is a little consideration which I wish to suggest most delicately. If the reader will refer to the places marked below,[1] he will find that the firstborn intended are כל פטר רחם, *each an opening of the womb*. Have we any means of knowing how frequently the womb of a virgin-wife is opened with a firstfruit born dead, or not brought to perfection? Will any medical man, who reads this defence of Moses, consider what difficulties attend first-births; and how often they perish, when either partial, or complete? Pardon me; Holy Scripture implies that the womb of the virgin mother must have been opened for the very first time, and with a perfect birth, having lived at least one month. There must have been no miscarriage, no failure of any kind. The womb must never have been opened with any birth. Will my readers consider whether this reflection does not materially affect the supposed deficiency of firstborn in Israel? The force, and soundness, of this argument is seen in a moment by asking ourselves the question—" Had a virgin mother in Israel brought forth a first son, stillborn, could she ever after have had a firstborn, in the scriptural sense of that term?" No; then, neither could she, if she had failed in a similar, though less, degree.

Lastly, as affecting the number of living firstborn sons, I shall

[1] Exod. xiii. 2, 12, 15, and xxxiv. 19; Num. iii. 12, and xviii. 15.

mention the fact that the numbering being from one month old, and upwards, without the higher limit, there can be no doubt but that many firstborn had died in the course of nature.

I venture to think that no necessity any longer remains for attempting to explain the seeming deficiency of firstborn sons in Israel at the time of the numbering. These several reasons assist in accounting for the fact: *first*, that the firstborn child, in a family, is usually a girl; *second*, that the firstborn, in a family, very often does not survive, and that from various causes; *third*, that in the case of Israel we have reason to fear that some of the firstborn *sons* had been slain by Pharaoh; *fourth*, that, of the older firstborn males, some would have died in the course of nature.

And, what is most important, we have not, in reference to any one of these four causes of diminution, any certain or statistical means given us of determining to what extent each, and every, of them might have operated. There is one question, which I would submit to Bishop Colenso, because I believe it affects his whole book,—" Is it safe to assail Holy Scripture by calculations based upon *hypothetical* numbers ?"

Yet I will call attention to one more consideration, which would tend very materially to affect the numbers of the firstborn. There is no sound reason for doubting that Hävernick is right when he suggests that the firstborn intended must be the firstborn both of the father and of the mother; and that Michaelis and Hävernick are right when they agree that, again, the firstborn intended is the firstborn in a whole family of the first virgin wife, as Reuben was, no matter how many other virgin wives, or virgin concubines, a man might have.

The expression כל פטר רחם, *each an opening of the womb*, is intended distinctly to intimate that the son intended by the sacred writer must be the very first that passes through the portal of life; but it by no means justifies Bishop Colenso's inference, at p. 84, " these were not the firstborn on the *father's* side, as Michaelis " supposes, so that a man might have many wives, and many children, " but only one firstborn, as was the case with Jacob himself. They " are expressly stated to have been the firstborn on the *mother's* " side—' all the firstborn that openeth the matrix.' (Num. iii. 12.) "
The cause of the Bishop's mistake is clear; he drops, like a firstborn baby, helplessly into the arms of the English translator, and supposes the Hebrew words must mean "all that openeth the womb" inclu-

sively of each firstborn male child, by every mother; whereas the words are more correctly rendered " each an opening of the womb," descriptively of each to be numbered, but not inclusively of all, born as to their mothers similarly. If the Bishop will consult the passages, already referred to at p. 138, above, he will notice (and he is fond of *points*) that the segholate noun is used and not the participle, in the word פטר. But, indeed, if he prefer the participle, the translation will still be " each opening the womb." And also, to the same effect, if we take the third person of the perfect verb. Or, at Exod. xiii. 2, כל בכור פטר כל רחם, *each firstborn opening each womb;* "each to each." That is, "each firstborn" the first produce of the womb that bears it.

Why does Dr. Colenso venture so broadly to contradict men like Hävernick, when any one may tell that he does not possess the information necessary for the purpose? Was he aware of what Bochart says[1] on this subject? "Here we must inquire what פטר " properly is, in these laws (Exod. xxxiv. 19); ' every פטר of the " ' womb is mine.' It is plain, indeed, that in this place, and " similar" (as already referred to) " the word פטר means *firstborn;* " but it is not equally plain in what sense the firstborn is called " פטר."

Nor is the idea that the *firstborn* means, in the scriptural sense, the firstborn both of the father and of a virgin mother, without probable Scripture authority. It will never do to permit the Bishop to say, as he does at p. 88, " The ' Hebrew usage ' has nothing to do with " the question." It has everything to do with it. And such a remark is of the very strangest kind to proceed from a Bishop, who professes to know Hebrew. Nor can we allow him to add, without calling attention to the error, " We are here only concerned with " ' all the firstborn, whatsoever openeth the womb ' (Exod. xiii. 2), " ' being males' (ver. 15)." Where, again, he falls into the superficial sense of the English words, without venturing to consider the possible force of the Hebrew, as above explained. " Each first-" born opening each womb," *i.e.*, " each firstborn opening each " a womb," " each to each." Nor can we help, again, referring to his extraordinary question, " What is the use of quoting such " passages as Gen. xlix. 3, ' Reuben, thou art my firstborn ' ? " To which we now reply.

[1] Bochart's Hieroz., vol. I., p. 298.

At Deut. xxi. 15—17, are clearly suggested two great considerations bearing upon this question of the *firstborn*, in direct refutation of Bishop Colenso. There we learn, 1. That polygamy was permitted, and provided for, as actually existing, which Dr. Colenso has denied (see p. 103, above). 2. That the two, or more, families were viewed as one, by the Levitical law, in respect of the *firstborn*. "If the "firstborn son be hers that was hated"—"he may not make the son "of the beloved לבכר (*to have the rights of the*) firstborn before the "son of the hated, the firstborn. But he shall acknowledge the son "of the hated the firstborn, by giving him a double portion of "all that he hath; for he is the beginning of his strength," כי הוא ראשית אנו. Whence results clearly the doctrine that, Levitically, in families of more than one wife, or of one wife and more women (whether concubines or wives), there was but one to be regarded, legally, as בכור *firstborn*, and to that one all the rights, and privileges, of the firstborn belonged. And, again, results the conviction that Reuben's is the exact precedent to be followed, though so despised by Bishop Colenso; for Moses represents the Almighty as here using part of the very words employed by Jacob, ראשית אוני, *beginning of my strength*. (Gen. xlix. 3.)

Now, in addition to this legal injunction, (Deut. xxi. 15—17), the words of Jacob's prophecy, here referred to, intimate to us the peculiar sense in which the Hebrew law spake of firstborn sons. They were regarded as the earnest, or firstfruits, of that worldly power and wealth which *all* the family represented. So that as *all* the family was regarded as *one* body of wealth and power, the first son of the first virgin wife was regarded as the *one*, and only, firstborn of all that *one* family. The English translation, (Gen. xlix. 3) is sublime as a grand expression of high sentiment, "Reuben, thou art my firstborn, my might, and the beginning of my strength, the excellence of dignity, and the excellence of power." But it scarcely represents the Hebrew, nor conveys literally Jacob's meaning. He intends to say that the birth of Reuben, by Leah, as the first living proof of his own productiveness, was the earnest of other children to be born of her, and of other women. And placing his worldly power and prosperity in the number of his children, the size of his household, and implied multiplication of his goods, he calls Reuben, as his firstborn son, "his strength, the beginning of his "substance, excess of dignity, excess of might." So that, in whatever the Patriarch considered *all* his wealth, and *all* his power to consist, of *all* that, Jacob saw but one בכור, or *firstborn*, viz., Reuben.

Also, the reader will not fail to notice that in the law, as laid down in Deuteronomy, the *firstborn* is reckoned to the man, or father; as is also the case in Jacob's prophecy, to which the law in Deuteronomy verbally refers. And, indeed, this was always the case among the Hebrews; their genealogies, as any one may see, are reckoned by the fathers. And such a question as "Abner, whose son is this youth?" (1 Sam. xvii. 55—58) could not be answered by giving the mother's name. "Thy servant is the son of Jesse, the Bethlehemite." So that Dr. Colenso is utterly at fault, and shows he has no powers of digestion for Hebrew idioms, when he says the firstborn "were not the firstborn on the father's side." He should have said "not the firstborn only on the father's side." They were sure to be reckoned to the father; but the expression "each opening a womb," added another condition, viz., that he must be the firstborn of the mother also, since he is said to open the womb, in the sense of being emitted from it. To these two conditions, necessary to Hebrew firstborn sonship, Hävernick has directed Bishop Colenso's attention.

If, then, polygamy and concubinage did prevail among Israel, in the desert, as we know they did, we know that though a man had several sons by several wives, he could have but *one* firstborn, viz., that by his first wife, being a virgin. So that several families, by different mothers, might be ranked under the head of only one firstborn; and Dr. Colenso's extraordinary idea that, according to the scriptural statement, every mother in Israel must have had, upon the average, forty-two children, comes to nothing, in this way also; as we have showed before, it does in another.

Now, as to the Bishop's reference to the slaughter of firstborn sons in Egypt, it is nothing to the purpose. Does he mean to say that there *must* have been a firstborn son in every house? God's threatened judgment was specifically against the *firstborn* sons (Exod. xi. 4, 5); and the assertion of its fulfilment, "There was a great cry in Egypt; for not a house, where not one dead!" (Exod. xii. 30) *must* be read accordingly. Not a house, where there was a firstborn, where that firstborn was not dead. Then, again, the social life of Egyptians was, wonderfully, like that of Hebrews. And we require, but have not given us, the Egyptian sense of the word *firstborn*. It may have been, and probably was, precisely that of Israel.

And, lastly, as to the marking of each Jewish residence with blood, the sections, if any, of entire Jewish families by wives and concubines, into separate residences, cannot be fairly held to change the sense of the word *firstborn*. But, once more, the threat was against the firstborn; and Dr. Colenso himself admits that we must not suppose there was a firstborn to *every* family; and, therefore, certainly not to every house marked. So that the *marking* will scarcely touch the question of the number of firstborn.

There is one more consideration, affecting this question of the firstborn, which I shall place before the reader, as deserving of some attention; although it is not necessary to my argument, nor do I attach any great weight to it. Indeed, there are difficulties, about the interpretation of the word *firstborn*, of which the Jews themselves appear to have been not masters; inasmuch as they say, traditionally, that Holy Scripture recognises two sets of firstborns;—one, those of the father, to whom the property-rights appertained; the other, those of the mother, to whom belonged the rights of priesthood. I can see no authority for this distinction; but, in reference to the firstborn generally, it may be worth while inquiring, whether any functional privileges limited their number. Had the word *firstborn*, in the Levitical law, a meaning which limited its application only to those, who had, for instance, priestly duties to discharge, for the rest of the family to which they belonged?

It is plain enough, from Moses' demand, " We will go three days' journey into the wilderness, and sacrifice," &c., &c. (Exod. viii. 27), that some sort of Divine worship, with religious rites, still continued among the Israelites in Egypt. That worship, doubtless, which each man discharged for his own family, in the days of Abraham, Isaac, and Jacob; that worship which would have devolved on Reuben, but for his sins; and which, we have reason to believe, did, in fact, devolve, through length of life, upon Levi, for all the house of Israel; then upon Kohath, probably through Gershon's early death; then upon Amram; and, through him, by God's especial intervention, upon Aaron, his firstborn, for the house of all Israel, through all time. Now, it is manifest that, in Egypt, no public, general, worship would be allowed to the Israelites, as a people, at least during the time of their persecution, or for about one hundred years before their deliverance. The functions of the head of the nation could not be publicly discharged; only the tradition of his rights, and office, could be held in memory. The people could not be generally assembled, and no priesthood had yet been appointed to their tribes. It is probable, therefore, that in sections, of various sizes, and not defined in the Scripture narrative, they did carry out the office of the firstborn, as the natural priest of the family; in various sections of families, including their own children, by wives, and concubines; and also the children of domestics.

We have a hint of this, at Exod. xix. 22, 24, where "priests" are mentioned, before the tribe of Levi had been consecrated. The Jews tell us, with one voice, that these were the "firstborn." But this is information, which, of course, Dr. Colenso despises. And even Bishop Patrick rejects their testimony,[1] because he thinks proper to maintain, they were the heads of houses, and elders! No doubt they were so; for these ante-Levitical priests were heads of "houses of families;" but all heads of tribes, or thousands, or elders, were not among the ante-Levitical priests. In other words, the "priests," thus mentioned, may have been heads of houses, and elders (as Bishop Patrick supposes), and firstborn too. The heads of houses (Num. ii. 1—31), the heads of thousands, hundreds, and tens, according to Jethro's suggestion (Exod. xviii. 25); and the seventy elders, who made the Sanhedrim; and the judges; are known in the Pentateuch, by their appropriate titles; and are never called "priests." But, before the consecration of Levi's tribe, there was a recognised number of men, heads of "houses of families," some of whom, no doubt, were also heads of tribes, or thousands, or filling various other offices; who, at the Exodus, and before, discharged, in various, but undefined, sections, the priestly, and patriarchal office. These, the Jews say, were the *firstborn*. Were these the firstborn numbered; and, among them, those infants, above one month old, who, by the death of others, were presumptively entitled to the office?

That some of these priests, as firstborn, were "young men" is clear, from Exod. xxiv. 5; and the traditions of this priesthood were never discontinued. On the contrary, it was perpetuated by the Levitical law, in the fact that laymen might slay their own Passover,

[1] Comment. on Exod. xix. 22—24.

and other sacrifices; and that, ages after, any number of laymen might be deputed, in certain cases, to assist the Levites, and the priests; only, that none but a priest could minister in the Sanctuary.

But, to conclude, without any such special limitation of the word, *firstborn,* we may feel assured that the several probable causes of the seeming deficiency—viz., those arising from death, under various circumstances, and from the great number of cases in which the firstborn would be a girl,—are sufficient to justify the Scriptural statement, or at least to save it from any successful assault, as to numbers. And, especially so, for two great reasons:—

1. Because the whole number of people, and of males, is mere matter of assumption;

2. Because we have no certain means of telling to what extent such preventing causes might interfere with the number of the firstborns.

§ XXIV. THE NUMBER OF PEOPLE.—THE EXTENT OF CANAAN.

It is hard to see what cause of attack upon the Pentateuch Bishop Colenso has found in the subject treated of in his thirteenth chapter.

Let the matter be stated in his own words:—

"91. '*I will send my fear before thee, and will destroy all the people to whom thou shalt come, and I will make all thine enemies turn their backs unto thee. And I will send hornets before thee, which shall drive out the Hivite, the Canaanite, and the Hittite, from before thee. I will not drive them out from before thee in one year, lest the land become desolate, and the beast of the field multiply against thee. By little and little I will drive them out from before thee, until thou be increased, and inherit the land.*'— Ex. xxiii. 27—30.

"The whole land, which was divided among the tribes, in the time of Joshua, including the countries beyond the Jordan, was in extent about 11,000 square miles, or 7,000,000 acres. (KITTO's *Geog. of the Holy Land, Knight's Series,* p. 7.) And, according to the story, this was occupied by more than two millions of people. Now, the following is the extent of the three English agricultural counties of Norfolk, Suffolk, and Essex, with the population, according to the census of 1851:—

	Acres.	Pop. in 1851.
Norfolk contains	1,354,301	442,714
Suffolk	947,681	337,215
Essex	1,060,549	369,318
	3,362,531	1,149,247

"By doubling the above results, we find that these counties of England are, at this very time, about as thickly peopled as the land of Canaan would have been, with its population of Israelites only, without reckoning the aboriginal Canaanites, who already filled the land, —'seven nations, *greater* and *mightier*' than Israel itself. (Deut. iv. 38; vii. 1; ix. 1; xi. 23.) And surely it cannot be said, that these three Eastern Counties, with their flourishing towns of Norwich, Lynn, Yarmouth, Aylsham, Cromer, Thetford, Wisbeach, Bungay, Beccles, Lowestoft, Ipswich, Southwold, Bury St. Edmunds, Sudbury, Woodbridge, Harwich, Colchester, Chelmsford, Romford, Maldon, &c., and their innumerable villages, are in any danger of lying 'desolate,' with the beasts of the field multiplying against the human inhabitants."

The cause of the Bishop's annoyance appears to be that God, in His goodness, made the gentlest possible provision for the settlement in Canaan of a small nation of *shepherd* people, whose flocks would necessarily be much exposed to the attacks of wild beasts; and who were utterly unused to, and therefore unprepared immediately to commence, the cultivation of land, at least to any great extent. The people, whom he chooses to select for comparison with Israel, being among the best cultivators in the world.

What is the use of comparing Canaan to Norfolk, Suffolk, Essex, Hertford, or any other English counties? But let us take up the Bishop's own idea, and suppose that any six of these counties lay on the borders of a vast continent, stretching away many hundreds of miles to the east, and overlapping it vastly on the north, and on the west. Let us suppose also that an extensive territory on the east and south was a wilderness, known to be the haunt of lions and other wild beasts, whose natural increase had been comparatively unchecked for long successions of years. Let us suppose, further, that there was a wild mountain range on the north, intersecting a country at that early date comparatively unpeopled, and full of fierce wild beasts; affording the great pleasure of hunting, whenever

Nimrods required a little active exercise. Let us conceive, that is, on the borders of any six English counties, vast preserves, not of hares and of pheasants, but of lions and wolves, *brown* bears, leopards, and hyænas,—and then how would their peaceful people feel if they had suddenly to colonise those counties, encumbered with large flocks and herds; being themselves utterly unused to the tillage of land, and all other people having been removed away? That Palestine was notoriously disturbed by these wild beasts, and that down to very late times, Holy Scripture assures Bishop Colenso.[1]

Or, again, let us imagine the inhabitants, of such six English counties, to be comparatively ignorant of agriculture; to be a small nation of shepherds, possessed of large flocks; and that the interior of Australia were tenanted by the fiercest wild beasts of Asia,—and then how would the inhabitants of these six counties like to be established on a strip of the sea-coast of Australia (all other people having been removed from that territory to which they went), with their flocks, and their herds, and their families, to be protected from the ravages of wild beasts; and no weapons with which to meet them but bows and arrows, unless they preferred hand-to-hand conflicts with sword and with spear? Let us suppose that, besides attention to their flocks, these people, unused to tillage, had to bring into cultivation, in one year, land enough to support themselves and all their families, amounting to about 2,000,000 of people. We may surely trust all the people of Suffolk and Norfolk, or any other English counties, for crying out, with one loud voice, that they thank God they are not likely to be exposed to any such danger.

Remembering how soon the sun withers up the lands of the East, so that in a very short time (let Dr. Colenso consider this) a fruitful land becomes a wilderness; remembering, also, how unused to agriculture the Israelites were, and how their flocks and herds had multiplied, it was surely a gracious Providence which said, "I will not drive them out from before thee *in one year*, lest the land become desolate, and the beast of the field multiply against thee. By little and little I will drive them out from before thee, until thou be increased, and inherit the land."

---

[1] Paxton's Nat. Hist., pp. 294, 352; Bochart's Hieroz, lib. iii., p. 829; Job xxxviii. 39; Prov. xvii. 12; xxii. 13; xxviii. 15; Cant. iv. 8; Jer. v. 6. *Tseboua*, the hyæna, Jer. iv. 7; xii. 8; Lam. iii. 10; Ezek. xxii. 27; Hos. v. 14; xiii. 17; Amos v. 19; Nahum ii. 12; Zeph. iii. 3.

I can see nothing in Bishop Colenso's objection, except this—that a man who could find, or imagine he found, any fair cause of objection against the Pentateuch, or its author, on this account, must be in a most extraordinary frame of feeling towards Holy Scripture —one from which we shall all pray that it may please the Almighty to deliver him, and protect ourselves.

§ XXV. THE WAR ON MIDIAN.

Before Dr. Colenso enters upon this subject, he takes a short and self-congratulatory review of the one hundred and thirty-eight pages he had previously written; and, in reference to them, believes, at p. 139, "that to the great majority of readers many of the above "facts will be new," as, he freely admits, they were .to himself, "till within a comparatively recent period." Unfortunately for Dr. Colenso, they are not facts, but imaginary difficulties, and mistaken objections, proceeding, for the most part, from false assumptions, and a serious lack of knowledge, with regard to the language in which the history of the Exodus has been recorded. What a pity it is that the Bishop did not take more time for reflection, and consult some of his Right Reverend brethren, some of whom are as good mathematicians, and most of them better scholars. Can there be any successful excuse made for a hasty assault upon God's Word, the mere result of views newly taken up "within a comparatively recent period?"

The Bishop, whose proper subject is the Pentateuch, cannot forbear insinuating objections against the books of Judges and of Samuel, before he enters upon the subject in hand. He is quite aware that these objections, at p. 141, turn chiefly, if not entirely, upon the round numbers, given in tens of thousands, of the "footmen," "war-chariots," "horsemen," &c., &c., mentioned in various places. He is also aware that "the ordinary supposition that there may be something wrong in the *Hebrew numerals*" (or, rather, in our mode of reading them), may have a considerable effect in showing the insolidity of such objection. But he carefully reminds us, that this cannot be the case in regard to the number, 603,550, of fighting men, continually alluded to, and "woven, as a kind of thread" (p. 143), all through the Exodus. Of this number, we have spoken, at p. 45, above; and there is no reason for our shrinking from it.

Yet, though that matter may not be affected by any misapprehension by us of the force of Hebrew numerals, why has Dr. Colenso not frankly acknowledged, that the brief account of the war on Midian may be? That was the question, on which he was about to enter. And he states his difficulty thus:—

"But how thankful we must be, that we are no longer obliged to believe, as a matter of fact, of vital consequence to our eternal hope, the story related in Num. xxxi., where we are told that a force of 12,000 Israelites slew *all* the males of the Midianites, took captive *all* the females and children, seized *all* their cattle and flocks (72,000 oxen, 61,000 asses, 675,000 sheep), and *all* their goods, and burnt *all* their cities, and '*all* their goodly castles,' without the loss of a single man; and then, by command of Moses, butchered in cold blood all the women and children, 'except all the women-children, who have not known a man by lying with him.' These last the Israelites were to 'keep for themselves.' They amounted, we are told, to 32,000 (ver. 35), mostly, we must suppose, under the age of sixteen or eighteen. We may fairly reckon that there were as many more under the age of forty, and half as many more above forty, making altogether 80,000 females, of whom, according to the story, Moses ordered 48,000 to be killed, besides (say) 20,000 young boys. The tragedy of Cawnpore, where 300 were butchered, would sink into nothing, compared with such a massacre, if, indeed, we were required to believe it. And these 48,000 females must have represented 48,000 men; all of whom, in that case, we must also believe to have been killed, their property pillaged, their castles demolished, and towns destroyed, by 12,000 Israelites, who, in addition, must have carried off 100,000 captives (more than eight persons to each man), and driven before them 808,000 head of cattle (more than sixty-seven for each man), and all without the loss of a single man! How is it possible to quote the Bible as in any way condemning slavery, when we read here (ver. 40) of 'Jehovah's tribute' of slaves, thirty-two persons *!*

"173. But it may be well at once to show that, besides involving the above incredible statements, the narrative itself, as it now stands, is unhistorical here as elsewhere.

"(i.) We are told that Aaron died on 'the *first* day of the *fifth* month' of the fortieth year of the wanderings (Num. xxxiii. 38), and they mourned for him a *month* (Num. xx. 29).

"(ii.) After this, 'King Arad the Canaanite fought against Israel, and took some of them prisoners;' whereupon the Israelites attacked these Canaanites, and utterly destroyed them and their cities" (Num. xxi. 1—3); for which two transactions we may allow another *month*.

"(iii.) Then they 'journeyed from Mount Hor, by the way of the Red Sea, to compass the land of Edom' (Num. xxi. 4); and the people murmured, and were plagued with fiery serpents, and Moses set up the serpent of brass (Num. xxi. 5—9); for all which we must allow, at least, a *fortnight*.

"(iv.) They now marched, and made *nine* encampments (Num. xxi. 10–20); for which we cannot well allow less than a *month*.

"We believe that, at every station, at least three days' rest must have been required. KURTZ, iii., p. 251.

"(v.) Then they sent messengers to Sihon, who 'gathered all his people together, and fought against Israel,' and 'Israel smote him with the edge of the sword,' and 'possessed his land from Arnon unto Jabbok,' and 'took all these cities, and dwelt in all the cities of the Amorites, in Heshbon, and in all the villages thereof (Num. xxi. 21–25); for which we may allow another *month*.

"(vi.) After that, 'Moses sent to spy out Jaazer, and they took the villages thereof, and drove out the Amorites that were there' (Num. xxi. 32); say, in another *fortnight*.

"(vii.) Then they 'turned up by the way of Bashan, and Og, the King of Bashan, went out against them; and they smote him, and his sons, and *all his people, until there was none left him alive;* and they possessed his land.' (Num. xxi. 33—35.) For all this work of capturing 'threescore cities, fenced with high walls, gates, and bars, besides unwalled towns, a great many' (Deut. iii. 4, 5), we must allow, at the very least, a *month*.

"174. Thus, then, from the '*first day of the fifth month*,' on which Aaron died, to the completion of the conquest of Og, King of Bashan, we cannot reckon less altogether than *six months* (and, indeed, even then, the events will have been crowded one upon another, in a most astonishing, and really impossible, manner), and are thus brought down to the *first day of the eleventh month*—the very day on which Moses is stated to have addressed the people in the plains of Moab. (Deut. i. 3.)

"And now what room is there for the other events, which are recorded in the book of Numbers, as having occurred between the conquest of Bashan and the address of Moses? The chief of these were—

"(1.) The march forward to the plains of Moab (Num. xxii. 1);

"(2.) Balak's sending twice to Balaam; his journey, and prophesyings (Num. xxii. 2; xxiv.);

"(3.) Israel's abiding in Shittim, and committing whoredom with the daughters of Moab (xxv. 1—3);

"(4.) The death of 24,000 by the plague (xxv. 9);

"(5.) The second numbering of the people (xxvi);

"(6.) The war upon Midian, above considered, during which they 'burnt all their cities, and all their goodly castles,' &c., and surely must have required a month, or six weeks, for such a transaction."

It is encouraging to observe, under iv., as quoted above, that Dr. Colenso quite admits, in this place, the fairness of our calculation made at p. 67 above, of the time probably required for the journey of Israel from Rameses to Pi-hahiroth. And he acutely quotes Kurtz as having made such an admission: "We believe that, "at every station, at least three days' rest must have been required." Why did not Bishop Colenso consider this when writing of "the "march out of Egypt"? Was it because he really did not understand, as he read it? or was it because his mind was so preoccupied, and his judgment so prejudiced, that he could see no probability which made against his theory? For, as we proved, it is clear enough from the narrative that Israel was not so "thrust out," nor so instantly pursued, as to prevent necessary halts, and encampments.

However, as regards all the above objections, the reader will perceive they naturally divide themselves into the following heads:—

1. The *moral question*, touching the fact that the Israelites did, as it is said, slay all the men, women not virgins, and all the boys; but "kept for themselves" "all the women-children who have not "known a man by lying with him." 2. That they did all this, "and took all the cattle," &c., &c., without the loss of a single man. 3. That "Jehovah's tribute of slaves" was thirty-two persons; as to which the Bishop asks, "How is it possible to quote "the Bible as, *in any way*, condemning slavery when we read of "this?" And, 4. That according to the historian's own statement there was really not time enough for the transaction of all the events, as he has recorded them. This last is the only serious objection made.

It is really astonishing to find one, whose mind has been disciplined like Dr. Colenso's, asking so illogical a question as "How is it possible "to quote the Bible as, in any way, condemning slavery," if Jehovah had His own tribute of slaves? Mark these words, *in any way.* Surely the Bible, or any book of law, may condemn slavery in some ways, and approve of it, or at least permit it, in others. The Gibeonites were slaves, (Josh. ix. 21); a Hebrew and his family might be slaves, in effect, for a time (Exod. xxi. 2—11; Deut. xxiii. 15, 16); in fact, the Bible does permit a certain kind of slavery. But it does not sanction kidnapping men, women, or children. (Deut. xxiv. 7.) It does not approve of bloody feuds for that purpose. It does not permit the horrors of a "middle-passage." Nor does it smile on lashing with cow-hides; hunting down with dogs; and pistolling the refractory. Many good "domestic institutions" may become intolerable by the certainty of abuse. All Englishmen hate slavery, because most Englishmen are fit for self-government and freedom, at least in these days. But there are people, even in Europe, and many more elsewhere, whose entire national history shows that they are not competent to self-government; nor ever so prosperous and happy; so truly dancing and fiddling; as when under despots. Dr. Colenso is here guilty of two gross fallacies: *first*, in the use of the words "in any way"; *second*, in using the word "slavery," with a latent peculiarity of meaning. *Hebrew* slavery may be biblical, and good; *American* may be sensual and devilish; though some will say that *West Indian* was not quite so bad.

By the way, the Bishop told us, see p. 132 above, that polygamy was not general among the Hebrews; and in his calculation of *numbers* he omitted any reckoning of *concubinage*. Will he now be so good as to inform us what the Hebrew soldiers did with these "women-children" whom they "kept for themselves"? And will he also be so good as to consider, what bearing Deut. xxi. 10—17 has upon this fact?

Now, with regard to the slaughter of the Midianites, irrespective of their numbers, I do not know that the objection deserves an answer. It is really so old, and threadbare. If the Midianites, and other people, as Amorites, Hivites, Girgashites—or Canaanites generally—were under the judgment of the Most High, it is a small matter, whether they were destroyed by fire and brimstone from heaven, or by burning slime-pits upon earth, or by fiery serpents and scorpions, or by wild beasts, or by famine, drought, or plague; in all such ways it has pleased the Most High to visit various people of the earth with judgment; and, even still, He chastens them by cruel and desolating wars. The sword of Israel was fierce and rapid, and was exercised against the Midianites, by especial direction of God. And Israel knew this. If the English people at Cawnpore had been a nest of corruption, and Nana Sahib had been the most chosen servant of God, and able to prove a Divine commission, the character of his act would have been changed; and Englishmen would have done well to submit to it.

As regards the round numbers, given in tens of thousands of Midianites, at Num. xxxi., and of other people, elsewhere, it is not that we suppose, as Dr. Colenso insinuates, at p. 142, only "an "error of the scribe," but that we suspect we do not rightly understand the principle upon which the Hebrews made use of words expressive of certain high numbers. This is quite a different matter. An error of a scribe may be but occasional; but a principle, or habitual idiom of speech, is constant, and may affect the entire current of a narrative, and is never likely to be more dangerous than when applied to *numbers*. So that Dr. Colenso has no cause to tell his lay readers, as if his fellow-clergymen were so guilty, that "it is an idle, or rather it is a sinful, paltering with the truth, "to attempt to explain away so many cases of this kind by "supposing, on every such occasion, an error of the scribe." Nor is he justified in charging "Hebrew writers," professing to be inspired of God, and implicitly referred to by Jesus, with "a systematic "habit of exaggeration with respect to Hebrew numbers." If Dr. Colenso, or any other scholar, would but send out a convincing treatise respecting the numerals, and some other matters of Hebrew philology, there are many of us who would feel deeply thankful; his time would be much better employed than it was at Natal, or has been of late, and some of us would be, *then*, right proud to have him for our Bishop.

Next, as regards the most serious objection made to the narrative of Midian's destruction, viz., that there really was not, according to the historian's own account, time for all the events recorded, it is easily seen—first, that Dr. Colenso's allowed periods are all suppositious, and may be all wrong; second, that some of the events alluded to may have been contemporaneous, or have overlapped each other.

Let us take, for instance, the second list of events referred to at p. 150 above, viz., those for which Dr. Colenso conceives there was, according to the historian, too little, or no time; then we cannot help noticing that three of them, viz., Balak's sending messengers to Balaam, and Balaam's arrival at Moab; Israel's abiding in Shittim, and committing whoredom with the Midianites; and the plague which slew 24,000, were, in part, contemporaneous; and were in other respects, very rapidly consecutive. Whilst Balak sent to Balaam, and "brought him from Aram, out of the mountains of the East," he was doubtless temporizing with Israel, then dwelling at Shittim; for Shittim lay to the west front of Pisgah (see *map* above). And no great time need be allotted to the whoredom, nor to the effectual working of the plague (Num. xxv. 9), nor to the subsequent numbering of the people (Num. xxvi. 2). What three days' pestilence, sent as a judgment from God, can do, we know (2 Sam. xxiv. 13, 14). If 70,000 died under David in three days, we can easily believe that 24,000 died under Moses in one.

It is not easy to estimate the time, which would be required, for Balak's two messages to Balaam, and his arrival at the camp of Moab. But we may fairly suppose that Balak's messengers, *to* and *fro*, and *to* again, for Balaam at Pethor in Mesopotamia, travelled at speed; and, instead of going north by way of Damascus, struck straight across the desert, by the site of what was afterwards Tadmor, or Palmyra. The swiftness of the best Arabian mares (mares are preferred) is wonderful; and the swiftness of the horses, in those parts, is continually referred to in Holy Scripture.[1] Sir John Malcolm, speaking of Turcoman horses, *Hist. of Persia*, vol. ii., p. 517, says " they have been known to carry their riders five " hundred miles within six days;" and De la Roque, *Voy. dans la Palestine*, cap. 11, p. 163, says that the Emir of Carmel had a mare which, on an occasion when flying for his life, carried him into the desert for three days and three nights without eating or drinking; and so saved him.

I submit to Dr. Colenso that, perhaps, Balaam travelled with episcopal dignity and state; but we must not suppose that, because, " he was riding upon his ass," (Num. xxii. 22), he was therefore travelling slowly. For, the ass thus used by Balaam, we have reason to know,[2] was of a breed drawn from the *onager*, or wild ass, and they were extremely swift and rapid. As to the speed of the *onager*, Mr. Morier tells us, (*Journey through Persia*, pp. 200, 202), that, in crossing the desert he and his friend chased two of them, but they quite turned up their noses at the horses; for " when they had got to " some distance," says Mr. Morier, smarting under the insult, " they " stood still, and looked behind at us, snorting loudly with their " *noses in the air.*"

I think, then, that, if we allow two months, or eight weeks, for Balak's messages to Balaam, we shall have shown ourselves very liberal to Dr. Colenso.

The journeys to Aram and back would occupy, say, fifty-six days. So that, assuming that Balak did not send until the war with Sihon was half over (Num. xxi. 23—26), and when Israel was settled at Shittim, we need suppose only sixty-three days for Balak's mission, Balaam's arrival, the spying out of Jaazer, (Num. xxi. 32), Israel's whoredom, the plague, and the numbering; *i.e.*, nine weeks.

[1] Paxton's Nat. Hist., pp. 206—211; Isa. v. 28; Jer. iv. 13; Habak. i. 18.
[2] *Ibid*, pp. 214—219; Gen. xvi. 12; Job xi. 12; xxiv. 5; Hos. viii. 9.

Further, there is not the slightest reason, given, or implied, in the narrative, why the conquest of Og, King of Bashan, (Num. xxi. 33—35), should not have been partly contemporaneous with that of the Midianites, and partly antecedent to it. Dr. Colenso is neglectful of localities. If, after defeating the Amorite, Moses with the Israelites took possession of, and encamped in his land, then, looking towards Jerusalem, Bashan, the territory of Og, would be on his right flank, in the north; and Midian and Moab, on his left, in the south. In short, the Israelites took up a commanding position at Abarim, on the slopes of Pisgah, (Num. xxi. 20), between two powerful foes. And we are expressly told two things, viz., *first*, that the Midianites were overthrown by a mere detachment of 12,000 men, (Num. xxxi. 5); and that Balak sent for Balaam, because he had heard of the overthrow of Sihon, the Amorite. (Num. xxii. 2.)

I infer, then, that while Balak was sending, and waiting for, Balaam, and temporizing with Israel, a part of those people were actively prosecuting the war against Og, King of Bashan; others were encamped, and of these, a detachment was sent against the Midianites, before the operations against Og were completed. The advance of the main body against Og, and the loss of 20,000 men, by the plague at Midian, may account for the fact that Moses was allowed to detach only so small a body of men, as 12,000, against the Midianites.

The historian clearly means to state, that the complete overthrow of Midian, without the loss of a man—" there lacketh not one man of us" (Num. xxxi. 49)—was by the miraculous intervention of God. The actual loss of the war on Midian ought to be reckoned, against Israel, in the 24,000 smitten by the plague. While, in the salvation of every man of the 12,000 (no doubt, men pure of the women of Midian), sent into the heat of battle, a deep moral lesson was conveyed.

Now, to the war against Og, Dr. Colenso assigns a *month;* and to the war on Midian, another month, or six weeks (p. 150, above); together, eight, or ten, weeks; whereas, I think it is clear, that one month, of four weeks, would do for both events. But, the reader will notice, we can afford to take Dr. Colenso's own time; because we believe the war with Og was partly over, when Balaam arrived at Moab.

Moreover, the Doctor asks, "What time is left for the march

" forward to the plains of Moab ? " *Answer:* No time. Because all the time they were defeating the Amorite, they were encamped on the north, close by Moab; see the map, above. The Bishop seems ignorant of sacred geography, as he is of many other sacred matters. For, to pass from Arnon (Num. xxi. 13), and conquer the territories of Sihon, King of the Amorites, would take them on to the river Jabbok, the border of the kingdom of Og, King of Bashan. So that, as soon as they had got possession of Sihon's territory, they were firmly fixed in a beautiful country, which intervened between the land of Og, and that of Moab.

Really, Bishop Colenso is extremely ill-informed. Burckhardt travelled the whole distance from Jabbok, the northern border of Sihon's land, to Kerek, a town somewhat east of the lowest part of the Dead Sea, in four days, at a leisurely rate of six hours a-day. The ground, thus passed over, includes all the land of the Amorites, and of Moab. So, it appears, that the armies of Israel, having occupied the land of Sihon, and having their head-quarters at Nebo, (Num. xxi. 20) it was two days' march, from the centre of that land to the territories of Og; and less than that to the land, and united forces, of Moab and of Midian. What, then, does the Bishop mean by the imposing question, " What time was " there left, for the march forward to the plains of Moab ? " It is clear enough, that an army of 500,000 light armed troops, inured to the toils of the desert, born and bred there, could, if stationed, as Israel was stationed, on the north border of Moab—*i.e.*, in the midst of Reuben's land—easily overrun all Palestine north, and all Moab south, in less than two months' time.

More than this, it should be observed, that when we are told that " Balak, the son of Zippor, saw *all* that Israel had done to the Amorites " (Num. xxii. 2, 3), and then sent messengers to Balaam, we are not required to suppose that Balak waited until the war with Sihon was completely ended. The word *all* does not require that. (See p. 19, above). It is enough to suppose that Balak waited until he saw that an irresistible tide of victory, against Sihon, had set in; and had thus become convinced that, since Israel so easily conquered Sihon, his own army of Moabites could not hope to stand against them. It is no wonder if the sons of Israel, hardy traversers of the desert, proved easily far more than a match for " the fat bulls of Bashan," as we may call the people of such favoured spots as the territories of Og, and of Sihon, and of Balak, king of Moab.

Dr. Colenso is content to allow one month, or four weeks, to the conquest of Sihon. Let us suppose that at the end of one fortnight Balak saw the necessity of sending to Balaam. Then the conquest of the rest of Sihon's land during the other fortnight, the mission to Balaam, the dwelling in the plain of Moab, at Shittim, where "Israel began to commit whoredom with the daughters of "Moab" (Num. xxv. 1), the smiting 24,000 people with the plague, and the numbering of all survivors, may be considered a close chain of events, not occupying more than nine weeks from the middle of the war with Sihon. For the two journeys of Balak's messengers to Balaam cannot be reckoned, reasonably, at more than eight weeks; the whoredom, and the plague, would require a very little time; and the making up of the regimental returns must have now become a mere piece of routine; give one week, to the three events.

When we are told, at Num. xx. 29, that "when all the con-"gregation saw that Aaron was dead, they mourned for Aaron thirty "days," we are not justified in assuming that no active duties were carried on by "all the house of Israel" during that time. And, even if we were, the narrative gives us reason to believe that very interesting events may have been forced upon Israel. For, although Bishop Colenso writes, "After this," viz., the mourning for Aaron, "King Arad the Canaanite fought against Israel," it is important to observe that there is no "after this" in the Bible (Num. xxi. 1); and also that Dr. Colenso leaves out the important, most important, words, "who dwelt in the south"—*most important*, because Arad's being quite to the south, throws him towards Mount Hor, and tends to abridge the time needed for his being conquered. It is strange, but the Bishop is always leaving out most important words (see pp. 12, and 85 above). The Bible says (Num. xx. 1), "And when King Arad "the Canaanite, who dwelt in the south, heard tell that Israel came "by the way of the spies; then he fought against Israel, and took "some of them prisoners." That is, Arad marched to the attack, and probably took them by surprise, when encamped.

Now, it was from Kadesh, in the wilderness of Paran, and to which the Israelites travelled through the [1] long valley El-Araba, that Moses sent out the spies; and Mount Hor (where Aaron died), being

---

[1] Paxton's Sacr. Geog., p. 258.

close to El-Araba, it is extremely probable that Arad attacked Israel when encamped there; and that, therefore, the attack made by Arad, and the destructive counter-assault upon him, were completely contemporaneous with the mourning for Aaron; and that, on that very account, the historian proceeds (Num. xxi. 4),—"And they journeyed "from Mount Hor, by the way of the Red Sea, to compass the "land of Edom." Then the month allowed by Dr. Colenso for the mourning over Aaron, and the other month allowed by him for the defeat of Arad, resolve themselves into one and the same, or, at any rate, but little more. We shall be liberal, and say five weeks.

Again, I fear we must notice another serious mistake of Dr. Colenso's. He allows (see p. 150, above) one fortnight for Israel's compassing the land of Edom; and another whole month for, what he supposes are, nine other distinct encampments, before they reached the valley of Moab, and the top of Pisgah, "which looketh towards Jeshimon." (Num. xxi. 20.) Here we have the very central position which the armies of Israel took up, having, when looking west, much the larger part of the land of Sihon on their right, and all the land of Balak, king of Moab, on their left. Now, Israel journeyed from mount Hor to the head of the gulf of Akaba, and on the eastern side of Akaba, at the head of the gulf, were smitten with serpents, because they murmured at the way. When Burckhardt was on the western side of Akaba, at a place[1] called Wasta, he noticed that "the sands on the shore everywhere bore the impres- "sion of the passage of serpents, crossing each other in many direc- "tions; and some of them appeared to be the marks of animals "two inches in diameter." And he adds,—"As serpents are so "numerous on this side, they are probably not deficient towards the "head of the gulf on its opposite shore, where it appears that the "Israelites passed, when they journeyed from mount Hor, by the "way of the Red Sea, to compass the land of Edom," and where "the Lord sent fiery serpents among the people." The question is, how long took they to reach the place where they were smitten with serpents? Dr. Colenso says *one fortnight;* but Burckhardt says[2] that, from Hebron, north of Mount Hor, "Akaba, or Ezion-gaber, "might be reached in *eight days* by the same road, by which the "communication was anciently kept up between Jerusalem and

[1] Burckhardt's Tour in Sinai, p. 499.   [2] *Ibid*, p. 443.

" her dependencies on the Red Sea." And the distance from Hebron to Akaba is to the distance from Mount Hor to Akaba as about eleven to four, taking Burckhardt's map. If, then, the journey from Hebron to Akaba required only eight days, as Burckhardt says, the journey from Hor to Akaba took *four-elevenths* of eight days, or about *seventeen hours and a-half*, *i.e.*, taking one day's journey to be six hours, the Israelites reached Akaba, in *three* days' journey, and allowing for the halts, as usual, we require *nine* days, and not *fourteen*, as Bishop Colenso supposes.

The nine encampments to Pisgah, or Nebo, are not known. It is at Wady-el-Araba that Burckhardt says, " I inquired in vain among " the Arabs for the names of these places where the Israelites had " sojourned during their progress through the desert; none of them " are known to the present inhabitants." But from Pisgah, or Nebo, to Kerek, Burckhardt took only two days, at a leisure pace; and from Kerek to Akaba is about three times as far, again taking Burckhardt's map. So that, possibly, the Israelites may have required far less time than the Bishop supposes. Since, however, there were nine encampments, let us close with Kurtz' allowance (see p. 150 above), and give three days to each encampment, or twenty-eight days, as taken by Dr. Colenso. Then it results that instead of six weeks, or forty-two days, from Hor, round Edom, to Nebo or Pisgah, as reckoned by the Bishop, we require only thirty-seven days altogether.

Or even less than this. For, at Num. xxxiii. 41—49, *all* the encampments from Hor to their camp at Shittim are given as *eight*,[1] viz., Zalmonah, Punon, Oboth, Ije-abarim, Dibon-gad, Almon-Diblathaim, Abarim before Nebo, and Moab-by-Jordan.

And the actual site, or extent, of their camp as follows :—" And they pitched by Jordan from Beth-jesimoth even unto Abel-shittim in the plains of Moab." So that their camp on the slopes of Pisgah rested on Beth-shemesh on the one side, and Shittim on the other, with their faces towards the west. And, allowing three days' halt to each encampment, as before, the march from Hor to Shittim and Beth-shemesh may have occupied only twenty-four days, and not forty-two days, as Dr. Colenso supposes.

[1] Robinson (*Researches*, vol. ii. 679) makes them several more; but, since the places are not known, it is manifest that, in the various passages he refers to, the same places may be called by different names.

A PLAIN REPLY

The result of our investigation, thus far, is as follows:—

1. The repulse of Arad, and the mourning for Aaron, to which the Bishop assigns two months, may be included in little more than one.

2. The journey from Hor, round Edom, to Pisgah, must be reckoned at thirty-seven days, instead of two months.

3. The attack on Sihon, the Amorite, had been made two weeks, when Balak first sent to Balaam; taking Dr. Colenso's allowance of four weeks for the whole conquest.

4. The completion of the conquest of the Amorites, the spying out of Jaazer, Balak's two messages to Balaam, Balaam's arrival, and part of the war with Og, may be looked on as contemporaneous events, occupying about eight weeks.

5. The whoredom at Shittim, with the Moabitish women, the plague which killed 24,000, the numbering of the people, may be considered rapidly consecutive events occupying one week.

6. The completion of the conquest of Og, King of Bashan, on the north, and of the Moabites and Midianites, on the south, may be considered contemporaneous events, occupying together not more than one month.

Suppose we submit the following distinct time-table:—

1. Aaron's mourning, and Arad's destruction . . . 5 weeks.
2. From Hor to the camp at Beth-shemesh and Shittim . 5½ ,,
3. Half the war with Sihon . . . . 2 ,,
4. Messages to, and arrival of, Balaam; the spying out and conquest of Jaazer, and other half of war with Sihon, and part of the war with Og, being contemporaneous events . . . . 8 ,,
5. Whoredom at Shittim, plague, and numbering; war with Og going on . . . . 1 ,,
6. War with Og, to the end, and war on Midian, being contemporaneous events . . . . . 4 ,,

And we find that we have a total of just . . . 25½ weeks; bringing us very easily within the time allowed in Scripture. The allowance in each case is ample; for I believe that about three weeks might be safely deducted from the allotted time, viz., one week on the *first* item, *Aaron and Arad;* and two weeks on the *fourth*, the *messages to Balaam*, &c.

Thus, instead of requiring the whole *six* months—between Aaron's death, on the first day of the fifth month (Num. xxxiii. 38), and Moses addressing Israel, on the first day of the eleventh month (Deut. i. 3), according to Dr. Colenso's hypothesis—we may require only little more than, at the outside, *five* months. And, thus, we see that there was ample time not only for part, but for all, of the events recorded.

But I object to these hypotheses, as altogether uncalled for, and, in Dr. Colenso's case, unfair, and unscriptural. It is evident that all through his history of the conquest of Eastern Palestine, Moses professes to have been guided, and miraculously assisted, by the Lord. He gives us no details, but, throughout his narrative, implies that the conquest of the people of Og, and of Sihon, of the Moabites, and of the Midianites, was made with miraculous rapidity and success, under the immediate auspices of the Most High. "All these cities fenced with high walls, gates, and bars; besides unwalled towns a great many" (Deut. iii. 5), fell as if by magic; and more rapidly than that. What panic fear seized the people we are not informed; but Bishop Colenso has forgotten God's promise. (Exod. xxiii. 27—30.) What places were evacuated? what stormed? Of these things we are not told. Nor does it require military genius to understand that, in a field of operations so limited as that part of the Holy Land, east of Jordan, the onslaught of some thousands of light armed troops, quick and fierce, conscious of their strength, and relying on the miraculous presence of their God, would speedily drive headlong into Jordan, or over it, such a depraved and doomed populace as then inhabited those territories.

Indeed, none of these particulars are given us. That there was time for the several operations, some of which were contemporaneous, we have seen. And the completeness of the result is expressly stated to have been miraculous. If the Bishop of Natal proposes to make a stand here, then we are at once carried away into another question, viz., the credibility of miracles; and that would ill become him. If, on the other hand, he professes not to deny the possibility, or credibility, of such miraculous success accorded Israel, then all ground of opposition as to the war on Midian, &c., &c., is cut from under him.

§ XXVI. ISRAEL IN THE DESERT.

It is strange, indeed, that a Christian Bishop, who knows that his God and Saviour conversed about the forty years' daily fall of manna in the desert, as of a well-known historical fact (see p. 7 above), referring to it in illustration of His own divine character, should call in question, even for one moment, the miraculous nature of Israel's sustenance in the desert. Of course, if Dr. Colenso does really believe that manna fell from heaven for forty years, to feed all Israel in Arabia Petræa, it is mere trifling on his part to pretend to raise a serious question about the maintenance of Israel's flocks and herds. The Bishop, alluding to the manna, does indeed venture to hint that it could not have been employed in the nourishment of sheep and goats. "The sheep and oxen could not live upon the manna" (p. 78). No, we do not say they could. But we do say that the Bishop has no right to say they could *not*. Does he know certainly what manna was? The Jews, who saw it, did not; מן הוא, *What is this?* (Exod. xvi. 15) speaking to one another in great surprise. Nor has it ever been satisfactorily ascertained what it was. At any rate, it was mingled with dew, and if at all like that which Burckhardt found at Wady-el-Sheikh[1] on the tamarisk trees, it might be eaten at least by camels, who loved to feed on the shoots of such trees. If, however, the Bishop really does believe in the miraculous fall of manna, and in the miraculous provision of water from the rock (Exod. xvii. 6), for any number of the people, even for a few thousands, then he is shut out from all argument as to the difficulty of finding support for Israel's flocks and herds, under conditions of life similar to those of their owners. For the same God, who by miracle preserved the people, could also lead them, beyond all expectation, to such pastures as were sufficient, and by providential retention of the rains and moisture in various places, have caused such pastures to grow. Only admit *one* miracle in the narration of the Exodus, and it becomes vain to call in question any other of its particulars.

It is important for the reader to remember that the author of the

[1] Tour in Sinai, p. 488.

Pentateuch distinctly records the circumstances of Israel's journeyings, with the plain avowal that he is engaged in narrating his people's history during one particular era, the daily experience of which was characterized by the immediate intervention and providence of the Almighty, miraculously applied. He does not wish any reader to accept his account, otherwise than as of a series of miraculous events. The miracles recorded are an integral and necessary part of the narrative. And to carry on arithmetical calculations, with entire disregard of the historian's constant assertion of miraculous agency, is, therefore, little to the purpose. The question between any objector to the Pentateuch and its author, may be reduced, in its simplest form, to this—Are you willing to admit the possibility of miracles?

All through his[1] narrative the writer asserts, again and again, the miraculous presence, and interposition, of the Most High. At the passage of the Red Sea, in the fall of manna and of quails, at the rock of Massah, at the giving of the law, by His appearance to Moses, in the fiery-cloudy pillar, by the Shechinah in the Tabernacle, in the journeys of the people, by the fire of Taberah, in the fall of Korah, and the staying of the plague, by the budding of Aaron's rod, at the waters of Meribah, and through the brazen serpent.

Perhaps we have no right to assume that the miracles recorded are all those which it pleased the Almighty to exhibit by the hand of Moses. This is the very question to which Canon Stanley's incorrect remark (referred to at p. 28, above), alluded; and which Dr. Colenso records as follows, at p. 70. "The question is asked, How " could a tribe, so numerous and powerful, as on any hypothesis the " Israelites must have been, be maintained in this inhospitable desert? " *It is no answer to say that they were maintained by miracles.* For, " except the manna, the quails, and the three interventions with " regard to water, NONE SUCH are mentioned in the Mosaic history; " and if we have no warrant to take away, we have no warrant to add." What damage is done to the Bible by some who profess to be its friends! How could Canon Stanley make such an observation as that? NONE SUCH! Let the reader consult the list I have just given him. NONE SUCH! Why the entire narrative professes to be miraculous. The manna was a *daily* miracle. The presence of the fiery-cloudy pillar, a daily miracle. The sudden emotion of the

[1] Exod. xiv. 21; xvi. 4, 13; xvii. 6; xix. 18; xxxiv. 5; xl. 35; Num. ix. 17; xi. 3; xvi. 32, 48; xvii. 8; xx. 11; xxi. 9.

Sanhedrim, by the Spirit, was a miracle. (Num. xi. 27.) And Moses avowedly professes, all through, to have been in constant supernatural, or miraculous, intercourse with the Lord. And it is not possible for us to determine how far the journeys of Israel *to pastures, and to consequent safety*, were directed in that intercourse, or by the guidance of the pillar. It would, possibly, be more correct to believe that the principle applicable to the life of Jesus, and recorded in St. John's Gospel (ch. xxi. 25); applicable, also, to the lives of the apostles; should be applied also to the life of Moses, viz., that the miracles recorded are not all those which were wrought; but were sample miracles of the whole. But, whether or not, it is plain that the miracles constitute the framework of the Mosaic account of Israel's life in the desert. Israel is preserved in the desert by an ark of miracles, as Moses in Egypt by a basket among the flags. The account must be taken, if at all, as a whole, modelled upon miracles; or else, as a whole, must be rejected. Bishop Colenso, and those who agree with him, have no other alternative. Either Moses must be believed without cavilling, or arithmetic; or else the Pentateuch must be entirely rejected; and we must take all the dreadful consequences, which that rejection implies to the religion of Jesus. For example, mere numerical embarrassments, like that of the war on Midian (Num. xxxi. 2) are of small consequence indeed, if we believe (as required of us) in the judicial plague at Shittim, and its sudden and miraculous cessation; with express intelligence from God that it was so surceased, in consequence of the unprecedented vengeance of Phineas. (Num. xxxv. 11.)

Moses maintains, and implies by his narrative, that, all through the desert, the support, and history, of Israel were miraculous. And it is beside the business for Dr. Colenso, or any one else, to write of it otherwise.

§ XXVII. THE SCRIPTURAL ACCOUNT OF THE DESERT.

Yet Moses does full justice to the natural character of this wilderness. And so do other sacred writers; who, being inspired of the Holy Ghost, believed in him. "For the Lord's portion is his " people; Jacob is the lot of His inheritance. He found him in a " desert land, and in the waste howling wilderness. He led him

"about, He instructed him, He kept him as the apple of His eye.
"As an eagle stirreth up her nest, fluttereth over her young,
"spreadeth abroad her wings, taketh them, beareth them on her
"wings: so the Lord alone did lead him, and there was no strange
"god with him." (Deut. xxxii. 9—12.) This one passage is
enough to refute Canon Stanley's observation; and to show that
Moses asserts that God's providence, and presence, with Israel were
miraculous, through all the journeys in the desert. Holy Scripture
does justice, no doubt, to the really terrible character of the desert;
and it behoves us all to bow, implicitly, to its statements. At the
same time we should be careful that we rightly understand them,
and should avoid drawing from them any conclusions which they will
not justify. The *particularly descriptive* references to the desert are
wonderfully rare in the Holy Bible. Of *general references*, there
are very many. I believe it will be found that none of these references
justify our thinking of the desert as being otherwise than provided
with continual sources of sustenance for men, and for cattle; and,
probably, with more such resources at that time than now. The
especial, *daily*, necessity plainly acknowledged in the Pentateuch, so
far as the desert is concerned, is that of *bread;* and that only. And
that, as we shall see, is its peculiar, characteristic, deficiency now.

It is wonderful how few are the *particularly descriptive* allusions to
the terrific character of the wilderness, of which Dr. Colenso has
been so carefully in search. I thought the Bishop was sure to be
right, on a matter of this kind, and sought information from his pages.
How surprised one may well be to find that all the places, cited by
him, at p. 66, as descriptive of the horrors of the wilderness, are
exactly *five;* viz., Num. xx. 4, 5; Deut. viii. 15; xxxii. 10; and
Jer. ii. 6. And he has quoted nearly all. At least, I am able to
add only the following *two:* viz., Deut. i. 19, and Hosea xiii. 5.

The Bishop has quoted such passages, as if they were descriptive
of the route, and tracks, of the Israelites, during all their forty
years' wandering in the desert. Close attention, however, will show
us, that several passages are not *general* descriptions of Israelitish
journeys and experience; but have *particular* reference to certain
spots on which they sojourned, during particular and corresponding
times of their travels. Thus Num. xx. 4, 5: "And why have ye
brought up the congregation of the Lord into this wilderness, that
we and our cattle should die there?" has particular reference to the

desert of Zin, in which, at Kadesh, the people then were. So Deut. i. 19 has reference to the specific route, which Israel took from Horeb to Kadesh, "by the way of the mountain of the Amorites," before the sentence of thirty-eight years' additional wandering, as a punishment for the mutiny of the people, after the return of the spies. (Num. xiv. 33.) Though, even here, we may notice, that they were in the immediate neighbourhood of a numerous and settled people (ver. 43). So, Deut. viii. 15: "Who led thee through that great, and terrible, wilderness; wherein were fiery serpents, and scorpions, and drought, where there was no water; who brought thee forth water out of the rock of flint," has especial reference to the same desert of Zin; to their being smitten with serpents, on the borders of the Red Sea, at the very end of their forty years' wandering; and as previously referred to, by Num. xx. 4, 5. Deut. xxxii. 10 has been already quoted; it is undoubtedly general, in the terms of its description, as applicable to various parts of Israel's wanderings, but not necessarily to all. And, as just now noticed, it is remarkable for containing the plainest assurance, conceived in most beautiful language, of God's daily, unceasing, special, protection of the people. "He found him," Israel, "in a desert land, and in the waste, howling wilderness. He led him about; he instructed him. He kept him as the apple of his eye." It seems strange that, when Dr. Colenso copied this passage, he did not let fall his pen, and conclude it was equally wicked, and hopeless, to attempt raising any prejudice against the Mosaical narrative; so far as any terrors of the wilderness were concerned. The passages, Jer. ii. 6, and Hosea xiii. 5, may be classed together. They are, undoubtedly, references to the frequent experiences of the Israelites, as of other wanderers, in the desert; that "land of great drought." But, even here, Scripture leaves us not without good reason to look, with certainty of success, for sources of hope, and safety, in the desert. Jeremiah's language is significant. He describes the wilderness, as a "land of deserts, and of pits," במדבר בארץ ערבה ושוחה; plainly implying that the מדבר, or *wilderness*, though it might be comparatively fertile, capable of culture, or furnished with water and pasturage, in many parts, was a land, having its ערבה, or *desert, i.e.*, chequered with spots absolutely barren; and, as a land of drought, overcast, in such places, with the shadow of death. It was a land, too, through which few men passed; a land which, being so comparatively unpeopled, and having so few to traverse it, is described as one, where "no man passed through, and no man dwelt," לא עבר בה איש ולא ישב אדם. It is amusing to see the Bishop taking these words in the strictest, most literal, sense possible:—" Besides, did the Amalekites live " in Sinai? On the contrary, we have the express statement of " the Prophet, that it was a land that 'no man passed through, and " 'where no man dwelt' (Jer. ii. 6)."—P. 74.

Or, again,—" As to their march generally, during the forty years, " it is described, as a march, ' through a wilderness, through a land " ' of deserts and of pits, through a land of drought, and of the " ' shadow of death; through a land that no man *passed through*.' " They met with no *caravans*, therefore; and where ' no man *dwelt*.' " (Jer. ii. 6)."—P. 77.

The *italics* are the Bishop's; and he takes the language thus, in the most literal sense; notwithstanding notorious historical facts; and the clearest intimations, from Holy Scripture, that, what with Amalekites, and Midianites, and Edomites, and Ishmaelites, and the sons of Sheba and Dedan, and the proximity of Egypt (then the most attractive country in the world), the peninsula of Arabia has been, daily, almost hourly, traversed, in all its parts; and, in many parts, numerously peopled, from the earliest dawn of history. And, particularly, was all that part traversed which lay between, and above, the heads of the two gulfs of the Red Sea, containing the wildernesses of Shur, and Etham, and Zin; in which Israel wandered for the greater part of their time. (See Map, above.) This mistake of the Bishop's, concerning "a land that no man passed through," is the old misapprehension of readers of Isaiah, when speaking of Idumea (Isa. xxxiv. 10), " None shall pass through it for ever and ever." In each case, the language conveys a powerful image of loneliness, and desolation, compared with other lands; but, by no means, implies, that *literally* none passed through.

There is nothing, in the references of Holy Scripture to particular spots in Israel's wanderings, to forbid our thinking that the desert then, was—what, in fact, it is now—capable, in many parts, of culture; furnished with frequent valleys; able to yield waters, at a low depth, fit for drink; and, in very many places, affording pasturage for sheep and oxen. Its present state, we shall proceed to exhibit; its past condition, was probably better still.

§ XXVIII. THE DESERT OF EL TYH.

All through his chapter on "Israel in the Desert," Dr. Colenso unfairly assumes, that the desert of Sinai was, three thousand years ago, exactly what we know it to be now; and, to this end, the accounts of Burckhardt, of Ruppell, Harmer, and others —especially of Stanley—are studiously quoted. But, not only is such an assumption opposed to all we know of the daily occurring phenomena of Arabia and the East, but it is also contrary to daily observation; and to the accounts of the most celebrated travellers, when fairly interpreted. For, continually, it may still be noticed, from the action of the elements in those countries, that the desolation of Arabia, and the adjacent parts, is even now increasing. The whole country between Euphrates and Syria is called a desert, and comparatively is such; yet in almost all parts it is capable of cultivation, and we can easily conceive that by neglect, arising from the want of a settled population, it may become more sterile still, even as much so as Arabia Petræa. The assumption that the desert of Sinai, or El Tyh, was as dreary and desolate 3,000 years ago, as now, is contrary to the expressed opinion of the ablest travellers. Volney,[1] than whom there never has been a better traveller, especially for Christian purposes (seeing that he was an Infidel), Volney says:—" The desert of Tih, which I have just men-
" tioned, is that into which Moses conducted the Jews, and kept
" them for a whole generation, to initiate them in the art of war, and
" transform a multitude of shepherds into a nation of conquerors.
" The name *El-tih* seems to have a reference to their history, as it
" signifies the country of wandering; but we must not imagine this
" to be in consequence of tradition, since the present inhabitants are
" foreigners, and men in all countries find it difficult to recur even to
" their grandfathers; the name of *El-tih* has been given to this
" tract by the Arabs from reading the Hebrew books and the
" Koran; they also call it *Barr-el-tour-Sina*, or the country of
" Mount Sinai. This desert, which is the boundary of Syria to the

[1] Travels, Vol. ii., pp. 290, 292.

"south, extends itself in the form of a peninsula between the two
"gulfs of the Red Sea; that of Suez to the west, and that of
"El-Akaba to the east. Its breadth is ordinarily thirty leagues,
"and its length seventy." (Note.—18,900 square miles.) "This
"great space is almost entirely filled by barren mountains, which join
"those of Syria, on the north, and, like them, consist almost wholly
"of calcareous stone; but, as we advance to the southward, they
"become granitous, and Sinai and Horeb are only enormous masses
"of that stone. Hence it was, the ancients called this country
"*Arabia Petræa*. The soil in general is a dry gravel, producing
"nothing but thorny acacias, tamarisks, firs, and a few scattered
"shrubs. Springs are very rare, and the few we meet with are some-
"times sulphureous and chemical, as at Hammam-Farouan, at others
"brackish and disagreeable, as at El-Naba, opposite Suez; this
"saline quality prevails throughout the country, and there are mines
"of fossil salt in the northern parts. In some of the valleys, how-
"ever, the soil becoming better, as it is formed of the earth washed
"from the rocks, *is cultivable after the winter rains, and may almost
"be stated fertile.* Such is the vale of Djirandel, in which there are
"seven groves of trees. Such also is the vale of Faran, where the
"Bedouins say there are ruins, which can be no other than those of
"the ancient city of that name. *In former times every advantage was
"made of this country that could be obtained from it.* M. Niebuhr
"discovered on a mountain, some tombs with hieroglyphics,
"which may induce us to believe the Egyptians had made settle-
"ments in these countries. *But, at present, abandoned to nature,
"or rather to barbarism, it produces nothing but wild herbs.* Yet,
"with such scanty provision, this desert subsists three tribes of
"Bedouins, consisting of about five, or six, thousand Arabs,
"dispersed in various parts. They are called by the general name
"of Towara, or Arabs of Ṭor, the best known and most frequented
"place in the country. It is situated on the eastern side of the
"branch of Suez, in a sandy, and low, ground, as is all the coast.
"Its whole merit consists in a pretty good road for shipping, and
"water which may be drank; *the Arabs also bring some thither from
"Sinai which is really good.* The ships of Suez lay in their pro-
"visions here when they sail to Djedda. There is nothing further
"to notice except that we find here a few palm-trees, the ruins of a
"wretched fort without a garrison, a small Greek convent, and some

"huts of poor Arabs, who live on fish, and serve as sailors for wages.
"There are also, to the southward, two small villages of Greeks,
"who are equally poor and miserable. As for the subsistence of
"the three tribes, it is derived from their goats, camels, some acacia
"gums sold in Egypt, and their robberies on the roads of Suez,
"Gaza, and Mecca."

Surely this is an admirable description, and does justice to the barrenness of the Sinaitic peninsula, and yet we cannot help reflecting upon the strange fact that the Infidel Volney, admits the past capabilities of the land, and attempts not to insinuate even that the sojourning of Israel for forty years in the desert was impossible; while the Christian Colenso, refuses to admit the one, and dares confidently to assert the other, in direct contradiction of Holy Scripture.

How curious, and how beautiful, is also the fact, which Volney plainly records in reference to his own times (1781—1786), that even then the Arabs brought "really good" water from Sinai. Elsewhere[1] he describes the aspect of the whole desert, "which
"extends 600 leagues in length, and 300 in breadth, and stretches
"from Aleppo to the Arabian Sea, and from Egypt to the Persian
"gulf," including *El-Tih*, or the wilderness of Sinai, the Hedjaz, or route to Mecca, and the Najd, or Great Desert. "If we
"examine," says he, p. 356, "the causes of the sterility and uncul-
"tivated state of the desert, we shall find it is principally to be
"attributed to the absence of fountains, and rivers, and, in general,
"to the want of water. This want of water itself is occasioned by
"the nature of the country, which being flat, and destitute of
"mountains, the clouds glide over its heated surface, as I have
"already remarked is the case with Egypt. They never rest there
"but in winter, when the coldness of the atmosphere hinders them
"from rising, and condenses them into rain. The nakedness of this
"country is also another cause of drought, since the air is for that
"reason more easily heated, and compels the clouds to rise. It is
"probable that a change of climate might be effected, if the whole
"desert were planted with trees; as, for example, with pine trees.
"The consequence of the winter rains is, that in those parts where
"the soil is good, as on the frontiers of Syria, a cultivation takes
"place very similar to that of even the interior parts of the province;
"but as these rains neither produce springs nor constant rivulets,

[1] Travels, Vol. i., pp. 355—359.

" the inhabitants are exposed to the inconvenience of wanting water
" the whole summer. *To remedy this, it is necessary to have recourse
" to art, and to form wells, reservoirs, and cisterns, in which they
" collect their annual supplies.* Such works require money and
" labour, and are, after all, exposed to a variety of accidents. War
" may destroy, in one day, the labour of many months, and the
" resources of the year. A drought, *which is but too common,* may
" cause the failure of a crop, and reduce the inhabitants even to a
" total want of water. *It is true that, by digging, it is almost every-*
" *where to be found, at from six to twenty feet depth,* but this water
" is brackish, as in all the desert of *Arabia* and Africa. This saline
" quality is so inherent in the soil, that it impregnates even the
" plants. All those of the desert abound in alkali and Glauber's
" salts; but it is remarkable that this salt diminishes *as we approach*
" *the mountains,* where it is scarcely sensible. It also frequently
" dries up, when thirst and famine succeed; and, if the Government
" does not lend its aid, the villages are deserted." .... " In those
" districts where the soil is stony and sandy, *as in the Tih, the Hedjaz,*
" *and the Najd,* the rains make the seeds of the wild plants shoot,
" and *revive the thickets, ranunculas, wormwood, and kali.* They
" render the lower grounds *marshy,* which then produce *reeds and*
" *grass; and the plain assumes a tolerable degree of verdure.* This is
" the season of abundance for the herds and their masters; but, *on*
" *the return of the heats,* everything is parched up, and the earth,
" converted into a grey and fine dust, presents nothing but *dry stems,*
" as hard as wood, on which neither horses, nor oxen, nor even goats,
" can feed."

No doubt it was at such a place and time as this that the young man went out to gather "sticks on the sabbath day. And they that found him gathering sticks brought him unto Moses and Aaron, and unto *all* the congregation" (viz., the *elders*), see p. 20, above. (Num. xv. 32). Showing us not only the duty of keeping the Fourth Commandment, but also that when Israel was "in the wilderness," they came *in winter* upon places then covered with growth, which in summer dried up into hard sticks, as Volney says. They must have contained, when living, considerable substance, to have become so stout and hard, when dead.

§ XXIX. DR. COLENSO'S AUTHORITIES ON THE DESERT.

Bishop Colenso's range of reading appears to have been extremely limited; as, indeed, is often the case with men eminent for mathematical attainments. Yet the authorities which he cites as to the nature of the Arabian desert, if he would but use them fairly, give him abundant reason for believing that the desert of Sinai once possessed much wider resources than at present. In reply, however, to every suggestion of this kind, by whomsoever made, Dr. Colenso has, as at p. 71, only one stolid answer,—" Whatever they may be, " they cannot do away with the plain language of the Bible, already " quoted, which shows that the general character of the desert was " as desolate and barren as now." An observation in which, as we explained, he misapprehends the meaning of Holy Scripture. Fearful as the desert was then, and more fearful as it is now, Scripture admits, in its most terrific account of it, that it was a country chequered with parts not wholly perilous to life, nor characterized by drought, and the consequent shadow of death. The Bishop's reading on this subject appears to be almost confined to Canon Stanley, one of the most recent, and, perhaps, not the most statistical of travellers. "There is no doubt," says Stanley, "that " the vegetation of the wadies" (or valleys of the desert) "has " considerably decreased." And there is no doubt of this, though Canon Stanley gives but a poor reason for believing it. No answer, bearing closely against the asserted fact, is given by Dr. Colenso. The reckless waste and destruction of the Bedouins is referred to; and we know that for many years the Towara, or Arabs of Sinai, have traded with Egypt in nothing but charcoal, to get which they have cut down all the wood and undergrowth they could lay hands on. But Dr. Colenso gives neither answer nor denial; he only attempts a reply concluding with this weak observation (at p. 73)— " Besides, the destruction of *trees* would not affect directly the " growth of *grass*, on which the flocks and herds depended in the " case of the Israelites: however (as Stanley suggests in the next " passage), it might, perhaps, indirectly, but surely to a very slight " and almost inappreciable degree, by diminishing the quantity of "moisture attracted to the land." Which last observation, most unfair in itself, does, in fact, admit the truth of Canon Stanley's assertion. The plain statement of the case being that, under a burning sun like Arabia's, the absence of trees does directly, and most seriously, affect the growth of grass. Says Stanley, " Charcoal is, in " fact, the chief—perhaps it might be said the *only*—traffic of the " peninsula. Camels are constantly met, loaded with this wood on " the way between Cairo and Suez." The Bishop flies away to Natal, as usual :—" It may be doubted if the ' probable ' labours of the " monks in burning charcoal during late years, are enough to account " for the disappearance of the trees. In Natal, trees of this kind " are cut down for firewood; and, by wasteful or excessive cutting, a " piece of good bush-land may be stripped of all the trees *which are* " *fit for such a purpose.* But there will still remain a multitude of " young trees and small *saplings,* which have sprung up from the " seed shed by the old ones, and have not been cut down, because " utterly useless as firewood." The Bishop ought not to have said, " probable labours of the monks," but " certain business of the Arabs of Tor." And, I think, we shall presently see that he is not acquainted with their mode of proceeding, for that they habitually use up the undergrowth and saplings. However, there is no doubt that, in Arabia, the destruction of the trees would materially reduce the quantity of vegetation, by exposing the surface of the land to the fierce rays of the sun, and by leaving whatever wells, or rivulets, or water-springs, there might be, to be speedily dried up. To all which considerations the Bishop can oppose only the same stolid answer, at p. 73, " The Bible speaks of the desert in exactly the same terms as " these, which would even now be used to describe it." An answer, as to which we have already pointed out his misapprehension.

Then comes a most important suggestion. It is derived from the fact that Shaw (quoted by Stanley) states that " *Though nothing that can be properly called soil is to be found in these parts of Arabia,* these " monks have, *in a long process of time* (N.B.), covered over with " dung and the sweepings of their convent, near four acres of these " naked rocks, which produce as good cabbages, salads, roots, and all " kinds of pot-herbs as any soil and climate whatsoever. They have, " likewise, raised apple, pear, plum, almond, and olive trees, not " only in great numbers, but also of excellent kinds. Their grasses,

" also, are not inferior, either in size or flavour, to any whatsoever.
" Thus this little garden demonstrates how far an indefatigable
" industry may prevail over nature." Yes; and it demonstrates
something more, viz., that whenever, and wherever, soil is laid in
Arabia Petræa, that burning land is capable of finest cultivation.
Now, the fact is, that other travellers give us cause to deny the general
correctness of Shaw's statement that nothing to be "properly called
" soil is to be found in these parts of Arabia;" but if it were literally so
now, it by no means follows it was so 3,000 years ago. Moreover, Dr.
Colenso, who marked the *italics* and the N.B. in the above extracts,
and dwells contentedly upon the " long process of time " required by
a few monks, forgets to calculate in how short a time the dung and
sweepings of the camp (to which the Bishop attended so minutely at
pp. 24, 25, above,) of 2,000,000 of people, with all their flocks and
herds, would produce fertility, in any spot of the desert of El Tyh; or
in that of Zin, or in that which Israel passed over, when compassing
the land of Edom. To this argument, it is necessary the reader should
remember, that we are absolutely ignorant of most of the encampments
of Israel, for thirty-eight years of the forty, during which they wandered in the desert; and that, for those thirty-eight years, only twenty-
eight journeys are recorded, viz., one to every year. (Num. xxxiii.
18—49.) They might, for aught we know, have hovered round spots
fertilized by themselves.

To a similar purpose Canon Stanley has said, "Even so late as
" the seventeenth century, if we may trust the expression of
" Maconnys, the Wady-el-Rahah, in front of the convent, now
" entirely bare, was ' a vast green plain,' *une grande champagne
"' verte.*" Dr. Colenso has none but the same stolid answer, " The
" desert was then, as it is now, a ' great and terrible wilderness,' ' a
" land of drought and the shadow of death.' " So it was, on the
whole, and who denies it ? The question is whether there were not
parts, which were then, and might be even now, reclaimed to verdure
and cultivation ? I verily believe that, speaking generally, if you
put a bundle of mere mathematicians under Bramah's press, you could
not squeeze ten bright thoughts out of them all.

§ XXX. DR. COLENSO'S STRANGE MISTAKE ABOUT THE DESERT.

Let us now give particular attention to the strange misapprehension under which the Bishop labours respecting the desert; and we shall then see that he is incompetent to give us correct information on this subject, most important, as it is, to the narrative of the Pentateuch. We will quote exactly his own words:—

"87. But it may be well now to quote one or two passages from other writers, which yet more plainly develop the absolute barrenness of this wild and desolate region, as it now appears, and as, we have every ground from the Bible itself to believe, it must *then* have appeared also.

"In *winter*, when the whole of the upper Sinai is *deeply covered with snow*, and many of the passages are choked up, the mountains of Moses and Saint Catherine are often inaccessible. Mr. FAZAKERLY, who ascended them in the month of February, found a great deal of snow, and the ascent was severe. 'It is difficult,' he says, 'to imagine a scene more desolate and terrific, than that which is discovered from the summit of Sinai. A haze limited the prospect, and, except a glimpse of the sea in one direction, nothing was within sight but snow, huge peaks, and crags of naked granite.' Of the view from Mount Saint Catherine he says, 'The view from hence is of the same kind, only much more extensive than from the top of Sinai. It commands the two gulfs of Akaba and Suez; the island of Tiran and the village of Tur were pointed out to us; Sinai was far below us; all the rest, wherever the eye could reach, was a *vast wilderness, and a confusion of granite mountains and valleys destitute of verdure*.'—CONDER'S *Modern Traveller*, Arabia, p. 159, 160.

"88. We have here another question raised, which is not generally taken into consideration at all. The Israelites, according to the story, were under Sinai for nearly twelve months together, and they kept the second Passover under the mountain before they left it. (Num. ix. 1.) As this was in the first month of the Jewish ecclesiastical year, corresponding to the latter part of March and beginning of April, they must have passed the whole of the winter months under Sinai, and must have *found it bitterly cold*.

"In the mountainous districts it is very cold in the winter nights. Sometimes the water in the garden of the monastery at Saint Catherine freezes even in February. And, on the contrary, in the summer months, the sun pours down his rays burning hot from heaven, and in reflection from the naked rocky precipices, into the sandy valleys. RUPPELL, quoted in HENGSTENBERG'S *Balaam*, Clark's Theol. Library, p. 338.

"Where, then, amidst the scanty vegetation of the neighbourhood, where at the present time there seems not to grow a single tree fit for firewood,—

and there is no reason to suppose that it was ever otherwise,—did the Israelites obtain supplies of fuel, not only for the daily cooking necessities of a population like that of London, but also for relief against the piercing cold of the winter season, or when, as Josephus says, *Ant.* iii. 7, 4, 'the weather was inclined to snow?' And the cattle,—unless supplied with artificial food, must they not also have perished in multitudes from cold and starvation under such circumstances? We find this to be the case even in the fertile colony of Natal, where in some winter seasons they die from these joint causes in great numbers, when the grass, though abundant, is dried up, and the cold happens to be more severe than usual, though not severe enough for ice and snow, except in the higher districts, and then only for about a month or six weeks in the year.

"89. If the last quotations describe the state of things in the depth of *winter*, the following (in addition to the words of RUPPELL, above quoted) will convey some idea of the general aspect of the country in the height of the *summer* season. It would seem that travellers generally choose the *most favourable season of the year* for visiting these desert regions. We must make due allowance for this fact also, in considering even their accounts of the desolate barrenness of the whole district, with reference to the story told in the Pentateuch.

"BURCKHARDT visited Um Shaumer, the loftiest mountain in the peninsula, and writes of the scene as follows:—'The devastations of torrents are everywhere visible, the sides of the mountains being rent by them in numberless directions. The surface of the sharp rocks is blackened by the sun; all vegetation is dry and withered; and the whole scene presents nothing but utter desolation and hopeless barrenness.' CONDER's *Arabia*, p. 199.

"He afterwards travelled from the neighbourhood of Sinai eastward, across the peninsula, to the gulf of Akaba. But, he says, 'the barrenness of this district exceeded anything we had yet witnessed, *except some parts of the desert of El Tih* [that is, the desert of Sinai]. The Nubian valleys might be called pleasure-grounds in comparison. Not the smallest green leaf could be discovered. And the thorny mimosa, which retains its verdure in the tropical deserts of Nubia with very little supplies of moisture, was here entirely withered, and so dry that it caught fire from the lighted ashes which fell from our pipes as we passed.' *Ibid*, p. 204."

Now, really, the Bishop is most unfortunate. When he ought not to have alluded to refuse, and other unpleasant matters connected with sacrifice, he did so; and made a very ridiculous mistake, as we saw at p. 23, above. Now, when he needs all that can be thought of, it seems never to occur to him. Besides sticks (when they can get any), the Arabs habitually burn dung, camel's dung, &c. And so, no doubt, did the Israelites. Moreover, Dr. Colenso entirely misapprehends the nature of the Arabian winter. This we shall presently explain. Meanwhile, be it noticed that fire is never needed there in the daytime, and only for a small part of the night.[1] "The Arabs endure the inclemency of the rainy season in a wonderful manner. While every thing around them suffers from the cold, they sleep barefooted in an open tent, where *the fire is not kept up beyond midnight.* Yet in the middle of summer an Arab sleeps wrapt in his mantle upon the burning sand, and exposed to the rays of an intensely hot sun." Besides which, the tents are snug; such tents as the Israelites would be able to obtain before winter set in, after their leaving Egypt at springtide (see p. 64, above). A description of these tents may be found in Burckhardt, as referred to below. The covering is of goats'-hair; "this goats'-hair covering keeps off the heaviest rain, as I know from experience." The sides of the tent, and the two divisions of it into men's and women's apartments, are partly of goats'-hair, partly of woollen stuff. Just as I suggested for Israel, at p. 41, above, "pieces of old *abbas*, or woollen cloaks, are stitched to the eight corners, where the poles are to be fastened; these pieces are called *Koum el beet.*" The Arabic *beet* being the Hebrew בית, or *house*, a *tent* being an Arab's house. See p. 38, above, on סכה, a *booth*. Again,—"The back part of the tent is closed by the *rowák*, a piece of goats'-hair stuff from three to four feet high, to which a *portion of some old cloak, or abba*, is stitched (called *sefále*), and hangs down to the ground. The *rowák* and *sefále* keep out the wind." Now, when an Arab, or Hebrew, family was shut into a tent like this, with a small fire of dung, there was not much danger of their catching cold.

For, once more, Bishop Colenso entirely misapprehends the character of winter in the desert. It is true that, at night, it is nearly cold enough to freeze to death any man, if exposed. But, in the daytime of that same winter, the sun glares on him all but enough to drive him mad. Even the head of a man, who was not a mathematician, might possibly permit of *coup de soleil*, if he ventured out without his turban. Read the following dreadful anecdote from Volney, invaluable Volney[2]:—

"In the year 1779, the Bedouin Arabs plundered an English caravan in the desert, between Suez and Cairo. Seven of the Europeans, stripped entirely naked by their inhuman spoilers, in

---

[1] Burckhardt's Bedouins and Wahabys, vol. i., pp. 37—50.
[2] Travels, vol. i., pp. 57, 58; or Paxton's *Geog.*, p. 403.

"the hope of reaching Cairo, pushed forward into the desert.
"Fatigue, thirst, hunger, and the heat of the sun destroyed one
"after another: one alone survived all these horrors. During
"three days and two nights, he wandered in this parched and sandy
"desert, *frozen at night by the north wind* (it being the month of
"January), and *burnt by the sun* during the day, without any other
"shade but a single bush, into which he thrust his head among
"the thorns, or any drink but his own urine. At length, on the third
"day, he was descried by an Arab, who conducted him to his tent, and
"took care of him for three days, with the utmost humanity. At the
"expiration of that time, the merchants of Cairo, apprized of his situa-
"tion, procured him a conveyance to that city, where he arrived in the
"most deplorable condition."

This took place in the desert between Suez and Cairo. I do not suppose that Dr. Colenso will object to take it as an illustration of what might happen in January, in a little lower latitude, in the desert of Sinai.

Now for one more mistake, by Dr. Colenso, regarding the desert. Most travellers choose to visit the desert of Sinai, as Robinson did, about the same time as the people Israel, viz., at springtide, or at early summer. The Bishop concludes that "travellers generally "choose the most favourable season of the year for visiting these "regions." Why! the *winter* is the most favourable season of the year for residence in the ¹ desert. "In spring and summer the Arabs "approach the cultivated parts of Syria, and quit them towards "winter." "The Aenezes, who live in the northern part of Arabia, "generally take up their winter quarters in the *Hammad* desert, or "the plain between Hauran and Heet, a position on the Euphrates. "The Hammad is without any springs; but in winter time the "water collects there in deep grounds, and the shrubs and plants of "the desert afford pasture to the Arab's cattle." "In these parts," viz., near inhabited grounds, "they spend the whole summer seeking "pasture and water, purchase in autumn their winter provision of "wheat, and barley, and return after the first rains into the interior "of the desert." "In spring, and winter, it is more difficult to "carry off the cattle, because in those seasons they find sufficient "food close to the tents, and are, therefore, easily protected." Which last quotation enables us to dispose, at least to some extent,

¹ Burckhardt's *Bedouins and Wahabys*, vol. i., pp. 1, 2, and 229.

of Dr. Colenso's anxiety for Israel's herds and flocks, during winter and spring.

In the above extracts, Burckhardt speaks more particularly of the great desert between Syria and the Euphrates; but, I shall have an opportunity of showing, that he speaks similarly of Arabia Petræa.

§ XXXI. THE ROUTE OF EUROPEAN TRAVELLERS.

Since we have referred so much to European travellers, it is well we should remember not only the time at which they visit the desert, but also the route they take. Now it is notorious that, for the most part, they follow a beaten track, and hurry through as fast as they can. The consequence is that such travellers really know very little, personally, about Arabia Petræa. Certainly not enough to justify Dr. Colenso, or any one else, in drawing from their accounts conclusions adverse to the credibility, or possibility, of Israel's sojourning in the desert, as narrated by Moses. Also, it is important for us to remember within how brief a period, say about 100 years, Europeans have travelled in the desert at all. However, of all modern travellers, the best, for statistical purposes, is, probably, Burckhardt; as for " long vacation " tourists, or dilettante divines, the less we refer to their ephemeral productions the better. For 3,320 years, viz., from .B.C. 1560, the year of the Exodus, to A.C. 1760, Arabia Petræa was little known to any Europeans; and visiting it, as they do, in haste, and following, so generally, in a beaten path, we have the best reason for doubting, whether they give us all the information which might otherwise be obtained for the elucidation of the Mosaic narrative.

It is only of late years, viz., in the year 1838, or twenty-four years ago, that " The important· fact of a spacious plain at the foot of " Sinai, which, from monkish traditions, *leads the generality of* " *travellers in one direction only*, and which represses in many minds " *the exercise of independent observation* and judgment, has lately " come upon the world, *with all the freshness of a new discovery.*" (Paxton, *Geog.*, p. 254.) That discovery may be read in Robinson's *Bibl. Researches*, vol. i., p. 130. So that, though Europeans have been deliberately searching for "discoveries" and information respecting the route of the Israelites in the desert, for about 100 years, it is but within twenty-four years that an American has made perhaps the most important "discovery" of all, because he did that which is so rare, viz., travelled out of the beaten track. With such excellent cause to suspect the possibility of fresh "discoveries," are we to reason about the desert, against the Bible, as if we were quite sure we knew all that would represent its condition more than 3,000 years ago? Dr. Colenso may trust such travellers' tales, but I will not.

And, in defending the Mosaic narrative, we must remember we have another sound motive for doubting the sufficiency of their evidence.

For thirty-eight years out of forty, the Israelites wandered we know not where. Soon after their being turned back from Kadesh-Barnea, as a punishment for their mutiny (Num. xii. 16, and xiv. 33), we lose all traces of their route. If the reader will refer to Num. xxxiii., and mark the verses 18—35, he will be able to note those places of Israel's encampment which we are not able to trace.[1] Burckhardt "inquired in vain among the Arabs for the names of "those places where the Israelites had sojourned during their "progress through the desert; none of them are known to the "present inhabitants." And, at that same time (1812), he says, "the "existence of the valley of El Araba, the *Kadesh Barnea*, perhaps, "of the Scriptures, appears to have been unknown both to ancient "and modern geographers, although it forms a prominent feature in "the topography of Syria and Arabia. It deserves to be thoroughly "investigated," &c., &c. Here was another modern "discovery."

Now we have seen, at p. 169, above, that the Arabian desert of El Tyh contains 18,900 square miles; and to these must be added the whole extent of the desert north of El Tyh (see map above); and we are utterly unable to trace out Israel's wanderings for thirty-eight years. Surely until these specific encampments are ascertained, we are in but a poor position to reason as to what were the probable resources of the wilderness in which the Israelites were wandering. Nor until that wilderness has been more thoroughly searched out, in all its parts, can we be sure that, even now, there do not remain resources of pasture and maintenance for man and beast, which indicate a more favourable condition still, in times so long gone by. Oh! that Dr. Colenso would retire to some lone spot in this desert, and there,

[1] Journey from Damascus to Cairo, in 1812, p. 443.

by the importation of guano, or anything else he pleases, carried on by the agency of others (see above, p. 23), see how green he could make that spot, even in the short space of twelve months!

§ XXXII. SCRIPTURAL ALLUSIONS TO THE ROUTE IN THE DESERT.

The journeys of the Israelites may be taken in three divisions (Num. xxxiii. 1—15, 16, 17, and 18—49) :—1. Those from Shur to Sinai. 2. Those from Sinai to Hazeroth. 3. Those from Hazeroth, for thirty-eight years, to places which cannot be identified. To which last we have just alluded.

Of all these, the most interesting are, perhaps, those from Shur to Sinai, being just ten journeys, of which I am about to speak. There were three journeys from Etham to Marah; at least one each from Marah to Elim, from Elim to the Red Sea, from the Red Sea to Sin, from Sin to Dophkah, from Dophkah to Alush, from Alush to Rephidim, and from Rephidim to Sinai. Even of these incipient journeys we know very little, except that which Scripture tells us; and which will be found of the utmost importance to our subject. People *think* they know where Marah is, *think* they know where Elim is, of Dophkah and Alush they know nothing, *think* they know where Rephidim is, and are *sure* they know where Sinai is; but, until the last twenty-four years, were unable to say where room could have been found for the people to encamp, and gather together into one plain, for the reception of the law.

If we turn to Exod. xv. 23, we shall notice that the people, and their flocks, journeyed three whole days in the wilderness, before they cried out for water; and when they came to Marah, they could not drink the water there, for it was bitter. Now, it is assumed that, during those three days, many of the cattle must have died of thirst. Even Kalisch is quoted by Dr. Colenso (at p. 78), as making this assumption. But why so? It is most important to remember that the time—viz., early spring, April 9th—when Israel entered the desert, was the very most favourable for their cattle. Then the effects of the winter rains were at their best; then the herbage, and plants, and shrubs, which they found, were full of moisture. And we have it upon the[1] testimony of Burckhardt, that, even "*in summer*, when rain water cannot be found in pools," the Arabs encamp near wells, "while their flocks and herds pasture all " around, at the distance of *several hours*, under the guard of slaves, " or shepherds, who bring them, *every second, or third, day*, to the " well, for water." Now, if cattle and flocks can thus go without water, for two, or three, days, in *summer*, in Arabia, Dr. Colenso can, perhaps, tell us how much longer they can go without, in *spring*.

Again:—" There are tribes which encamp in *spring time*, far " from any streams or wells, in fertile plains, where they remain " *for several weeks, without tasting water*, living wholly upon " milk; and their cattle *can dispense with water*, as long as green " and juicy herbage affords them nourishment."

There is, therefore, no justification for the assumption, that in three days, at spring time, many of Israel's cattle *must* have died of thirst. And, as regards the people themselves, we ought to bear in mind, the Egyptian mode of carrying water. The waterskins, to which Wilkinson alludes,[2] may be found particularly described in Lane. A camel carries two ox-hides full; an ass, or a man, a goat's-skin full. And assuming, as we fairly may, that each family of Israel was provided with the smallest means of carriage, viz., that by one man in each family, we can account for their having had, at least, a short allowance of water, enough for more than two days.

At Marah they found the water so bitter that they could not drink it. *So* bitter, because brackish water they could drink, as the Arabs do now. They had been accustomed to Nile water; and, like true Egyptians, hated all that was brackish, for wells in the neighbourhood of Cairo are now, and probably were then, as brackish as those in the desert. The water at Marah was so bitter that they could not drink it, and the Lord showed Moses a tree (Exod. xv. 25), by means of which " the waters were made sweet." Whether Moses was previously acquainted with this tree, but did not expect to find it in that locality, and was, therefore, providentially led to it; or whether it was a new piece of knowledge, miraculously conveyed to

---

[1] Burckhardt's Bedouins and Wahabys, vol. i., pp. 228, 229.
[2] Wilkinson's Ancient Egypt., vol. ii., pp. 141, 364. Lane's Modern Egypt, vol. ii.. pp. 15—17.

him; are questions. But for our present purpose we may, probably, venture to infer that the presence of one tree indicated that of many more; and that there was pasture in the neighbourhood of Marah. Also, it is far from improbable that the miracle thus wrought at Marah was frequently repeated elsewhere. Though it matters not what we think on that point. Water is found, almost anywhere in the desert, by digging to a certain depth; "water, in fact, is[1] readily "found by digging in every *fertile valley* in Arabia, and wells are "thus easily found, which are quickly *filled up again by the sands.*" This mention of the *sands* shows us in what sense we are to take Burckhardt's words "every fertile valley." And the fact that such water might be brackish does by no means imply that it is not drinkable. Thus, in the desert between Cairo and Suez, "the water is brackish, but it serves for drinking," says Burckhardt, and the people fill their water-skins there rather than pay " a higher price for the sweet water" of Suez. It is plain enough, the Israelites might have filled their waterskins the very day before the night, on which they passed through the Red Sea. Again, says Burckhardt, when in the desert of Sinai, the ships lying in the harbour of Tor "might fill their casks at the well Abou Szoueyra, about seven hours "south of Ayoun Mousa, and about half-an-hour from the sea shore, "*where the water is good;* but Arabs will seldom give themselves so "much trouble for water, and will rather drink what is at hand, "though bad, than go to a distance for good."

Thus the present condition of the desert clearly intimates that the Israelites might have habitually found water good enough for themselves and their cattle, though by no means like the water of the Nile, to which they had been accustomed. When at Howarah, *i.e.*, Marah, Burckhardt says, "The complaints of the bitterness of the water by "the children of Israel, who had been accustomed to the sweet water "of the Nile, are such as may daily be heard from the Egyptian "servants and peasants who travel in Arabia."

Their next station was at Elim, (Exod. xv. 27); "where were "twelve wells of water, and threescore and ten palm trees; and "they encamped there by the waters." This station was of far more importance to them, than even the twelve wells of water so plainly indicated. The treasure of those seventy palm trees was invaluable. Dates were given to camels, and other quadrupeds (*etiam quadru-*

[1] Burckhardt's Tour in Sinai, pp. 465, 468, 473, 474.

pedum cibus, Plin. 13, 4) in the East; and one tree can produce as much as four cantars of dates, or 440 lbs., on about eight branches, though generally it bears much less. And besides the food it provides, the tree is useful also, among other things, for every purpose for which laths or any thin woodwork is required; for wicker baskets, caps, mats, and brooms.[1] It is scarcely possible to magnify the utility of the palm, thus found at Elim by the people. Now[2] Burckhardt identifies Elim, in the end of Wady Gharendel; and says it contains date trees, tamarisks, acacias of different species, and the thorny shrub *Gharkad*, which is extremely common in the peninsula of Sinai, and bears a small red berry of which the Arabs make a conserve, of which they are particularly fond. It seems, that the Israelites may not only have had necessary food in the desert, but jam besides! Burckhardt suggests that the berry of this tree may have been used to sweeten the waters at Marah. However this may be, it is certain that date trees, tamarisk, and acacias, abounded in the desert of Sinai, and could furnish food both for man and for flocks and herds. The Arabs told Burckhardt that Wady Gharendel extended north-east, being one mile in breadth, through the whole desert, as far as El Arysh on the Mediterranean; and that it was full of trees. He had no means of verifying this statement. But, allowing for exaggeration, it is manifest enough that we can scarcely magnify too much the importance, to Israel, of this encampment, as a situation for pasturing the flocks and herds; and also for providing themselves with a multitude of articles conducive to their comfort in the desert. Niebuhr, as well as Burckhardt, considers Gharendel to be Elim; and says expressly, that his companions obtained water by digging to a very small depth.

The great want of the desert, the greatest known to Arabs, is that of bread. Unleavened bread is the bread of Arabs,[3] and such bread Israel had been taught to provide before they entered upon Arab life; probably, too, they had some "parched corn." But of all wants to a person in the desert, the most certain, and most distressing, is that of bread. "It is the want of corn that obliges all " Bedouins to keep up any intercourse with those who cultivate the " soil; and it is a mistake to imagine that the Bedouins can ever " be independent of the cultivators." This want the Israelites felt,

---

[1] Wilkinson's Anc. Egypt., vol. ii., pp. 177, 178.   [2] Tour in Sinai, pp. 472—475.
[3] Burckhardt's Bedouins and Wahabys, vol. i., pp. 57, 239, 240.

(Exod. xvi. 1—4); and as soon as manna was provided for them, the sustenance of the people in the desert, irrespective of any intercourse with other people, was secure. Dr. Colenso thinks to raise a prejudice against the Mosaic narrative by persistent allusion to the flocks and herds: "But even if the people were supported by miracles, yet " there is no provision whatever made in the Scripture for the sup- " port of the cattle," (p. 70); " the question is how were the flocks " and herds themselves supported?" (p. 71); and he perseveres in assuming, that they had to be " sustained in the desert without " miraculous help." (p. 71.) I say *assume ;* for what proof has he of that? Nay; we have proof to the very contrary. The drawing of water from the rock of flint was a miraculous intervention not only conducive to the sustenance of man, but also to that of the flocks and herds. So, also, was the miraculous, providential, leading, by Him who dwelt in the fiery-cloudy pillar, through their forty years of wandering. He, doubtless, conducted them to those particular spots, best adapted for the support and encampment of themselves, and also for their cattle. I cannot doubt but that many a rich wady, then existing, was pointed out by Him; which, even if now existing, European visitors would overlook, or prove incapable of discovering. Besides, we know that both men, and cattle, would feed on dates; and, how often they happened upon these palm trees, we are not told. Elim was, it seems, at the entrance of Gharendel, a vast, and beautiful, wady abounding in trees; how many such may have existed, or do exist, on the route of Israel we cannot know; because in truth we are not certain of by far the larger part of that route itself. The cattle would find some nourishment from palms, and tamarisks, and acacias, which (Burckhardt is[1] authority) are still plentiful in various parts of the desert. Says Burckhardt, when in the desert of El Tyh (Dr. Colenso will be aware that this is our *very* desert) " Wherever the rain collects in winter, vegetation of trees and " shrubs is produced;" and in Wady Rouak, in the same desert, " the rain water from the inequalities of the surface collects, and " produces a vegetation of low shrubs and a few Talh trees; " *the greater part of the wadys from hence to Egypt are of this* " *description ;*" and, again, when at Nakhel, a station on the north of El Tyh, " the appellation Nakhel (*i.e.,* date-tree) was probably " given to this castle at a time *when* the adjacent country *was covered* " *with palm trees,* none of which are *now* to be seen. At Akaba "

[1] Tour in Sinai, pp. 448, 449, 450.

(*i.e.*, close by the station of Israel, when they were bitten of serpents, Num. xxi. 6) "on the contrary, *are large forests of them*, belong-"ing for the greater part to the Arabs Heywat." Yes! the Arabs know their value, and make property of them. Yet "the ground "about Nakhel is chalky, or sandy, and is covered with loose "pebbles." And, while such information respecting the desert was open to him as much as to others, Dr. Colenso can be capable of writing thus, "That palm trees are found, washed up on the "shores of the Dead Sea, into which they found their way, no "doubt, from the river Jordan, gives surely no shadow of ground for "believing that *such trees or any other* (!) grew in the wilderness "of Sinai." We have seen Dr. Colenso wrong about the Hebrew; we have seen him wrong about sheep; wrong about pigeons; and now he is wrong about a question of physical geography.

Again, Dr. Colenso will assume that the flocks and herds could not have been fed on *manna*. "But the *sheep and oxen* could not live "upon the manna, nor could the people drink it." (p. 78.) We may admit, with perfect safety, that they did not. But, what right has Dr. Colenso to assume this? Can he tell us what that *manna* was? If so, he is the first person who ever decided the question. While, if it were like that which is still to be gathered from tamarisk trees, which camels love to nip, it is clear that they, at least, would probably eat the manna too. It is extremely possible, that the flocks and herds, as they sipped the dew, derived also much nourishment from the manna, which lay with that dew upon the ground: "And when the dew that lay was gone up, behold, upon the face of the wilderness, a small round thing, small as the hoar frost on the ground. And when the children of Israel saw it, they said one to another, It is manna; for they wist not what it was." (Exod. xvi. 14.) Now, in his considerations for the cattle, has the Bishop calculated the value of that dew? For forty years, they had manna; and, where manna was, there was dew; and, wherever dew was, there was moisture, which must have tended to the refreshment of the cattle. This description of the appearance of the manna, in the morning "when the dew that lay was gone up," leads us to think that it settled in a *liquid* state, and hardened as it lay; and, if so, the cattle might well be nourished by it.

Volney speaks[1] of the "excessive dews of the Delta;" and, though he adds, "which are less considerable in the Thebaid and

[1] Travels, vol. i., p. 323.

"the desert, as I am well assured;" the phenomena of such dews did not escape his notice. Nor should they ours, when speaking of Israel's flocks in the desert.

Burckhardt informs us,[1] that, near Elim, or Wady Gharendel, rock salt abounded. And Israel's first journey from this place was along the shore of the Red Sea: "And they removed from Elim, and encamped by the Red Sea." (Num. xxxiii. 10.) In the Red Sea, there were fish; that, at least, Dr. Colenso will admit. Also, by the Red Sea, God covered the camp with quails: "And it came to pass, that at even the quails came up." (Exod. xvi. 11—15.) Now, in Egypt, the Israelites had learned, not only how to catch fish and birds, but to salt them also.[2] "The "birds taken in nets, were principally geese, ducks, *quails*, and "some small kinds, which they were in the habit of *salting*, especially "in Lower Egypt" (*i.e.*, Goshen), "where Herodotus tells us, "they 'ate *quails*, ducks, and small birds, *undressed;* having merely "*'preserved them in salt.*'" It is interesting to observe, that the *geese* were caught in nets; and here is fair authority for what I said, at p. 57, above,—viz., that the Egyptians were fond of *goose and onions;* and now, we have ducks and quails, with a new mode of cooking them. Also, we see, why quails were wanted by Israel, just where salt was. Fish, too, were salted; "Salted, as well as fresh, fish, were much "eaten in Egypt, both in the Thebaid and the lower country," *i.e.*, Goshen. And, as to catching them—for we must catch fish and other things, before we cook them—they were skilful both with rod and net. As for boats, or rafts, we have no reason to doubt that, as now, so then, there were Arab fishers, tenanting the shores of the Red Sea. To their getting fish, at some time, Moses seems to allude, when he says, "Shall all the fish of the sea be gathered together for them, to suffice them?" (Num. xi. 22.) But we need not be anxious about the fish. Probably, the people, when they had fowl, cared not much about them. Yet, it is worth while noticing, that, to this day, the Bedouins on the coast of the Red Sea, are active fishermen,[3] and "sell their *dried* fish to the "crews of ships."

[1] Tour in Sinai, p. 475.
[2] Wilkinson's Ancient Egypt., vol. iii., pp. 47—58.
[3] Burckhardt's Bedouins and Wahabys, vol. ii., p. 21.

§ XXXIII. THE RESOURCES OF MOUNT SINAI.

When the people left the shores of the Red Sea, they entered the desert of Sin (Num. xxxiii. 11); and pitched at Rephidim, in Horeb. It was there that God, in His mercy, gave them water from the rock to drink. And, at Rephidim, they fought with Amalek. (Exod. xvii. 6, and Num. xx. 1—13.) Of which last event, I shall take no notice, until presently speaking of Israel's intercourse with other nations, when in the desert. It is now more important to observe, that Sinai was part of Horeb; that no limit is set to this miraculous supply of water from the rock; that it, probably, continued all the year they dwelt at Sinai; that the Israelites, who had learned the mode of conducting the Nile water, in rills, in all directions of Goshen, for purposes of pasture and cultivation, would do the same with water at Horeb; and seeing (as we do from abundant authorities) that wherever water is in the desert, there is verdure, vegetation, pasture, and life; we also see, that, as long as they stopped at Sinai, Israel, and their flocks and herds, were abundantly found with all that they required. Moreover, as we told Dr. Colenso, at p. 54, above, every breeding ewe would produce, at least, two lambs in that same year, so that abundant provision was being made for holding the second grand Passover—viz., that in the second year—at Sinai. Israel reached Sinai in June—the very time when drought was setting in.

Nor must we suppose that half a million of men, under God's chosen servant, remained long idle. One plan of securing water, well understood by Arabs, is its lodgments in the ledges, and cavities, of rocks; and they continue residing in certain[1] spots, "as long as they can find rain water remaining in the rocks." Dr. Colenso learns from Mr. Fazackerly, that the tops of Horeb are covered with snow in winter; and Burckhardt teaches us, that heavy rain sometimes falls as early as autumn;[2] so, the most ordinary prudence would have suggested that, soon after their arrival at Sinai, in June, the men of Israel should appoint some of their

---

[1] Burckhardt's Bedouins and Wahabys, vol. ii., p. 19.
[2] Burckhardt's Tour in Arabia Petræa and El Tyh, p. 417.

number to discover and examine the natural reservoirs in the mountains; and, by labour, to enlarge, or make perfect, any that required it. Besides which, Moses was no stranger to this locality. The rock at Horeb found them with water enough, at a moment, to prevent fatal drought; but there is not the slightest difficulty in conceiving how the people should have been abundantly provided with water, in the winter, and succeeding spring. They quitted Sinai, early in the following summer, B.C. 1561.

Still, as Bishop Colenso is incredulous, and rather derides Kalisch, we shall explain this more at large. The Bishop quotes Kalisch in the following manner, at p. 76,—" Nearly a whole year the Israelites " encamped in the fertile (!) region around the Sinai, where the air " is pure and refreshing, where fountains abound (!), and a variety " of game is found (!). See Num. xi. 31 [where we find an account of the *miracle* of the gift of quails]." I proceed to show that, in substance, Kalisch is correct; and that Bishop Colenso's notes of admiration are marks of ignorance.

On April 20, A.D. 1816, Burckhardt left Cairo for the desert of El Tyh, and Sinai. The Israelites left Rameses on April 9, B.C. 1560 (see p. 64, above); and the following are some of his observations [1]:—He travelled over an unfrequented route to Suez, a route now covered with *petrified trees*, and considers that he was upon the ancient road between Clysma and Memphis; and that the water requisite to produce this great vegetation, of which such remarkable remains are found, was procured " from deep wells, and from " reservoirs of rain water, as is done in the equally barren desert " between Djedda and Mecca." It was just at the end of this route that he met with ostriches from the desert of El Tyh. This desert of Suez, he says, is still " full of rich pasture and pools of water " during winter and spring." The Israelites journeyed through it in *early* spring (see p. 64—66, above). As he draws near Suez, he observes,—" Rains are much more frequent in this desert than in the " valley of Egypt, and *the same remark may be made in regard to all* " *the mountains to the southward* " (*e.g.*, El Tyh, or Sinai), " where a " regular though not uninterrupted rainy season sets in." He notes the date trees, then still at Ayoun Mousa; and the Wady Gharendel, a great valley for them, as already mentioned (p. 184, above). He

[1] Tour in Sinai and El Tyh, p. 460, &c , &c.

remarks on the *withered* date, acacia, and tamarisk trees at Wady Oswaita, yet nearer Sinai, showing what the site once had been. He finds a well of "excellent water" at Wady Naszeb, farther on. And now, having reached El Dhelel, a portion of the range of El Tyh, he describes "these chains" as forming "the northern " boundaries of the Sinai mountains," and being "the pasturing " places of the Sinai Bedouins;" and adds, "The valleys of these " mountains are said to afford *excellent pasturage*, and *fine springs*, " though not in great numbers." And at the *southern* foot of El Tyh (*i.e.*, towards Sinai), he finds "a broad *sandy* plain" continuing " for two days' journey *eastward*," *i.e.*, right into the desert, "afford-" ing good pasturage in spring," (Israel passed there in spring,) "but " it has *no water*, and is therefore little frequented by Bedouins." Burckhardt was there on April 28,—about the same time as the people Israel.

A little further on the road, and on April 29, he arrived at Djebel Leboua, and in the Wady Genne, which he describes as "a fine valley, " *several miles in breadth*, and *covered with pasturage*." Here it was he found "Bedouins occupied in collecting *brushwood*, which they " burn into charcoal for the Cairo market;" and adds, "They " prefer for this purpose the thick roots of the *shrub* Rethem, " *Genista Raetam* of Forskal, which grows here in abundance;" giving us an opportunity of pointing out, by reference to p. 172, above, that Dr. Colenso is quite mistaken as to his notions of making charcoal; and that brushwood, or broom, or saplings, or undergrowth can be employed for that purpose, at least by Bedouins, contrary to his expectations. It was here, also, that the Israelites got soap to wash their linen with; a lucky thing for the priest, if he had had to do what Bishop Colenso supposes (see p. 23, above). For Burckhardt adds, "The Bedouins collect also the herb Adjrem, which they " dry, break in pieces, and pound between stones, and then use as a " substitute for soap to wash their linen with. I was told that *very* " *good water* is found at almost two miles to the east of this valley;" of which, no doubt, the women were very glad. He ended this day of useful discoveries at Wady Osh, looking towards Sinai, and observes, "In the Wady Osh there is a well of *sweet water*. From " hence upwards, and *throughout the primitive chain of Mount Sinai*, " the water is *generally excellent*, while in the *lower* chalky moun-" tains *all round* the peninsula, it is brackish, or bitter, except in one "or two places." Yet, remember, brackish water could be drunk, see p. 182, above.

On May the 1st he arrived near *the central summits of Mount Sinai*, and "came to a *thick wood* of tamarisk trees, or Taifa, and " found many camels feeding upon their thorny shoots;" adding, " it is from this *evergreen* tamarisk, which grows abundantly in *no* " *other* part of the peninsula, that the manna is collected." Here, again, I am happy to say, they found more soap. For there is a substance there called Tafal, a feldspar of granite, which has all the appearance of pipeclay. "The Arabs sell it at Cairo, where it is in " request for *taking stains out of cloth*, and where it serves the poor " instead of soap for washing their hands." But, in connection with this subject, our considerate traveller adds, "It is chiefly used to rub " the skins of asses during summer."

On this same day, May 1, he arrived in a broad valley, " at the " termination of which he was agreeably surprised by the beautiful " verdure of a garden of almond trees belonging to the convent. " From thence, by another short turn to the left, he reached the con- " vent in seven hours and a half."

There we shall leave him. He deserves his rest. He travelled the route of Israel, just at Israel's time, from April to May. And I leave the reader to consider whether there was not, even in A.C. 1816, water enough and pasture enough for Israel and their flocks on their road to Sinai. And if so much in A.C. 1816, how much more in B.C. 1560?

§ XXXIV. ISRAEL'S INTERCOURSE WITH INHABITANTS OF THE DESERT.

It is important to remember that Burckhardt's whole journey, made quite leisurely and for purposes of careful observation, occupied only ten days. In that time he journeyed from Cairo, round the head of the Gulf of Suez, to Sinai. But the people of Israel crossed the bed of the Red Sea, landed at Shur, and had only about half the way to walk. Now the Amalekites dwelt from Havilah unto Shur (1 Sam. xv. 7); that is, they occupied the country between the Dead and the Red Seas, skirting the borders of Canaan. They were, in fact, people of the desert; people of that very desert of which Sinai is the south part. They attacked Israel at Rephidim, by Horeb (Exod. xvii. 8), and were repulsed. The cause of their attacking Israel is not mentioned. There must have been some cause, and we are left by the historian to imagine what it could be (see p. 27, above). Now, if we remember that they dwelt between Canaan and Egypt, were extensive pastors of cattle, and that it was the custom to drive cattle to the very desert of Sinai for that pasture, which Dr. Colenso says was never to be found there, we have instantly suggested three causes for their attack:—1. The probability that they were urged on by the Egyptians, in hatred and revenge for the loss of their slaves, of their firstborn, and of their king and his army; 2. That they were urged on by the Canaanites, who had heard that the people Israel were bound for Canaan; and 3. That they could not be reconciled to so numerous a people, with their flocks, and herds, journeying into, and on, the precious pastures so much needed by themselves.

This rapid attack by Amalek suggests to our reflection the speedy communication which might be, at that time, established between Sinai and Egypt; and one reason, therefore, why Israel was detained, by the will of the Almighty, so long at Sinai.

I said, and at p. 178 above have shown, that it was the habit to drive flocks and herds into the wilderness for pasture, especially in winter. And, accordingly, if we refer to Exod. iii. 1, we shall see that, in winter, the chief Midianitish flocks were pastured at Horeb, where Bishop Colenso says pasturage was not to be had:—" Now " Moses kept the flock of Jethro his father-in-law, the priest of " Midian; and he led the flock to the backside of the desert, and " came to the mountain of God, even to Horeb." This must have been in winter—the depth of winter. For Israel left Egypt in April, 1560 B.C.; after the tenth plague, and, as we said at pp. 31, 51, above, we can scarcely allow less interval than one week between two plagues, so that, allowing for Moses' journeying back to his father-in-law, his arranging to leave him (Exod. iv. 18), and his then going on to Egypt, Moses could not have arrived at Pharaoh's court much before February, nor have left Horeb much before the middle of January, 1560 B.C. In the depth of winter, therefore, Moses pastured the principal flocks of Midian, round about Horeb, where Dr. Colenso says no pasture was. But where Kalisch says, and Burckhardt justifies him, that excellent pasture could be found.

Now[1] the Amalekites dwelt in the desert between the Dead Sea and the Red Sea, down to Shur, where Israel landed; and the Midianites dwelt in the desert from the Red Sea to Sinai; two considerable families of people living habitually, and pasturing their cattle, in that very desert of which Dr. Colenso, misunderstanding Scripture, says that, *literally*, no man passed through (see p. 167 above). On the west of the desert were Amalekites and Midianites; on the east of the same desert were Edomites; and throughout the desert Ishmaelites, or Hagarenes.

The whole journey between Cairo and Sinai can be done comfortably, we have seen, in about ten days. Surely Jethro's visit to Moses was not without significance. Exod. xviii. 1—6:—" And Jethro, Moses' father-in-law, came with his sons and his wife unto Moses into the wilderness, where he encamped at the mount of God." Surely this event is recorded, because it was of the very greatest importance, not only to Moses personally, but also to the whole people whom he led. It is in reference to matters of this kind, that we are justified in applying to Holy Scripture the principle of interpretation, explained before at p. 27. Conceive Moses and the elders of Israel, soon after the battle with Amalek, noticing from a distance the approach of a large cavalcade of men and of camels. Who are here? Are they friends or enemies? And, behold, 'tis Jethro! The very man, of all others, that Moses and his elders would like to see; the very man, of all others, able and likely to be of most service to them. " Now we can get *good* tents! Now we can get *more* camels! Now we can obtain an infinite variety of articles conducive to our safety in the desert! Now we can send away, sell, or otherwise dispose of, all useless encumbrances! Now we have a certain chain of intercourse established between ourselves and Egypt, by which we may receive supplies of various commodities once a fortnight, or oftener!" And we may imagine this going on for a whole twelvemonth. For the Midianites were travelling merchants, who carried on a lucrative trade with Egypt, even in the days of Joseph. (Gen. xxxvii. 28.) It is impossible to over-estimate the importance of Jethro's visit to the camp of Israel.

[1] Paxton's Sacr. Geog., p. 518.

§ XXXV. GENERAL ASPECT OF THE DESERT.

After so clear a picture of the desert of Sinai, as that conveyed in the foregoing extracts, I shall deem it unnecessary to allude particularly to those few other journeys which the Israelites took before they arrived for the first time at Kadesh-Barnea, and sent out the spies. (Num. xiii. 2.) I would merely observe, in regard to them, that from Deut. i. 33, I infer, as already intimated at p. 185, that Israel was conducted by an abiding miracle, through the fiery-cloudy pillar, to those particular spots best suited for an encampment; as being most furnished with those various local resources of the desert, conducive to the maintenance of themselves and their flocks and herds. "And they departed from the "mount of the Lord three days' journey; and the ark of the "covenant of the Lord went before them in the three days' journey, "to search out a resting-place for them. And the cloud of the "Lord was upon them by day, when they went out of the camp;" and whether it were "two days, or a month, or a year," (Num. ix. 21, 22, and x. 33), the pillar of cloud and of fire directed them to move forward, or to halt, as was best adapted for their welfare at the time.

But we are particularly interested in knowing the character of the desert around the land of Edom, for Israel "compassed Mount Seir "many days" (Deut. ii. 1); where the ימים רבים, many *days*, may mean, and probably does, many *years*: (a common use [1] of ימים, of which Dr. Colenso seems perfectly unaware, see p. 76); and, though we are quite unable to discover the places of their encampment, we are also concerned to know the general aspect of the desert more to the west of Edom, and to the north of El Tyh (see map, above).

In 1812, Burckhardt travelled "through the mountains of Arabia "Petræa; and desert of El Tyh to Cairo," and on August the 14th, was passing through Wady Ghoeyr, or Little Ghor, along the mountains of Shera. "These are the mountains called in the "Scripture *Mount Sin*, the land of Edom." The traveller was,

---

[1] *Dies*, pro anno, quando videlicet ימים *dies, sine additâ voce numerali* ponitur (Gen. xl. 4; Exod. xiii. 10; Lev. xxv. 29). Glassius, Philolog. Sacr., p. 1276.

therefore, outside the land of Edom. The valley, through which he was thus passing, he describes as " intersected by numerous wadys of " winter torrents, and by three or four valleys *watered by rivulets* " which unite below, and flow into the Ghor." And he adds, " The " Ghoeyr is famous for the excellent pasturage, produced by its " numerous springs, and has, in consequence, become a favourite " place of encampment for all the Bedouins of Djebal and Shera." A little farther south, on the same route, he reached an encampment of Fellahein Bedouins, *i.e.*, Bedouins who were *cultivators*, and says, " their herds of cows, sheep, and goats, are very numerous." And from this place all through his route to Aaron's tomb, he speaks of " vestiges of former cultivation," of the " country hereabouts " as " woody," and of springs and rivulets. " Ain Mousa is a copious " spring, rushing from under a rock at the eastern extremity of Wady " Mousa ; " or, again, in another place, " the rivulet joins with " another descending from the mountain to the southward." And, when at Wady Mousa, examining ruins which he believed to be those of Petra, " the river has worked a passage through them, and " runs underground, as I was told, for about a quarter of an hour." And, lastly, in reference to the plains round Aaron's tomb, " The " plain of Haroun, and the neighbouring mountains, have no springs; " but the rain water collects in low grounds, and in natural hollows " in the rocks, where it partly remains *the whole year round*, even " on the top of the mountains."

With such a description of the country around Edom, during the hot month of August so recently as 1812, and when Idumea is comparatively desolate, and uninhabited, we need be at no loss to imagine how Israel, and their flocks and herds, were sustained in the desert, during the " many days," or years, that they " compassed the land of Edom."

Let us trace the neighbourhood of their encampments, more southward in the desert. That we are considering the state of a country fairly representative of the worst parts of the desert, we may be sure ; for when drawing towards " Maan " somewhat north of the Red Sea, (we remember that Israel left Mount Hor to approach the shores of the Red sea, p. 158, above) he observes, " We have thus a natural " division of the country, which appears to have been well known to the " ancients, for it is probably to a part of this upper plain, together "with the mountains of Shera, Djebal, Kerek, and Bilka, that the name of *Arabia Petræa* was applied, the western limits of which must have been the great valley, or Ghor. It might with truth be called *Petræa*, not only on account of its rocky mountains, but also of the elevated plain already described, which is so much covered with stones, especially flints, that it may with great propriety be called a stony desert, *although susceptible of culture*. In many places it is overgrown with wild herbs, and must once have been thickly inhabited, for traces of many ruined towns and villages are met with on both sides of the Hadj road between Maan and Akaba."

It is not improbable that this Hadj road from Maan southward, to Akaba, or Ezion-gabir, on the eastern gulf of the Red Sea, may denote the very route which Israel followed from Mount Hor.

"At present all this country is a desert, and Maan is the only inhabited place in it." Yet although he states that "Maan is situated in the midst of a rocky country, not capable of cultivation," and that "the inhabitants therefore depend upon their *neighbours* of Djebal and Shera for their provisions of wheat and barley," he adds, that "the pomegranates, apricots, and peaches, of Maan are of the finest quality." How rapid, too, is the communication between Hebron (see p. 159, above) and this place on the road to Akaba may be judged by the fact that the inhabitants buy all sorts of provisions at Hebron, and even Gaza, to sell to the pilgrims on their way to Mecca.

Take his description of a fearful wady, Wady Gharendel (another than that referred to above, at p. 184), leading westward into that of El Araba:—"At five hours the valley opens, and we found ourselves upon a sandy plain, interspersed with rocks; the bed of the wady was covered with white sand. A few trees of the species called by the Arabs Talh, Tarfa, and Adha, grow in the midst of the sand, but their withered leaves cannot divert the traveller's eye from the dreary scene around him." Could there be, indeed, a more dreary scene? And yet six hours and a-half, viz., one day's journey farther on, he says of the mouth of this wady, "A few hundred paces above the issue of the wady are several springs, called Ayoun Gharendel, surrounded by a few date trees, and *some verdant pasture ground*. The water has a "sulphureous taste, but these being the only springs on the borders of the great valley, within *one day's* journey to the north and south, the Bedouins are obliged to resort to them."

Verifying still the general character of this terrible desert, this waste, howling wilderness, viz., that, even in its worst parts, there are frequent *springs* of water drinkable, though bad; and *verdant pasture grounds*.

This dreadful Wady Gharendel leads into Wady El Araba, which Burckhardt believed to be the *Kadesh-barnea* of Holy Scripture. Now it is a curious fact, quoted with great animation by Dr. Colenso, at p. 74, that Stanley says of El Araba, "The first thing that struck me, in turning out of the Arabah, up the defiles that lead to Petra, was that we had suddenly *left the desert*. Instead of the absolute nakedness of the Sinaitic valleys, we found ourselves walking on grass, sprinkled with flowers, and the level platforms on each side were filled with sprouting corn. And this continues through the whole descent to Petra, and in Petra itself." Yet of this very El Araba, Burckhardt, though doing the fullest justice to its horrors, as " in summer entirely without water," as " an expanse of shifting sands," adds, " Numerous Bedouin tribes encamp here in the winter, when the torrents produce a copious supply of water, and a few shrubs spring up from their banks, affording *pasturage to the sheep and goats*."

Again verifying the general character of this terrible wilderness, this waste, howling wilderness, " this land of deserts " (ערבה, *Araba*) " and of pits," viz., that spots of fearful desolation, terrific to European summer travellers, are nevertheless *in winter* the chosen resting-places of *numerous tribes* of Bedouins, because affording them *a copious supply of water*, and *pasture for their sheep and goats*.

So, too, of Wady el Lahyane, eight hours W.N.W. of El Araba, he says, " In this desert the water collects in a number of low bottoms and wadys, where it produces verdure *in winter time;* and an *abundance* of trees with green leaves are found throughout the year. *In the winter* some of the Arabs of Ghaza, Khalyl, as well as those from the shores of the Red Sea, encamp here. The Wady Lahyane is several hours' in extent; its *bottom is full of gravel*."

Now, from this spot it is eight days' journey to Gaza, in Palestine; and, in these eight days' journeys, there are three watering-places.

Also the distance from Hebron to Akaba is nine days (see above, p. 159); and, in these nine days' journeys, there are three springs. This, again, gives us a clear and lively picture of the nature of the desert in its worst parts; water every two or three days. Often enough, for the flocks and herds (see above, p. 182), and, remembering their abundant means of transport, made perfect, probably, by means of Jethro's visit, not too dangerously infrequent for the people Israel.

From Wady Lahyane the traveller entered El Tyh, and it is of that desert, peculiarly the desert of which we wish to form correct ideas, he says, "Wherever the rain collects in winter, vegetation of trees and "shrubs is produced."

We need scarcely pursue this subject farther. Wherever Burckhardt wanders in this desert, there he finds some sources of encouragement, some resources for men and cattle. In one place, "a level plain, consisting of rich red earth *fit for culture,* " and similar to that of the *northern* Syrian desert." Agreeably to what I have stated, at p. 178, above. At another, a wady, " overgrown with green shrubs, but without trees." At a third, "in " a valley of the Sheghar, we found an abundance of shrubs and " trees." In the very midst of this terrible desert, " this land of " drought, and of the shadow of death," " good water, but in small " quantities, is found everywhere on digging to the depth of ten or " twelve feet. There were about half-a-dozen holes, five or six feet " in circumference, with a foot of water in each; *on drawing up the* " *water, the holes fill again immediately.*" It was here he found a tribe of Bedouins watering a large herd of camels.

Surely we have now [1] a very clear idea of the general aspect of the desert in which Israel wandered for forty years. We have taken it in two divisions,—first, that which they lived in, and passed over, during the first two years of their wanderings; *second*, that about which, and in the neighbourhood of which, they were wandering and encamping for thirty-eight years; and we see that, while the language of Holy Scripture is exactly correct, and the wilderness was a land subject to fearful drought, a land studded with terrific deserts (or Arabas) and pits, it was also provided throughout with capabilities for verdant pasture; was furnished, very frequently, with water, sometimes

[1] Burckhardt's Tour through Arabia Petrea and Sinai, pp. 377—455.

bad, sometimes good; was, and is, in some spots even capable of cultivation; and, in fact, did, and does, supply very considerable natural resources for the support both of men and cattle.

So that, while we entirely acknowledge the wonderful hand of the Almighty in preserving Israel miraculously, we do see that there were also certain, and abundant, natural sources of maintenance, to which God's kind providence led the people with surety at their times of need; and which leave the infidel but small room to question the possibility of a numerous people being kept alive for forty years in the desert.

§ XXXVI. MODE OF LIVING IN THE DESERT.

It may be of some service to notice, very briefly, the mode of living in this desert, as enabling us to form a clearer idea of the natural probabilities that a numerous people could be sustained there.

The diet of the Arabs is, first, *unleavened* bread, such as that which Israel carried with them out of Egypt. On their journeys the Bedouins live almost wholly upon unleavened bread baked in the ashes, and mixed with butter. And they use butter to excess,— showing no deficiency of pasturage for their sheep and goats, of whose milk alone that butter is made. Throughout the desert there is a great sameness in the Bedouin dishes, for they everywhere consist chiefly of flour and butter. I have already observed, at p. 184, that the great want of the Bedouins is corn. In the case of Israel this deficiency was supplied by the forty years' fall of manna. Their butter is made only of goats' and sheep's milk. The milk is put into a goat-skin, and for one or two hours is constantly moved backwards and forwards; the buttery substance then coagulates, the water is squeezed out, and the butter put into a skin. Some tribes live almost wholly upon *dates* and milk.

There is also a kind of truffle, which *grows* in the desert. It is a favourite dish with the Arabs. It has no appearance either of roots or seeds; consists of three sorts, red, black, and white; and if the rain has been abundant during winter, this food is found in the end of March. It lies about four inches under ground, and is sometimes so plentiful that each family in a tribe may gather *four or five camel loads* of it. While this stock lasts the Arabs live exclusively on it, without tasting bread in any shape. The Israelites were better off, for whatever truffle there was, they had new bread every day.

Inhabitants of the desert require, and habitually take, but little food. Their daily universal dish is flour made into a paste with camel's milk, and boiled. Sometimes they eat a paste made of bread, butter, and dates. An Arab rarely indulges in luxuries, and that only upon the arrival of a stranger. Burckhardt says that " wherever dates grow, that excellent fruit constitutes their chief " diet. The quantity of butter they use is extraordinary, showing " no fear of deficiency of milk from their goats and sheep ; " and therefore, I suppose, no fear of deficiency of pasture for their sheep and goats. Although Burckhardt notes, on August 16, " There was " not a drop of milk to be got, for, at this time of the year, the ewes " are dry." Whoever can get butter swallows every morning a large cup full before breakfast, and snuffs up as much into his nostrils. All their food swims in butter. From one hundred ewes or goats (the milk of which is always mixed together), the Arabs expect, in common years, about 8 lbs. of butter a-day, or about 7 cwt. in the three spring months.

It is a curious fact, worth noticing, in connection with the second Passover, as held at Sinai (see p. 54, above), that the Arabs habitually kill their male lambs and kids, except two or three, which they keep for breeding. They are, of course, aware of the fact, to which we called Dr. Colenso's attention, at p. 54, viz., how very few male lambs or kids are required for that important purpose. They kill the rams and he-goats (so habitually offered in Levitical sacrifices) in order to economise pasture; and they keep the ewes for the purpose of securing milk.

But enough on this subject. Having thus the general character of the desert before us, and, particularly, the character of El Tyh ; having noticed, also, the moderation of the people of the desert in their diet; remembering that Israel was provided miraculously with daily bread ; and directed miraculously by the fiery-cloudy pillar to their encampments; we need be at no loss to consider in what way God's people Israel were kept alive, with their flocks and herds, for forty years in the wilderness.

§ XXXVII. CONCLUSION.

I have now done with Dr. Colenso's book, and hope that, in some particulars, at least, it has been refuted to the reader's satisfaction. Surely we are not mistaken; but have found Dr. Colenso wrong in his Hebrew; incorrect in the interpretation of separate phrases, some of such a kind, as, *e.g.*, "the fourth generation," and "between the two evenings," that a large part of his book depends upon them; inaccurate in matters of natural history, as, for instance, such as refer to sheep, and goats, and pigeons; curiously unknowing on points of physical geography, as, for example, upon the general physical aspect, and resources, of the desert; wonderfully misapprehensive of the correct meaning of certain entire passages of Holy Scripture, *to wit*, those which concern the institution of the Passover, the time and mode of the Exodus, and the institution of Levitical Sacrifices, and the numbering of Levitical families; and are laymen to have their minds unsettled by a Bishop, who writes like this?

We have even found him wrong on subjects pertaining to his own peculiar department, viz., those which demand the application of numbers, and require the capacity to strike fair averages, and to tell at a glance what acknowledged conditions are necessary to the solution of his problem. And, extraordinary as such a fact may be, it is one of the utmost consequence in determining our estimate of his book. Dr. Colenso's strength is prostrated, when attacking the Pentateuch, as if Samson had aimed a vile blow at the High Priest of God, and dropped dead in doing so. After this, what confidence can any reasonable man have in the value of what he has written, and has, unhappily, published; or in anything more, which he may think proper to write upon a similar subject at some future day?

Bishop Colenso proves himself strangely incompetent to carry on an argument, or to conduct an investigation. He assumes that the Israelitish families, born in Canaan, can be taken as a fair average of their families born in Egypt, in which country their social condition had become entirely changed. He assumes that the facts recorded of a particular family, Levi's, in Egypt, are a fair index to the probable multiplication of a whole people. He hunts all through the Bible for family pedigrees to justify his interpretation of the expression "fourth generation," and having found only eleven, which are, in fact, reducible to two (see p. 116, above), from these eleven, or, rather, two, cases, he ventures to draw conclusions respecting the procreations, in separate families, of a people, which he admits to have numbered about two millions and a-half.

Surely, we cannot be wrong in thinking that, in conducting arithmetical, or mathematical, calculations to anything like a certain and satisfactory result, we ought to be quite safe as to the *data* upon which these calculations are based; and fully informed as to the collateral influences which may nullify, or render inaccurate, those calculations. Dr. Colenso proceeds in a very different way from this. He finds the number of Israel's firstborns stated at, what he believes to be, far too low a figure; and proceeds to reason severely upon its inaccuracy, without producing, or attempting to produce, any statistical estimate of four disturbing influences, which may seriously affect the number of the firstborn; viz., the frequency of the cases in which the firstborn child is a girl, the frequency of the cases in which the firstborn perishes naturally, the frequency of the cases in which, (as to the people Israel,) the firstborn boy may have been killed by Pharaoh, and, lastly, the number of the firstborn who may, possibly, have died in the course of nature.

Nor is it less remarkable how, sometimes, the Bishop states propositions plainly illogical. Thus, as to the tribe of Levi, he tells us, that either they were included in the sentence of death, before entrance into Canaan, passed upon all the other tribes; or they were not; forgetting that they *may* have been included partially, though not entirely. So, again, observing that the Midianitish girls were to be reduced to a certain kind of slavery among the Hebrews, he asks, How is it possible to quote the Bible, as condemning slavery, "in any way," if such a statement be historically true? forgetting that the Bible *might* condemn slavery, in some ways; and, yet, permit it in others.

Similar inaccuracy, or even unfairness, characterizes his refusal to make certain admissions, which cannot rationally be denied to those who differ from him. Thus, he will not believe that polygamy, or concubinage, prevailed among the people Israel; whereas, we find, that they were specifically provided for in the Levitical law; and such provision implies their existence at the time, and also contemplates their permission in the future. He refuses to admit this, also, in direct opposition to the known character, and behaviour, of Israel, before their descent into Egypt; and after their departure from it; and, also, in direct opposition to all probability, gathered from the known character of Egyptian women. Again, in reference to the families of Israel, Dr. Colenso will not admit the probability of Jacob's having had, in conjunction with his twelve sons, a large, or indeed, any, number of servants. And, yet, it is certain, that the Patriarchs, Abraham, Isaac, and Jacob, must have had a considerable body of retainers, at various periods in their history. And it is also certain, that, if, as stated, they took down a considerable number of oxen, sheep, and goats; and, probably, of camels, and asses; it is difficult to understand how they could have done so, without the aid of some number of servants.

Moreover, the Bishop is not only illiberal, in allowances to his opponents; but also, on, at least, three most important occasions, misquotes the Scripture, by leaving out words of great consequence to the argument. In the question concerning the native place of Hezron and Hamul, he leaves out the word, "were;" upon which, especially in the Hebrew, the whole argument turns; in the inquiry concerning the Levitical sacrifices, he leaves out, in respect to one serious class of sacrifices, the words, "Behold the blood of it was not brought in within the holy place," and, in reference to the attack, and overthrow, of the Canaanites of Arad, where everything, as to the *time*, in question, depends upon their proximity to Israel at Hor, he leaves out the all-important words, "which dwelt in the south."

Also, the Bishop not only misquotes: he misinterprets Scripture; and, when doing so, manifests a very thorough ignorance of the Hebrew language. Now, though the "rule of three" is notoriously of golden value, it is of no use to apply the "rule of three" to an author's statements, until you are sure you understand what he really says. Dr. Colenso's sums may be quite correct; but the very first necessity, in arithmetically computing the probability, or possibility, of Moses' statements, was, that he should be certain he quite understood the language in which Moses made them. Dr. Colenso does not understand. He was, evidently, quite unaware, what questions *might* be raised upon the presence of the word, "were," in the historian's statement of Hezron and Hamul's parentage. He strangely misapprehended the meaning of "all the congregation," "the whole assembly," &c., &c. He seems to have been quite unmindful of the mode in which the law was read to the people. He made an extraordinary mistake in thinking that the priest himself had to carry out of the camp the skin, and inwards, &c., &c., of a whole bullock. He misrepresented (but not intentionally) Aben Ezra, as to the meaning of "between the two evenings." He seems not to have known the varieties of interpretation possible for that phrase. Or (and that would be worse), if he knew them, he disingenuously passed them by. He entirely misconceived the force of the little pronoun, translated, "this," in the account of the institution of the Passover. He misapprehended the whole statement regarding the periods intervening between the plagues. He failed to see in what way Israel had abundant time to prepare for their departure. He misapprehended the *then* state of Goshen, between Memphis and the Red Sea. He took the Israelites, by a route of sixty miles, in three days, viz., twenty miles a-day; when, it has been demonstrated, it need be only thirty-six, or twelve miles a-day. He omitted to say, or did not know, that, taking the slowest rate of travelling, on camels, or, little more than two miles an hour, the Israelites might be encamped eighteen hours, out of twenty-four, and have abundant time for casualties. And he plainly stated, that there were no indications of the people halting, given us in Holy Scripture, when it is distinctly asserted, that they did camp, make booths, and cook; and, even by express order of the Almighty, quietly encamped at Pi-hahiroth, as if they were waiting for Pharaoh.

It is a fact, most destructive of Dr. Colenso's work, that he does not give the writer of the Pentateuch credit for common-sense. The "impossibilities, contradictions, and inconsistencies," which the Bishop believes he has detected, are such as no writer, or compiler, of average intelligence, could have been guilty of; and such, as, if they really existed, must certainly have been detected, and exposed, long ago. No one, for example, will believe, that the historian meant to say, that Hezron and Hamul were born, in Canaan, of Pharez, when that person must have been a child, only four or five years old. Nor will any one believe, that the lawgiver meant to say, that each priest had to eat eighty-four pigeons a-day, besides other food, "in the holy place," or anywhere else.

None could possibly imagine the sacred writer guilty of the absurdity of saying, that, to hear the law, or for any other purpose, 600,000 men had to stand in a tail, nearly twenty miles long. Such ideas cannot effect any serious assault upon the Pentateuch.

But, worse than all, is the fact, that a Christian Bishop ignores the miraculous features, which the writer professedly imparts to his history. He, again and again, asserts, that the increase of the people, and their preservation, in Egypt, were peculiarly miraculous. The Bishop goes closely to work with his figures, and thinks he proves that they could not have increased so. The writer studiously records that the people were miraculously preserved in the desert, and he there alludes particularly to their flocks and herds. The Bishop at once proceeds, by reference to some half-dozen modern travellers, to show that such a thing could not have been. Assuming that the desert was, more than three thousand years ago, much the same as it is now. Mistaking the statements of Holy Scripture, upon the subject; and, being apparently ill-informed as to the actual character of that desert, as even now existing. This character is clearly exhibited from the writings of various travellers, as likely to have furnished very considerable resources for the maintenance of a numerous people, with large flocks and herds; even had no miraculous means been provided for their preservation. Although the tenour of the whole narrative is, to the effect that they were miraculously preserved.

Surely, we have glanced at reasons enough for doubting the solidity of Dr. Colenso's book; and for concluding, that his method of attack, and the way in which he has carried it out, are not such as to give Christian Laymen any alarm concerning the historical veracity of the Pentateuch; nor, by having done so, to shock their Christian faith, which, to a considerable extent, depends upon it.

FINIS.

A BRIEF GENERAL INDEX.

ABARBANEL, his division of sacrifices Levitical, 87
Acacia, and other trees, *withered*, near Sinai, 190
All Israel, Moses and Joshua addressing, 20
"All the congregation," meaning of this expression, 16, 19
Amalekites, where they dwelt, 189
Amram, his family, no fair test for all Levitical families, 125
Apostles, testimony of the, to Pentateuch, 9
Armed, and dwelling in tents, Israel, 29
—————, Israel may have been so, at the Exodus, 31
—————, proper rendering of word so translated, 33
—————, Dr. Colenso's mistake in arguing on, 34
Arms, how obtained by Israel at the Exodus, 32

Balaam, Balak's messages to, 154
Benjamin, probable reason of small number of his tribe, 114
"Between the two evenings," meaning of this phrase, 68
————————————, authorities referred to, for, 69
————————————, various explanations of, 71—74
Births, Israelitish, on the road to Pi-hahiroth, 66
Bochart, his Hierozoicon referred to, 41, 140, 147
Booths, Dr. Colenso's limited knowledge of word so translated, 38

Borrowed, the Israelites, explanation of this fact, 35
Bread, the great want of people in the desert, 182
—————, unleavened, habitually eaten by Arabs, 182
Buffon, his "Natural History" referred to, 54, 111
Burckhardt, his "Travels" referred to, 158, 177, 178, 180—186, 198
Butter, great quantity habitually eaten by Arabs, 199

"Came with Jacob" into Egypt, meaning of, 13
Camp, the extent of; and the priest's duties, 22
Canaan, extent of and number of the people, 145
Charcoal, Dr. Colenso knows not how made by Arabs, 190
—————, brushwood, and saplings, used in making, 172
Charges, Dr. Colenso's against the Pentateuch, improbability of, 2
Chief pastor, of a flock, Dr. Colenso as, 52
1 Chron. xxiii. 6—23, compared with Exod. vi. and Num. xxvi., pedigrees in, 121
Concubinage, existing among Israel at the Exodus, 103
Concubines, children of, how regarded, 104
Criticism, Dr. Colenso's mistakes in, 27, 34, 38, 50, 70, 77, &c., &c.

Danites, the number of, at the Exodus, 113

Danites, probable reason for large number of, 114
Darkness, important use of the three days of, in Egypt, 51
Dates, and date-trees, use of in the desert, 184
Desert, Scripture allusions to Israel's route in, 181
———, Israel's intercourse with inhabitants of, 191
———, general aspect of, 194
———, Israel led by miracles in, 185
———, general resources of, according to Burckhardt, 195
———, mode of living in, 199
———, capable of cultivation, 174
———, Dr. Colenso's mistakes concerning, 175—178
———, Dr. Colenso's authorities on, 172
———, European travellers in, 179
———, Scriptural account of the, 164
Deut. xxi. 15—17, explanation of, as to firstborn, 141
Dew, value of in the desert, for sustaining flocks and herds, 186
———, in the Delta, and in the desert, 186
Divorce, permitted by Egyptians, to any extent, 104

"Each opening each womb," phrase descriptive of firstborn, 138
Edom, or Seir, Israel compassed, many days or years, 194
———, aspect of desert around, 195
Egypt, what time Israel left, 64
———, Israel's march out of, 56
———, Israelites were prepared when they left, 51
———, time of Israel's sojourn in, 91
Egyptians, children of, by marriage with Hebrews, 104, 105
El Araba, terrific nature of, yet a pasture ground in winter, 197
El Tyh, the desert of, 168
———, Volney's description of, 169
———, desert of, vegetation easily produced in, 185
Encampment, Israel's at Abel-Shittim, 159
European travellers in the desert, 179
Exodus vi., Hebrew families mentioned in, no fair standard for others, 105

Exod. vi., Dr. Colenso's strange misapprehension of, 116
———, explanation of pedigrees in, 119

Family, cost of keeping in Egypt, 109
Families, principle of division of tribes into, not known, 101
Fish and geese caught in nets and salted in Egypt, 187
Firstborn, Hävernick and Michaelis right concerning, 139
———, question concerning, not affected by the *marking* of doorposts in Egypt, 143
———, means first son, of first wife a virgin, of whole family, 140
———, number of the, 132, 138
———, probable priestly functions of, 144
Flocks, possible size of, Israelitish, at the Exodus, 54
———, Egyptian, and probably Israelitish, very great, 57
Fourth Generation, the Exodus in the, 90
———————, patriarchal family was to be the test of the, 98

Gen. xlvi. 12, word *were* most important in, 12
———————, translation proposed for, 15
Gen. xlix. 3, explanation of, as to firstborn, 141
Generation, natural, Scripture hints on, 94
———, ———, in sense of *begetment*, 95
———, ———, as a cycle of time limiting a life or race, 96
Gesenius, his Thesaurus referred to, 45
——— his Heb. Gram. referred to, 16
Glassius, his Philolog. Sacr. referred to, 16, 194
Goats, some particulars about breeding, 55
Goshen, land of, where, 57
———, ancient cities of, now a desert, 58
Grazing, extent of land required for Israel's flocks in, 56
Gresswell, his "Three Witnesses" quoted, 41, 64

Halts and encampments of Israel, when leaving Egypt, 64
Hamul and Hezron, birth of, in Egypt, 10
Hebrew families in Canaan, no standard for in Egypt, 104
—— ——, Scripture furnishes no sufficient *data* concerning, 105
—— numerals, difficulties concerning, 153
Hebrews, their fruitfulness in Egypt, Scripture testimony to, 106
——, their fruitfulness in Egypt, heathen testimony to, 106
Holy Bible, Dr. Colenso's opinion concerning. *generally*, 4
Horeb. how the Israelites probably conducted water at. 185
——, Israel did not live in idleness at, 186
Hurry, in what sense Israel left Egypt in a, 51

Israelites, their increase in Egypt, miraculous, 91, 112
——, their number at the Exodus, 100
——, possible number of, at the Exodus, 110
——, variation in number of the several tribes of, 130
——, variation in number of the several tribes of, various ways of accounting for, 131
——, number of, and extent of Canaan, 145
—— in the desert, miraculous preservation of, 163

Jerem. ii. 6, explanation of, as to the desert, 166
Jethro, what time Moses fed flocks of, at Horeb, 193
——, value of his visit to Israel, in the desert, 193
John iii. 1—21, important reference to, 7
John v. 46, 47, important reference to, 6
John vi. 30—58, important reference to, 7
Joseph, the Patriarch, his death as marking a generation, 97

Kadesh-Barnea, or El-Araba, in 1812, comparatively unknown, 180

Kalisch, as quoted regarding Sinai, by Dr. Colenso, 189
Kings, Egyptians mourned their, 72 days. 65

Lane, his "Modern Egyptians" referred to, 41, 104. 109, 182
Law, the reading of the, by Ezra, 21
——, giving of the, at Sinai—Robinson's discovery of the plain, 179
Laymen. important offices of, 26, 83
Lee, his Hebrew Grammar referred to, 16
Levi, family of, probably avoided Egyptian concubinage, 107
Levites, great continency intimated on the part of, 125
——, may have increased much more than stated, 126
——, number of, at the Exodus, 115
——, proper duties of the, according to Ezra, 24
——————, according to Chronicles, 25
——, why not popular in Israel, 128
Leviticus iv. 11, 12, mistake by Dr. Colenso on, 27
Lindsay, Lord, his "Travels" referred to, 62

Maan, in the desert, between Araba and Hor, 196
Macdonald, referred to on the Pentateuch, 5
Maimonides, his account of killing the Passover, 77
Mana-seh and Ephraim, why number small in each tribe, 114
Manna, the Saviour refers to fall of, as to historical fact, 7
Marriage, at what age contracted, in Egypt, 109
Married men. Dr. Colenso's mistake in counting. at Sinai, 136
Messiah, or Christ, descended from Hezron, 14
Midian, the overthrow of, was miraculous, 155
——, the war on, 148
Midianites, where they dwelt, 193
——————, and others, slain *judicially*, by command of God, 152
Midwives, their answer to Pharaoh a concerted evasion, 105

P

Miracles, in the desert, continuous, 163
Misquotations, by Dr. Colenso, 11, 85, 157
Moses' writings, Christ, as SON OF GOD, testifies to, 6, 8

Nakhel, or *date-tree*, place so called in the desert, 185
Noldius, his "Concord. Hebr. Partic." referred to, 16, 50
Numbered, those, only men fit for war, 46
Numerals, Hebrew, difficulties concerning, 153

Officers, Hebrews were provided with, at the Exodus, 34
Og, King of Bashan, the conquest of, 155

Palm-trees, numerous in the desert now, and more so formerly, 186
Passover, institution of the, 47
————, celebration of, matter for historical evidence, 79
————, time for slaying, and sprinkling of the blood, 76
Patriarchs, the twelve, had probably more sons born in Egypt, 107
————————————, relative ages of, 108
————————————, sons of at the Eisodus, 108
Patriarchate vested in Amram's family at the Exodus, 99
Paxton, his "Scrip. Illustrations" referred to, 40, 58, 62, 147, 157, 177, 193
Pedigrees, no *data* for judging of, in Holy Scripture, 101
————, selected from the Bible, by Dr. Colenso, 92
————, women not included by Scripture, in Jewish, 101
Penalty for Israel's rebellion, in refusing to enter Canaan when told, 129
Pentateuch, references to Christ in, 8
————, itself claims to have been written by Moses, 5
————, object of Dr. Colenso's book against, 3
Petrified trees, marks of former vegetation, between Cairo and Suez, 189
Pharzites, distinct from Hezronites and Hamulites, 13

Pigeons, Dr. Colenso's ideas on sacrifice of, 87
————, were birds of the Arabian desert, 88
Polled, the Israelites, at Sinai, 42
Polling, and taxing, Exod. iii. 11; xxxviii. 25; and Num. i. 1—46; explained, 44
Polygamy, did prevail among Israel at the Exodus, 103
Prejudice in argument, proofs of Dr. Colenso's, 133
Priests, their number and perquisites at the Exodus, 79, 82
————————————, and extent of the camp, 22

Quails and other birds salted in Egypt, 187

Rams, habitually killed by Arabs, 200
Regimental returns, Israelitish, matter of routine, 157
Reserves, the clergy, 89
Reservoirs, natural in cavities of the rocks, 189
Robinson, his "Biblical Researches" referred to, 40, 61—67, 179

Sacred Geography, Dr. Colenso's mistakes in, 156
Sacrifices, Levitical, not all observed in the wilderness, 81
————————, how disposed of, 83
————————, optional, not compulsory, 86
Scriptures, on reading the Holy, 27
Servants, Israelitish, Dr. Colenso refuses to allow for, 110
————, at least a few at the Exodus, 111
Sheep, some hints on breeding, 55
Sicard, Abbé, his calculation at Pi-hahiroth, 60
Sihon, war on, and war on Midian, harmony of events between, 153, 160
Sinai, natural resources of Mount, 188
——, period of Burckhardt's arrival at, 191
——, still good water at, 169
——, second passover kept at, 78
Slavery, difference between scriptural and other kinds of, 151
Story, an offensive title applied to the Pentateuch by Bishop Colenso, 3

Substance, Israel's, at the Exodus, 42
Succoth, probable reasons why place so-called, 40
———, journey from Rameses to, 59
Suez, desert of, its present condition, 189

Tents, the Israelites in, 37
Time-table of events between war on Sihon and on Midian, 160

Volney, his "Travels" referred to, 41, 61, 63, 168, 170, 186

Wady'el Lahyane, verdure of, 197
———Genne, Burckhardt's description of, 190

Wady Gharendel, near Sinai, divers sorts of trees in, 184
———, at Araba, terrible desert, 196
Water, cattle can go without, a long time, under certain conditions, 182
———, mode of carrying in Egypt, 182
———, brackish, may be drinkable, 182
———, excellent at Sinai, 190
———, found everywhere in the desert at a low depth, 183
"Whole Assembly," the, meaning of this expression, 16, 19
Wild beasts, Canaan peculiarly exposed to attacks of, 147
Wilkinson, his "Ancient Egyptians" referred to, 39, 41, 54, 65, 104, 109, 182, 184, 187

BY THE SAME AUTHOR.

NOTES on the RESTORATION and CONVERSION of ISRAEL. One Vol. Demy 8vo. 14s.

ISAIAH'S CALL to ENGLAND: a Critical Exposition of Isaiah xviii. One Vol. Demy 8vo. 10s. 6d.

THE CHRISTIAN VERITY STATED: being a Summary of Trinitarian Doctrine, especially adapted for Present Times. One Vol. Post 8vo. 5s.

N.B.—A WELSH EDITION, by the Rev. HUGH OWEN. Aubrey's, Llanerchymedd, Anglesea.

www.ingramcontent.com/pod-product-compliance
Lightning Source LLC
Chambersburg PA
CBHW021831230426
43669CB00008B/938